BLOOD FOR DIGNITY

BLOOD FOR
DIGNITY

THE STORY OF THE FIRST INTEGRATED COMBAT UNIT IN THE U.S. ARMY

DAVID P. COLLEY

ST. MARTIN'S PRESS ✄ NEW YORK

www.stmartins.com

Book design by Jonathan Bennett

ISBN 0-312-30035-2

First Edition: February 2003

10 9 8 7 6 5 4 3 2 1

This book is dedicated to the members of the 5th Platoon, K Company, 394th Regiment, 99th Infantry Division, and to all the black infantry volunteers of the 5th Platoons, whose courage and patriotism have never been recognized by the country they served during World War II.

And to Mary Liz.

CONTENTS

ACKNOWLEDGMENTS

I am especially indebted to the veterans of the 5th Platoon, K Company, 394th Infantry Regiment, 99th Infantry Division, who spent many hours with me on the phone and in person, going over details of their lives, their service during World War II, and their combat experiences in March, April, and May of 1945 in Germany. I include among these men Arthur Holmes of Alta Loma, California, who was particularly gracious during my visit with him; Lawrence Boris of Mount Vernon, New York; Waymon Ransom of Burlington, New Jersey, who also invited me into his home; Harold Robinson of Buffalo, New York; the late Clayton Des Journette of Los Angeles, California; and former 5th Platoon leader Lt. Richard Ralston of Portland, Oregon, with whom I spoke many times on the phone and who sent me an abundance of information and personal recollections.

I want to thank Mrs. Hattie Des Journette for interviews about her husband after his death in 1999, and Mrs. Margaret Scobbie, of Cwmbran, Wales, Clayton Des Journette's daughter.

There are many other veterans of black infantry platoons to whom I am indebted. Among these men are James Strawder of Washington, D.C., whose memories of his wartime experiences, especially those in combat, are still vivid. Willfred Strange of Washington, D.C., gave me great insight into the struggles of black troops during World War II, as did Bradford Tatum, also of Washington, D.C. I appreciate the time given me by the Honorable Bruce Wright, and his wife, Elizabeth Davidson, in their home in Connecticut. J. Cameron Wade of Irving, Texas, who founded the Association of the 2221 Negro Volunteers, also provided me with information.

I thank my agent, Richard Curtis, for his unflinching faith in *Blood for Dignity*. He has been a great supporter of my work. I also appreciate the enthusiasm of my editor, Marc Resnick of St. Martin's Press, and his guidance and enlightening comments about the manuscript. And I thank Adam Goldberger, copy editor, for his diligent work.

No author could survive without a library. I wish to acknowledge Mrs. Dottie Patoki and the Easton, Pennsylvania, Area Public Library reference staff for making available to me a stream of books through interlibrary loan. The Lafayette College Library also was a valuable source, particularly its collection of books on World War II. Dr. Richard Sommers, assistant director of patron services at the Center for Military History in Carlisle, Pennsylvania, and his staff were extremely helpful in gathering information on the black volunteers, specifically the written recollections and memoirs of members of the 99th Infantry Division. Richard Boylen and Wyman Bailey were also helpful in obtaining records from the National Archives in Maryland.

Above all, this book could never have come to fruition without the love, support, and editing skills of my wife, Mary Liz, who always offered sound advice and took the time to read the manuscript numerous times. Our sons, Padraic and Christopher, offered their encouragement and interest throughout the writing process.

The decision from the High Command is the greatest since enactment of the Constitutional amendments following the emancipation.

> —*Brig. Gen. Benjamin O. Davis, America's first black general, concerning Eisenhower's decision to integrate black infantry platoons into all-white combat divisions along the Rhine in March 1945*

We used to discuss segregation in high school. Our history teacher told us that we could expect to gain our dignity as human beings in this country when we put our blood on the line in combat.

> —*James Strawder, 5th Platoon, Company E, 393rd Regiment, 99th Division—a black volunteer*

INTRODUCTION

In early March 1945 more than two thousand African-American infantrymen entered the front lines in Germany to fight alongside white soldiers
in infantry and armored divisions engaged in the final battles of World
War II in Europe. Today black combat troops go unnoticed in an American army that has been integrated since the 1950s.

But in 1945 the appearance of these black volunteers in all-white
fighting units was a radical departure from military practices dating back
to the birth of the nation. For 162 years, from the end of the Revolution
in 1783 until the last three months of World War II, blacks served prin-
cipally in noncombat service units, and the few who fought were relegated
to segregated combat units. The psychological impact of this exclusion on
black men was profound. They were deprived of the fundamental right
to be men among men.

In the closing months of World War II the army took the first mean-
ingful steps to integrate its combat units by calling for black volunteers
and assigning them to various divisions in the European theater. The high
command originally planned to integrate the black infantrymen individually with whites, but because of feared political repercussions stemming
from long-standing policies of segregation, they were formed into all-black
platoons that were integrated into white infantry companies. In March
1945 the first of fifty-two platoons, comprising about fifty men each, went
into action along the Rhine as the Allies began their final push to defeat
Nazi Germany.

American military doctrine had long held that blacks were inferior
fighters who fled under fire and who lacked the intelligence, reliability,
and courage of whites. The combat record of the black platoons in March,
April, and May 1945 dispelled this notion. The majority of black troops
who fought in the integrated infantry and armored companies did so with
an élan and courage that deeply impressed their white superiors and comrades. In some cases white officers regarded the black infantrymen as superior fighters to whites. One former white soldier who fought alongside
blacks in K Company, 394th Infantry Regiment, 99th Division, characterized these African-American warriors as "courageous to the point of

foolishness." He was not alone in his observations. A white officer saw them as more aggressive than whites in combat, more willing to kill or be killed.

After the war the army conducted a study of the performance of the black volunteers entitled "The Utilization of Black Platoons in White Companies." In interviews with 1,700 white soldiers, including 84 percent of the black platoons' white officers, those queried said the blacks had performed "very well." There was not one instance in which the performance of black troops was rated as poor.

Another surprising aspect of this postwar study was that the color line and racial enmity that had existed between whites and blacks in civilian life, and in much of army life during World War II, disappeared at the front. Relations between whites and blacks in combat units were judged to be "excellent." By war's end many of the white infantrymen and officers who served with blacks "endorsed the idea of having colored soldiers used as infantry troops."

After V-E Day, however, segregation once again prevailed in the American army. Most of the black volunteers were separated from their infantry and armored divisions and returned to segregated service units prior to being shipped home. In at least two cases black volunteers mutinied and demanded that they be allowed to remain with their infantry units. One incident required the intervention of Brig. Gen. Benjamin O. Davis, America's first black general, to defuse the crisis.

The pressure for equality in American life following World War II proved irresistible, and in 1948 President Harry S. Truman ordered the integration of the armed forces. It would be a number of years before Truman's executive order was fully implemented, but the American army, particularly its combat formations, became fully integrated by the mid-1950s. Integration in army combat units began in earnest during the Korean War. Ironically, during the Vietnam War there were complaints of disproportionate numbers of blacks in the infantry.

It is hard to quantify the impact of the black platoons on the later integration of the American army. Did it speed the process of integration in the military and later in civilian life? Many of the black platoon members believe their service helped the cause of racial equality. Postwar commissions studying the problems of segregation in the military looked to the black platoons as examples of how integration had worked in the U.S. Army.

Blood for Dignity is the first chronicle of the black platoons, told mostly by surviving members of 5th Platoon, K Company, 394th Infantry Regiment, 99th Infantry Division. The story of the "5th of K" is supplemented by accounts of black platoon members in the two additional regiments of the 99th, and in other combat divisions. The 5th of K went into the line on March 12, 1945, and was put to the test in its first hours of combat. The platoon was engaged in both heavy combat and in mopping-up operations in the final months of the war.

While focused mostly on three months of combat, the story of the men of the 5th of K transcends war. It also relates the story of their courage and determination to achieve success and acceptance before and after World War II. Platoon members began life in a segregated culture that relegated them to the status of second-class citizens. Through the postwar years they struggled and persevered, and today many are successful and aging warriors of the Great Crusade. Above all, they are proud African-Americans.

This is the story of the men of the black platoons, mostly in war, but also in peace.

1

•

HEALING OLD WOUNDS

"YOU PROMISED MOTHER YOU would go," Harold Robinson's daughter, Debbie, reminded him in the spring of 2000. Robinson, an eighty-two-year-old retired autoworker from Buffalo, New York, had never attended a reunion of his old infantry outfit, the 99th Division that fought in Belgium and Germany in World War II. The 99th had won fame and glory during the Battle of the Bulge in December 1944, as it doggedly fought off the German onslaught. The division later advanced through the Ardennes into Germany, and, in early March 1945, was one of the first divisions to cross the Rhine River at the town of Remagen.

Robinson was a member of the 5th Platoon attached to K Company, 394th Regiment, which joined the 99th in the spring of 1945 in the Remagen bridgehead. The "5th of K" was formed as part of an "experiment" initiated in late 1944, in which the army asked for black volunteers to integrate white infantry companies. Robinson answered the call along with 4,561 other black troops who had been serving in segregated noncombatant units. The army, hitherto segregated, was bowing, in part, to mounting pressure for integration from the black community in America. But the military was also desperate for new infantrymen to replace mounting casualties, and blacks constituted an untapped manpower pool. In 1945 there were hundreds of thousands of African-American soldiers stationed behind the lines in Europe, many of whom had previously begged to fight but had been turned away. The army now gave them a chance.

Robinson's introduction to combat was abrupt and violent, and, like so many soldiers new to combat, his initial reaction was terror. He witnessed a comrade's brains blasted from his head and heard the snap of German machine-gun bullets even before the 5th got to the front lines. In its first hours in combat the 5th of K was shelled by enemy and American artillery and was attacked from all sides by enemy troops. Robinson was amazed at his naïveté in thinking combat would be heroic.

Robinson and his buddies endured days and nights of combat in the hills above the Rhine in the Remagen bridgehead and in the nearby city of Honningen. Then came weeks of guerrilla-style fighting as they marched through Germany to the Ruhr, did an about-face, and fought their way south through Bavaria to the Danube River. The enemy faced imminent defeat in the last weeks of April 1945, but German soldiers often turned to fight sharp and deadly engagements when they gathered enough strength to challenge the advancing Americans. Many of Robinson's buddies were killed and wounded.

Robinson and his wife, Shirley, planned to attend the reunion of the 99th in Philadelphia in July 2000, but Shirley's death that winter dampened Robinson's desire to see old comrades and relive the war. He decided not to go. But Debbie urged him on and reminded him that the journey would be a long-overdue pilgrimage to silence the demons of the past, particularly those of World War II.

For years after World War II the veterans have gathered annually to renew old friendships forged by war. These are the "bands of brothers" who defeated Hitler before returning home to a grateful nation, to raise families and move to the suburbs. As the years passed, their ranks thinned, but those who remained were fervently loyal to old units.

Harold Robinson had never attended a reunion of the 99th because he never felt welcomed by old comrades, even many years after the war. White men attended World War II unit reunions almost exclusively, and Harold Robinson is an African-American whose heritage as a man and soldier was segregation. He grew up in a segregated society, and all but three months of his three-year army stint was in segregated units. He was middle-aged before integration was fully implemented in the United States. White Americans had scorned his race, and he never understood why.

After the war no one from the 99th reached out to the men of the division's three black platoons to invite them to reunions, nor had the veterans of other divisions with 5th Platoons approached their black veterans. The whites and the army forgot the African-American volunteers. The military had never issued many of the black platoon members their combat medals and still listed some as having served only with their old service units. As far as the army's records were concerned, these men were still truck drivers and laborers, not combat veterans.

Robinson wasn't the only black veteran with ambivalent feelings about wartime service or about attending a division reunion. James Strawder, who served in 5th Platoon, E Company, 393rd Regiment, 99th Division, was equally uncertain about reestablishing old ties. Then came the invitation to attend the reunion of the 99th.

For Strawder, the sight of the division's shoulder patch, an insignia of a blue, black, and white checkerboard that brought pride to white 99th veterans, reminded him of the painful discrimination he had experienced in the army during World War II. More tormenting, however, was the recollection that all the black volunteers in the 99th had been hustled out of the division at the war's end and reassigned to segregated service outfits. Instead of remaining with the 99th for a triumphal return to the United States, Strawder and his black comrades were shipped home separately. He was convinced that the army had purposely and callously disregarded the valor and sacrifice of the black infantry veterans and reimposed segregation to maintain the all-white veneer of its combat forces for home front consumption.

Even as a proud, wounded combat veteran, Strawder viewed his military experience as so humiliating and degrading that he left the army vowing never to look back. He refused to admit even having served in the 99th. Then one day in the mid-1990s he encountered a group of aging white men at a public golf course in Washington, D.C., where he often played. One was wearing a windbreaker with the familiar checkerboard patch of the 99th Division.

"I served in that sorry-ass outfit during the war," Strawder said, barely disguising his disgust. One of the men was surprised and extended his hand to Strawder: "We've been looking for you guys for a long time," he said. The irony was palpable. Forty years before, these men might well have prevented him from playing golf on this same course. And welcoming a black man as an old comrade would have been unthinkable for many of the "coal crackers" from Appalachia and "rednecks" from the old Confederacy, who had made up much of the 99th. "I felt strongly at the end of the war that whites classified us as nothing. We were just absolutely nothing. We were the lowest heap," Strawder said, the anger still vivid in his voice.

Harold Robinson had similar feelings. He constantly wondered why the white man had so despised the black man. "What did we do to make them hate us so much?" he often mused.

Robinson nevertheless fulfilled his promise to Shirley and attended the reunion of the 99th held at the Adams Mark Hotel in Philadelphia. He would be there with black comrades James Strawder, and Lawrence Boris of Mt. Vernon, New York, who had served in the 5th of K alongside Robinson.

The former young men and boys of the 99th, now old men, gray and some frail, pressed around the black veterans. Robinson chatted amiably with his old white comrades, some from K Company, and listened to their belated praise.

Bill Meyer, editor of the 99th Division Association newspaper, told the assembled vets how proud the association was to have these blacks as members in attendance and said that he had never heard anything but praise for their performance in the battle for Germany. Meyer had published letters and articles in the association newspaper asking veterans to help locate the men of the 5th Platoons. The division did not see them as African-Americans but as members of the 99th. Meyer added that whites and blacks were all part of the same unit regardless of race.

Strawder had always assumed the division was responsible for separating out the black volunteers at the end of the war. Now he knew this wasn't so, and he expressed his gratitude to his old comrades. Finally, he felt accepted as a member of the 99th Division.

"They were glad to see us," said Robinson, who also was surprised at the warm reception. He stood among his white comrades and took them back fifty-five years to a day in mid-March 1945. K Company, 394th Regiment, was in trouble in the hills above the Rhine. The company was almost surrounded by enemy, its ranks were being whittled away, and wounded men in need of medical attention could not be evacuated. Its commander had been wounded and K Company was virtually leaderless. The black platoon, dubbed the 5th Platoon because it was one more than a company usually carried, trudged up the hills of the Erpeler Ley on the east bank of the Rhine through enemy fire to reinforce the beleaguered infantry company. When the black troops arrived the welcome they received from the men of K Company was wild. They greeted the newcomers with cheers and smiles wide with relief. These black men had assured their survival.

In the calm of the Adams Mark Hotel, Harold Robinson spoke to his former white comrades: "I came to this reunion to determine if you were as glad to see us now as you were back then when we reinforced you on that hillside. You didn't care then that we were black. You just saw us as soldiers, and human beings, men who had saved your lives. I truly believe now that you are genuinely as happy to see us today as you were in 1945."

2

•

I THOUGHT I WAS GOING BLIND

MARCH 13, 1945—REMAGEN bridgehead, Germany. The men of K Company had fought all night, sometimes hand to hand, against bands of enemy troops from an assortment of German divisions counterattacking up the deep-cut draws and over the forested ridges above the Rhine River town of Erpel. The GIs strained to see into the enveloping blackness that danced with demonic apparitions inching furtively through the trees toward the American positions. The blinding flash of grenade explosions intermittently cast the surrounding forest in unearthly hues. Sometimes the ghostly specters materialized and the night was pierced by the guttural shouts of Germans rising to rush the American outpost line. Other enemy troops infiltrated silently between the hastily dug foxholes to swarm through K Company's perimeter, and the Americans found themselves fighting in all directions.

The GIs sent up flares that burst in a blue-white brilliance and lingered before descending, hissing and flickering in a searing light that revealed dark and vague forms amid the shadows thrown by the enveloping forest. The desperate Americans called for artillery fire, and within minutes the smudged and black sky to the west across the Rhine was splashed yellow-red with flame as U.S. batteries of 155- and 105-mm guns blasted out their projectiles. The concussive roar of the artillery echoed off the bluffs above Erpel and reverberated up the steep ravines to the ridgeline where K Company was dug in. The avalanche of explosions was repeated when the shells rained down around the American positions, driving the men to the bottom of their holes as each shell burst with a deafening blast or a metallic clang.

Relief came mercifully at dawn as the Germans left their dead and retreated into the forests that covered the steep hillsides of legend and folklore. It was in these rugged hills that the mythical Teutonic knight, Siegfried, slew the dragon and bathed in his blood. It was here also that corpulent burghers and their families before the war had strolled peacefully above the Rhine to gaze down on the Ludendorff railroad bridge that connected Erpel, on the east bank, with the town of Remagen on the west bank some forty miles south of Cologne. But the men of K Company were too weary and frightened to muse about legends and holiday pursuits.

K Company had crossed the Rhine on the Ludendorff Bridge during the night of March 11 as shells exploded with a deafening clatter into the sagging superstructure and sent up frothy plumes from bursts in the river. The company took several casualties as the men advanced toward the Erpeler Ley, the rocky uplands that rise in places five hundred feet above the river in sheer cliffs at the east end of the bridge. Wood planking and slippery steel plating made treacherous by jagged shell holes covered the bridge's rail tracks. Once across, K Company went immediately into the attack with the 394th to drive the Germans from the rugged hills where enemy troops waited and German forward observers directed artillery fire on U.S. positions.

In the first several hundred yards of their attack K Company and the 394th met light resistance as they advanced southeastward along the Rhine toward the small industrial town of Honningen. They soon ran into pockets of determined Germans dug in on ridgelines and in the woods that covered the Erpeler Ley. Late in the day the 394th, with K Company in the vanguard, had smashed its way through the enemy resistance and taken a ridge running northwest and southeast. But Honningen remained beyond their grasp.

By the evening of March 12 the 99th Division's 394th and 393rd Regiments were abreast on a strip of high ground that dominated much of the area in the division sector. The 99th's front formed an arc about four and a half miles in length from the east bank of the Rhine some five hundred yards north of Honningen to the flank of the 9th Infantry Division, which was also fighting to secure the bridgehead. The 394th measured its gains in yards, and the fighting seesawed back and forth as the Germans fought in near desperation. By the second day of hard combat in the Remagen bridgehead casualties had depleted the 394th and its men were exhausted.

Daylight on the thirteenth after the night of bitter fighting brought more shells on K Company's position, this time both German and American fire. Heavy artillery rounds exploded around and amid the company perimeter and the men dodged the hail of enemy 20- and 37-mm antiaircraft shells that were spewed out in a rhythmic, staccato thumping to explode in short, coughing blasts. Enemy snipers kept the Americans in their holes, and the casualties mounted and soldiers bled as they waited for medical care.

The Germans were determined to throw the Americans back across the Rhine, the last barrier protecting the German heartland in the west, and launched a daylight counterattack along the battalion front. Their antiaircraft batteries resumed a sweep of American positions, and well-hidden nests of machine guns opened up as enemy troops moved forward. The line of GIs bent as Germans penetrated 150 yards into American ground. The Americans fought back with a fury, and the enemy was stopped and driven back to lick their wounds and prepare for another attack. In the meantime the enemy continued aggressive patrolling all along the line.

Battalion ordered a general advance for the 394th, and K Company was directed to attack in support of L Company's right flank. The men of L Company set out, weaving up through the thick, forested hillsides, engaging enemy snipers and machine guns. But K Company was nowhere to be seen. Lt. Neil Brown, L Company commander, frantically called battalion.

"Where's K Company?"

"On your right flank," replied Capt. Charles Roland, battalion executive officer.

"That's bullshit!" Lieutenant Brown roared into his radio. "K Company is not there and the Germans are."

Lieutenant Brown asked Captain Roland for mortar fire on K Company's assigned sector to prevent his troops from being outflanked. Captain Roland demurred and studied his situation map. He was the de facto battalion commander because the commanding officer was pinned down by enemy fire somewhere in the hills nearby and two senior battalion officers had been killed by enemy artillery fire that same day. Lieutenant Brown was asking Roland to rain bombs on their own men. Lieutenant Brown persisted, and Captain Roland ordered the fire. "I had a lump the size of a basketball in my stomach because I was not absolutely sure we would not be firing on our own people," Captain Roland said.

The situation was aggravated by American artillery fire from across the Rhine that was hitting U.S. positions with almost greater frequency than German shellfire. Captain Roland heard it roaring in from across the river, and every American knew its signature as it came in from the west. But the enemy and American forces were so closely intertwined that to aim at the Germans meant shooting at Americans as well.

Roland had been amazed earlier in the day as the battalion's artillery liaison officer, Capt. Henry Reath, stood in the village of Ariendorf, just northwest of K Company's position, and ordered the American batteries to cease firing. "We were taking heavy salvos from our own artillery and Reath actually stood at his radio and got that fire stopped," Roland said. "I thought that at any instant he would be killed."

K Company had not attacked, because it was leaderless and was pinned down by the volume of German fire. Seventeen men had been killed or wounded. Their commanding officer, Capt. Wesley Simmons, was away on leave for a much-needed rest, and the replacement commander, Lieutenant Wilson, was among the wounded. K Company, 394th Regiment, 99th Division, desperately needed a new leader as well as reinforcements.

Captain Roland made his way up the hill to the K Company perimeter to sort out the command problem and found Lieutenant Wilson badly dazed from a head wound. "A bullet had hit his helmet and gone in the front and out the back and grazed his head deep enough to leave a bloody streak all the way across his head above one ear, and his bell was really rung. I sent him back to the aid station under escort and placed another lieutenant in command."

"K Company was in a real bad situation," Captain Roland remembered. "There was firing going on all the time. It was steady, small arms and occasional artillery salvos. The worst weapons were those 20- and 40-mm AA guns. They fire like a machine gun except their projectiles explode when they hit."

The entire front was being peppered by flak-gun fire. "They'd just aim those sons of bitches at ground level as far as they would deflect and sweep around. If you didn't have a crevice to get down in you didn't do well," Lieutenant Brown said. "They stopped us from moving at all and we just concentrated on securing our positions. This wasn't any afternoon tennis match. The Germans were pretty damned serious about not welcoming us to their area."

During the late afternoon of March 13, as the men prepared for another onslaught in the coming night, sounds of a sharp engagement broke out on the steeply wooded hillside below the company position. The men peered anxiously down the slope toward the Rhine to ground they had already won and cleared of enemy. The short popping bursts of American M1 fire and the dull crump of grenade explosions indicated that there was a gap somewhere in the line and that the enemy had infiltrated back into the woods behind K Company's position in and around the village of Leubsdorf. The American fire was answered by shrill bursts from a German MG 34 machine gun and the sharp crack of an enemy flak gun and the blast of mortar explosions. The fighting reached a crescendo and then trailed off to occasional shots until there was silence in the forest.

"Evening was drawing near and we were afraid the enemy would infiltrate into town," recalled Ralph Treadup, a veteran K Company infantryman holed up in Leubsdorf.

The exhausted men of K Company warily peered from their foxholes through the dense woods and heard the banter of approaching infantry and shouted commands, but the oncoming force was too distant and obscured by trees to determine whether it was friend or foe. K Company troops had become accustomed to the harsh-sounding commands of

German officers exhorting their troops during the nights on the hill.

A ragged line of men began emerging from the trees in small groups, ducking under the low branches of the firs and hardwoods. K Company troops gripped their weapons and released their safeties as these strange-looking soldiers advanced. There were glimpses of approaching men clad in American OD (olive drab) brown and potlike helmets, but the oncoming ranks did not seem filled with typical U.S. troops. They had no faces, and the brown of their uniforms merged with the mud color of their helmets. Everything was brown. As the line approached, only two men stood out: a white-faced and stocky lieutenant, a platoon leader, and a white-faced platoon sergeant. The officer signaled greetings to the soldiers in the defensive perimeter, and the men of K Company looked at one another in amazement as the approaching troops neared and finally reached K Company's line.

"Their eyes got as big as Eddie Cantor's," remembered Pfc. Harold Robinson, a grenadier with the newly arrived 5th Platoon sent to reinforce K Company. "They were all southern boys but they sure were glad to see us. They welcomed us black troops."

Arthur Holmes, another member of the newly arrived 5th of K, glanced around. He saw men lying about and heard the moans and cries of wounded soldiers. "One of the boys in K Company says to me, 'Where are you guys from?' I said, 'We're supposed to be with Company K,' and he said, 'Thank God you're here.' The white guys were just as friendly and nice and you would have thought we were all black guys," Holmes said.

"You couldn't tell the guys to come out of their foxholes and introduce themselves," said Pfc. Lawrence Boris with the 5th of K. "There was firing going on all over and those flak guns opening up."

"There was quite a bit of mortar fire," recalled Pfc. Waymon Ransom. "When we approached, the guys in K Company kept saying, 'Get down, get down!' "

The white troops broke into muted cheering and hailed the oncoming troops even as they urged them to take cover from artillery and flak-gun bursts and snipers who lurked in the woods. Lt. Richard Ralston, platoon leader for the newly arrived 5th of K, recalled the reception. "They were overjoyed and greatly relieved to see a new additional platoon join them. I imagine a lot of the white men were incredulous at having blacks join them. It would be natural."

Incredulous they were! "Christ, I thought I was going blind," one K Company white soldier said for all to hear. "I thought I was seeing things." Private Ransom was used to such comments, as were all the men in the 5th of K. But this comment was said without the usual bite.

The K Company soldier was seeing something American soldiers had not seen for more than 150 years. The approaching troops were black Americans from the newly attached 5th Platoon and they had been sent to join and reinforce K Company and fight the Germans alongside their white mates. The last time blacks had served shoulder to shoulder with whites in infantry units was in Washington's Continental army.

The whites of K Company experienced a strange transformation. No longer were these reinforcements regarded as "niggers," "smokes," or "coons." Now they were just ordinary GIs putting their lives on the line, and their K Company comrades were grateful. One white mortarman from K Company, Sgt. Jack Dufalla, expressed the feelings of the men of K Company that day on the ridge above the Rhine: "They saved our ass."

3

•

WE STARTED SOMETHING

THE ARRIVAL OF 5TH Platoon (5th of K) to reinforce K Company on the Erpeler Ley, and the assignment of other black volunteer infantry platoons to various infantry and armored divisions on the western front in March 1945, was a turning point in American history. These black infantrymen were in the vanguard of a movement that would gather momentum and lead to the integration of the American army and American society and ultimately transform the United States over the next generation.

Ironically, it was the U.S. military that led the way in the arduous and momentous process of integration after World War II. Initially the armed forces resisted integration during the war largely because the generals perceived blacks as inferior soldiers. But commanders also believed their primary duty was to win the conflict and not engage in a social experiment to test the parameters of integration in American society. They argued that integrating the military would be so controversial and disruptive that it could severely cripple the fighting effectiveness of America's armed forces.

While the integration of the black platoons in 1945 was a temporary measure—more a passing expedient—and was based as much on manpower needs as on a genuine rejection of the traditions and policies of segregation, some people saw great significance in the action. Brig. Gen. Benjamin Davis recognized the weight of the change when he asserted: "The decision from the High Command [to integrate the black platoons] is the greatest since enactment of the Constitutional amendments following the emancipation." He was referring to the Thirteenth, Fourteenth, and Fifteenth Amendments, adopted in 1865, which prohibited slavery and granted African-Americans their civil rights and citizenship along with the right to vote.

Bruce Wright, a volunteer infantryman who served with the 1st Infantry Division, and who rose to become a justice on the New York Supreme Court, believed that the new policy opened a door that could never again be closed. "I was doing something for a dream. I was living to see partial integration coming to be a matter of fact." Volunteer Arthur Holmes, who was an officer in the Army Reserve for many years after serving with the 5th of K, believed the integration of the black platoons was a turning point. "The platoons had a lot to do with the later integration of the army in 1948," Holmes said.

"We knew the black platoons were a first," said Clayton Des Journette, also a member of the 5th of K. "You could feel a change. We started something."

World War II was a white man's war and is still remembered and portrayed as such. Of the hundreds of photographs, films, and histories of the conflict, few depict blacks. Bill Mauldin's famed cartoon characters, Joe and Willie, were white. In the mind's eye, white men in loose-fitting uniforms and casually tilted helmets and garrison caps won the war and returned home to rebuild America. The blacks were merely adjuncts to victory who went back to the ghetto or the sharecropper's plot.

This perception persists into the twenty-first century in such films as *Saving Private Ryan* and *Band of Brothers*. Only once, and for hardly more than a second, does the camera pan on the face of a black man in either of these films, a truck driver transporting the 101st Airborne Division into Bastogne in *Band of Brothers*. Yet, hundreds of thousands of blacks served in the European theater of operations (ETO) and performed tasks essential to the final victory.

It is a surprise to many younger Americans today, who don't remember segregation, to learn that until the mid-1950s the American army was segregated. Prior to the Revolutionary War the American armed forces, particularly the militias, had been integrated. During the period from the first settlements in America up to and including the Revolution, blacks were accepted into white infantry units. To be sure, there was great ambivalence among some Colonial leaders and legislators about permitting African-Americans to serve alongside whites in the militias. But in many areas it was simple necessity to arm all able-bodied men regardless of race. Colonial America was a frontier society subject to attack by hostile marauders and, until the end of the French and Indian Wars in 1763, by French forces operating in Canada, along the Ohio River, and in the Lower Mississippi region.

Military records dating back to the 1600s show black men serving with whites in many Colonial militia units. The Dutch armed slaves, and in the 1640s blacks in the Massachusetts Bay Colony were called on to fight against hostile Indians.

Blacks participated in the French and Indian Wars from 1689 to 1763. One such African-American militiaman was Barsillai Lew, a six-foot cooper from Chelmsford, Massachusetts, who later fought with distinction at Bunker Hill and at Ticonderoga during the Revolutionary War.

It is difficult to determine the number of blacks who served during the American Revolution, but estimates suggest that as many as five thousand fleshed out the ranks of the three-hundred-thousand-man Continental army. "Negro" militiamen were among the Minutemen who responded to Paul Revere's call to arms and stood against the British at Lexington and Concord. There were blacks in the ranks of Ethan Allen's troops who captured Fort Ticonderoga in New York State. As many as seven hundred are estimated to have served in Washington's army at the Battle of Monmouth, New Jersey, in 1778.

Blacks also served in Gen. John Glover's Marblehead Regiment, which fought with Washington's army. In fact, had it not been for the Marbleheaders, the United States might not exist today.

Glover's troops were Massachusetts fishermen and used their nautical skills to rescue Washington's battered army in the summer of 1776 after the Battle of Long Island. With the Continentals surrounded and pinned against the East River in Brooklyn, the British leisurely waited for the Americans to surrender and end the rebellion. But Glover's seamen-soldiers gathered boats and ferried the American troops to safety across the river from Brooklyn Heights to Manhattan during a nighttime operation.

Six months later Glover's troops, including blacks, once again saved the Revolution when they carried the remnants of Washington's army across the Delaware River on Christmas night, 1776. They then joined the troops on the march to Trenton, where they overwhelmed three regiments of Hessian mercenaries in the employ of the British. Ten days later they repeated the operation and marched with Washington to the Battle of Princeton, where the Continentals defeated a contingent of British troops garrisoned in the town. While these victories were little more than skirmishes, they must rank among the greatest in American history. Washington's army was demoralized and disintegrating, and the Battles of Trenton and Princeton revitalized the American cause and brought in thousands of new enlistments.

Life in the Continental army was not easy for blacks. From the beginning of the Revolution there were many government and military leaders opposed to their enlistment. A week after his appointment on July 3, 1775, to command "all Continental forces," Washington's adjutant general, Gen. Horatio Gates, issued a command, with Washington's approval, denying blacks the right to enlist in the army.

Benjamin Franklin also opposed the enlistment of blacks, and Congress agreed to eliminate them from the military. But expediency prevailed, if only for the duration of the war. Washington and the Continental Congress soon reversed themselves and began accepting blacks into the army. Washington, like Eisenhower nearly two centuries later, needed all the manpower he could muster and knew his small, ill-trained, poorly armed

Continental army could not afford to exclude willing volunteers. Blacks continued to serve.

The fledgling Continental army was also mindful that denying blacks the right to fight with whites ran counter to the ideals of the Revolution—freedom and equality for all. More critical, however, was the fact that the British actively recruited African-Americans for the king's army with the promise of freedom when their service was completed and the war was over.

Once the Revolution ended, blacks were virtually eliminated from America's armed forces. A few remained in service to complete their tours of duty, but most were prohibited from duty by the Militia Act of 1792, which restricted service in the militia to able-bodied white males.

There were a number of reasons for the exclusion. Foremost was the inborn prejudice against African-Americans, which was taken to new heights in the United States, where whites believed themselves superior, particularly since most blacks were uneducated slaves.

But after the Revolution, there was little need for additional manpower in the military. The army was whittled down to a force of some three thousand men, and there was no room for blacks. Additionally, the old state militia units became important social and political groups in their communities and did not accept blacks.

The Haitian Revolution was also a major factor in the exclusion of blacks from the military. Considered the greatest slave rebellion in modern history, the revolt racked the island during the 1790s and early 1800s. A black guerrilla army under Toussaint-Louverture defeated several British and French expeditionary forces. The rebellion influenced American state legislatures, particularly in the South, to make service in the militias almost exclusively white.

The treatment of blacks following the Revolution established a government pattern in which blacks were called to serve in time of war but were ignored and excluded once hostilities ceased. This was the case during the War of 1812, when the fledgling United States again fought Great Britain. Necessity compelled the Americans to turn to all able-bodied men to fight the British, who attacked on several fronts. The redcoats organized an invasion of the United States from Canada. A British force landed in the upper Chesapeake Bay and marched on Washington, D.C., to burn the White House. And, late in the war, the British attacked north through Louisiana to capture New Orleans.

Just before the Battle of Lake Erie, where the Americans won the engagement by turning back the British invasion from Canada, Oliver Hazard Perry, the victorious U.S. commander, asked Commodore Isaac Chauncey, Great Lakes naval commander, for reinforcements to meet the oncoming British force. Chauncey sent him a number of Negro seamen, and when Perry complained about "this motley set of blacks, soldiers and boys," Chauncey replied: "I have yet to learn that the color of the skin or the cut and trimmings of the coat can affect a man's qualifications or usefulness. I have fifty blacks on board this ship and many of them are my best men." Perry sailed with his diverse crew and won one of the decisive battles of the War of 1812. Some 45 of his 432 men were black.

As the British closed on New Orleans in 1814 many citizens feared that a militia battalion of free Negroes, established under French rule prior to the Louisiana Purchase of 1803, would side with the British. Gen. Andrew Jackson, commander of U.S. forces gathering to counter the British, wrote the governor of Louisiana and stated: "Distrust them and you make them your enemies, place confidence in them, and you engage them by every dear and honorable tie to the interest of the country, who extends to them equal rights and privileges with white men." The Negro battalion performed admirably at the Battle of New Orleans, and Jackson singled them out as having "manifested great bravery."

The Battle of New Orleans essentially was the last time that blacks served their country in the army for many years, despite their courage and willingness to fight for their country during the War of 1812. A general order from the adjutant and inspector general's office of the United States Army stated: "No Negro or Mulatto will be received as a recruit of the Army." None were called until midway through the Civil War.

During the Civil War it took the better part of two years before blacks were permitted to fight. When war was declared in 1861 President Abraham Lincoln issued a call for volunteers, and blacks flocked to recruiting stations. The call was intended for whites only and the blacks were turned away. Despite the fact that the Civil War was a conflict to abolish slavery and that blacks had fought heroically in the Revolution and the War of 1812, whites believed that no black man would stand to fight against a white man in battle regardless of the cause.

Denied the right to fight, blacks lobbied Congress, the president, and state and local governments. They organized volunteer military units and began drilling in preparation for war. It wasn't until 1863 that states were permitted to raise volunteer Negro regiments and a special bureau for black soldiers was established in the Adjutant General's office to handle the recruitment, training and disposition of "United States Colored Troops." The army developed a special manual for training black troops during the Civil War, as they would do again during World War II.

The bulk of the black troops who served during the Civil War were organized into 163 federal regiments and two state regiments. Altogether their numbers totaled 178,985 men, and most served in the infantry. The black units were, for the most part, led by white officers. Fewer than 100 officers were black.

The black infantry units of the Civil War served in 449 engagements, 39 of which were considered important battles, and suffered 36,847 casualties. Secretary of War Edwin Stanton reported that these troops were engaged in some of the heaviest fighting of the war, and Adjutant General Lorenzo Thomas praised them for their fighting qualities, particularly their proficiency at hand-to-hand combat. Gen. Benjamin Butler commended the black troops who served under his command:

> In this army you have been treated as soldiers, not as laborers. You have shown yourselves worthy of the uniform you wear. The best officers of the Union seek to command you. Your bravery has won the admiration of those who would be your masters. Your patriotism, fidelity and courage have illustrated the best qualities of manhood. With the bayonet you have unlocked the iron barred gates of prejudice, and opened new fields of freedom, liberty and equality of right to yourselves and to your race.

Many black veterans must have thought that they would now be accepted as equals among their white brethren. Like James Strawder eighty years later, they assumed that by spilling their blood they would gain their dignity as men. It was not to be.

The period after the Civil War did bring some measure of respect to black soldiers. Congress authorized the creation of six Negro regiments, later reduced to four: the 9th and 10th Cavalry and the 24th and 25th Infantry, whose men came to be known as the "Buffalo Soldiers." While segregated, these regiments were established to recognize and reward the valor of the black soldiers in the Civil War. Their reputation was such that many white officers vied to command these units, which were proficient and famous as Indian fighters on the American frontier. General "Black Jack" Pershing, who later commanded the American Expeditionary Force in France during World War I, got his start and nickname commanding Negro troops in the 10th U.S. Cavalry.

The future General of the Army praised his black cavalrymen: "It has been an honor, which I am proud to claim, to have been at one time a member of that intrepid organization of the Army which has always added glory to the military history of America—the 10th Cavalry."

During the Spanish-American War in 1898 and 1899 a number of additional Negro regiments were raised. The four regular "Buffalo Soldier" regiments conducted themselves well under fire, with the 9th and 10th Cavalry joining Teddy Roosevelt's Rough Riders in their charge up San

Juan Hill. The four regular black regiments, along with the newly raised all-black 48th and 49th Infantry Regiments, were later deployed against guerrillas in the Philippines from 1899 to 1902 during the American occupation of the islands following the Spanish-American War.

Like their counterparts in the black platoons forty-five years later, the African-American troops who fought in the Philippines believed their service "would enhance rather than degrade their manhood . . . and hoped that a display of patriotism would help dissipate racial prejudice against them," wrote Willard B. Gatewood Jr., in his collection of letters from black troops during the Spanish-American War entitled *Smoked Yankees*.

Many blacks serving in the Philippines, however, found the conditions of their service intolerable and their treatment by white officers and enlisted men reprehensible. "Throughout their tenure in the Philippines, Negro soldiers were subjected to insults and discriminatory treatment by their white comrades. The men of the Twenty-fifth Infantry had scarcely landed in 1899 when, as they marched into Manila, a white spectator yelled: 'What are all you coons doing here?' White troops not only refused to salute black officers but also delighted in taunting Negro soldiers by singing, 'All coons look alike to me,' and 'I don't like a nigger nohow,' " Gatewood wrote.

The Buffalo Soldiers serving in the Philippines rebelled against subduing a people of their own color, and some were so angered by their treatment by white army comrades that they deserted and joined the guerrillas fighting the Americans. "Of all Negro soldiers who deserted the most famous was David Fagan of the Twenty-fourth Infantry. He accepted a commission in the insurgent army and for two years wreaked havoc upon the American forces," Gatewood states.

The next military engagement for the black regiments was in 1916 during the expedition along the Mexican border to subdue the Mexican bandit Pancho Villa. The 10th Cavalry joined U.S. forces hunting down Villa under the command of "Black Jack" Pershing.

With the turn of the twentieth century racial hostility and discrimination toward blacks in the United States became increasingly virulent, and by the time America entered World War I in 1917, the army's policy of segregation had become even more hardened. Despite the acceptance of blacks in the Civil War and in the Indian Wars of the later nineteenth century, the white military establishment during World War I had nothing but contempt for black troops. The seasoned black cavalry and infantry regiments that could have been used in France sat out the war guarding U.S. possessions.

The vast majority of the 367,410 blacks drafted into the military during World War I were assigned to service units or were used as laborers.

Blacks generally were excluded from combat service and the few who saw action were in the newly established 92nd and 93rd Divisions, which were commanded by white officers. Both divisions served on the western front and the white American officers of the 92nd Division reported that their troops performed poorly. Ironically, the four regiments of the 93rd Division served under French command and were highly praised by experienced French officers for their fighting abilities.

The effectiveness of the 92nd and 93rd Divisions in the trenches in World War I was long debated after the war. Whites saw the deficiencies in the divisions whereas blacks saw the strengths. During the war, however, newspapers carried accounts of the bravery and fighting qualities of the black soldiers on the western front. In one account the writer stated: "American Negro troops have proved their value as fighters in the line east of Verdun on June 12. . . . The Germans attempted a raid in that sector but were completely repulsed by the Negroes. The Boches [Germans] began a terrific bombardment at one minute after midnight . . . In the midst of this inferno the Negroes coolly stuck to their posts, operating machine guns and automatic rifles and keeping up such a steady barrage that the German infantry failed to penetrate the American lines."

The French army thought enough of the black troops' performance to award the croix de guerre to three regiments of the 93rd Division, to one company of the 4th Regiment, and to the 1st Battalion of the 376th Infantry Regiment of the 92nd Division.

The *Literary Digest* lauded one of the regiments: "Exceptional tho [*sic*] the award of the coveted French War Cross may be, the deeds of valor by which this Negro regiment won it are less exceptional than typical of the way in which all our colored troops measured up to the demands of the war. . . . They proved their valor on countless occasions, and it was one of the common stories that Jerry feared the 'Smoked Yankees' more than any other troops he met."

But white commanders in the U.S. Army discounted these reports. Many observers, however, believed that if there were deficiencies in the black divisions, much of the blame had to be attributed to the army itself. Black troops consistently received inferior training and equipment, and their officers were less motivated, since most did not choose their commands. These attitudes continued through the 1920s and 1930s and prevailed at the start of World War II. Army historian Ulysses Lee quoted the former white commanding officer of the black 368th Infantry Regiment, 93rd Division: "I consider the Negro should not be used as a combat soldier."

Lee also quoted the former white commander of the 367th Infantry Regiment, 92nd Division, also an all-black unit led by white officers: "As fighting troops, the Negro must be rated as second class material, this due primarily to his inferior intelligence and lack of mental and moral quali-fications."

"It was clear that most commanders of Negro combat troops in World War I had little to recommend for the employment of Negro troops in a future war except labor duties under white supervision," wrote Ulysses Lee in his work *The Employment of Negro Troops,* part of the U.S. Army's official history of World War II.

4
·
BLACKS IN WORLD WAR II

WORLD WAR II BROUGHT little change of attitude toward race in the army although by war's end there were signs of change. For the most part African-American troops continued to serve in segregated service units. Their work went largely unrecognized, but their performance in these noncombatant roles was invaluable. Blacks built airfields, cleared mines, maintained roads and rail lines, served as medics, and drove the trucks that supplied the armies.

The Red Ball Express, the famed military trucking line manned largely by blacks, was established in late August 1944, after the Allies finally broke the enemy's grip on Normandy in late July. The pursuit of the German armies across France by the Americans was so rapid that the U.S. armies outran their supplies. Allied bombing had destroyed the French rail network, so the only method of supplying the combat troops was by truck.

Black Transportation Corps troops drove thousands of two-and-a-half-ton trucks, nicknamed "Jimmies," in the night-and-day Red Ball operation that kept critical supplies rolling to the front. Most military observers believe that the Red Ball maintained the momentum of the Allied advance in the late summer of 1944 by delivering gasoline, ammunition, rations, and medical supplies to frontline troops. Without Red Ball the war in Europe would have been prolonged.

But most young African-Americans were still denied the right to fight; while many would have volunteered for the infantry had they been given the opportunity, they couldn't join white combat units, and there were few infantry slots available in black fighting units. Young men such as James Rookard, an African-American growing up in Cleveland in the 1930s, idolized the Buffalo Soldiers of the frontier and dreamed of one day being a combat soldier, especially a cavalryman. "That uniform! Every young fella wanted to be in the cavalry," Rookard mused. But he was sadly disappointed when assigned as a truck driver during World War II.

"I always wanted to be in combat from the time I was a teenager," recalled James Strawder. "I was always fighting. I've been fightin' all my life." Strawder was educationally and physically qualified for the infantry but spent most of his army career during World War II as a laborer.

The irony was that while many blacks yearned to be in the infantry, most whites wanted no part of this combat arm but had no say about their assignment. The army's Research Division, Special Services Branch, surveyed white soldiers in infantry divisions in 1943 and found that only 5 percent would choose the infantry while only 2 percent said they would choose the armored forces. The army tried to make the infantry attractive to whites and the research branch noted that the army was making "a broadside attempt to raise the prestige of the infantry among our soldiers."

The 761st Tank Battalion was one of the few black combat units to serve in World War II, and it was the first black tank unit ever organized in the U.S. Army. From the outset the men in its ranks carried a heavy burden, and they knew that if they faltered in combat their behavior would confirm racist notions of inferiority and cowardice. The responsibility of these tankers was reinforced when Lt. Gen. George S. Patton Jr., commander of the U.S. Third Army, under whom the 761st began service in Europe, addressed them when they arrived at the front.

Lee quoted General Patton: "Men, you're the first Negro tankers to ever fight in the American Army. I would never have asked for you if you weren't good. I have nothing but the best in my Army. I don't care what color you are, so long as you go up there and kill those Kraut sonsabitches. Everyone has their eyes on you and is expecting great things from you. Most of all, your race is looking forward to you. Don't let them down, don't let me down!"

It was a tall order for the 761st during its first days in the ETO. The battalion was committed to combat on November 7, 1944, and during 183 days in action the 761st was variously attached to the 26th, the 71st, the 87th, the 95th, the 79th, the 103rd, and 71st Divisions, the 17th Airborne Corps, and the XVI Corps. It fought in France, Belgium, Holland, Luxembourg, Germany, and Austria.

Lee noted that the performance of the 761st with the 26th Division elicited special commendation from the corps commander: "I consider the 761st Tank Battalion to have entered combat with such conspicuous courage and success as to warrant special commendation.

"The speed with which they adapted themselves to the front line under most adverse weather conditions, the gallantry with which they faced some of Germany's finest troops, and the confident spirit with which they emerged from their recent engagements in the vicinity of Dieuze, Morville les Vic, and Guebling entitle them surely to consider themselves the veteran 761st."

Several all-black field artillery units fought well and gained recognition in Europe. The first of these units landed in France in June 1944 and immediately supported beleaguered ground forces in Normandy. In December 1944, during the Battle of the Bulge, black artillery units heavily engaged the Germans.

The 578th Field Artillery Battalion demonstrated the courage and tenacity of black troops. During the Bulge, the 578th fought off attacking enemy forces and then joined white artillery battalions in the retreat to Allied lines. Lee stated that their white commander lauded their valor under fire: "The steadiness and determination of all concerned in this trying moment when a heavy artillery battalion was fighting a rear guard action is worthy of the highest praise."

The black 969th Field Artillery Battalion supported the 101st Airborne Division at Bastogne during the Battle of the Bulge. Gen. Maxwell D. Taylor, commander of the 101st, praised its performance.

"The Officers and Men of the 101st Airborne Division wish to express to your command [the 969th] their appreciation of the gallant support rendered by the 969th Field Artillery Battalion in the recent defense of Bastogne, Belgium. The success of this defense is attributable to the shoulder to shoulder cooperation of all units involved. This division is proud to have shared the Battlefield with your command. A recommendation for a unit citation of the 969th Field Artillery Battalion is being forwarded by this headquarters."

The army's two resurrected all-black infantry divisions, the 92nd and 93rd, didn't fare nearly as well and turned in what commanders judged to be mediocre performances. Once again, the leadership qualities of the white officers were suspect, since many considered it an insult and a mark of failure to command blacks. The 92nd Division fought in Italy, while the 93rd Division fought in the South Pacific but was used more as a labor force than a combat group.

As the war progressed, black leaders demanded a greater share of the combat action, and the army made concessions. Blacks, for example, were given their own fighter squadron because the Air Corps was segregated. The 99th Pursuit Squadron, the "Tuskegee Airmen," initially under the command of Lt. Col. Benjamin Davis Jr., son of the elder General Davis, won high praise for its performance in Europe. But the accolades came only after much hardship for "the Lonely Eagles," as the Tuskegee Airmen were initially called. In the beginning even the NAACP opposed the creation of a separate and segregated flying unit, fearing that it would continue the precedent of a segregated military. But the squadron was formed in 1941 and took wing in combat in 1943. As was the case with most other black units, initial reports of its combat proficiency were poor, and the Air Corps seriously considered disbanding the fliers.

Once again there were questions about whether the black pilots were being unfairly judged because the standards to which they were held were tougher than those for whites. In the end, however, the 99th found itself and turned in such a good performance that the Air Corps sent several more black squadrons to the Mediterranean theater to join the 99th and form the 332nd Fighter Group. Today the Tuskegee Airmen are regarded as heroes in the pantheon of World War II.

The men of the 99th Squadron carried a heavy burden to prove the worth of the black man in combat. Lt. Col. Benjamin O. Davis Jr. spoke to them of their burdens in 1943. Lee quoted excerpts of his speech:

It is a very significant fact, I believe, that all members of this organization were impressed at all times with the knowledge that the future of the colored man in the Air Corps probably would be dependent largely upon the manner in which they carried out their mission.

Hence, the importance of the work done by this squadron, the responsibility carried by every man, be he ground crewman or pilot, meant that very little pleasure was to be had by anyone until the experiment was deemed an unqualified success.

However, he [the individual airman] had the good sense to realize that the best means he had to defeat the end of supporters and philosophers who relegated him to a subsidiary role in the life of the United States was to do the job in such a way that the world would know that he was capable of performing a highly specialized and technical piece of the work in a creditable manner.

At all times every man realizes that the pleasures and relaxations that are available to men in other organizations are not available to him because his task is far greater, his responsibility is much heavier, and his reward is the advancement of his people.

Davis could have been speaking of the black platoons.

5

•

TRAINING IN THE UNITED STATES

IN 1940 THE AMERICAN army numbered about a half million men but contained only 4,700 black enlisted men and two black officers. The military was so segregated that when patriotic African-American civilians flocked to enlist in 1940 as they had at the outset of the Civil War, they were turned away because there was no place for them to serve.

Ironically, the government sensed the patriotism of its black citizens. A 1944 manual entitled *Leadership and the Negro Soldier* reported: "Negroes have been notably a loyal and patriotic group. One of their outstanding characteristics is the singlemindedness of their patriotism. They have no other country in which they owe or feel any degree of allegiance. They have neither cultural nor economic ties with kindred in any other lands. Therefore they have built in America a fine record of loyalty and willingness to support and defend their native land."

Nevertheless, at the beginning of the war blacks could not join such branches as the Tank Corps, the Army Air Corps, or the Signal Corps. When finally they were able to enlist, black recruits discovered that it was almost impossible to join the infantry. The ranks of the all-black 92nd and 93rd Divisions were quickly filled, and the all-black 2nd Cavalry Division was disbanded in North Africa in 1943 and its troops turned into laborers and stevedores.

Waymon Ransom, from Detroit, an infantryman with the 5th of K, had hoped to be an infantryman. "I had not intended to volunteer in nobody's army," Ransom recalled. "But I saw a series of ads in the paper about the last chance to volunteer and pick your branch of the service."

Ransom went to a Detroit recruiting office to enlist in the infantry. "All right," the recruiter said, "come back on Monday." Whether it was a setup, Ransom will never know, but Monday was "immediate induction day," when draft dodgers were rounded up and forcibly inducted into the army; Ransom was dragged in with everybody else. "You were under guard by MPs and we went up the stairs and you weren't getting out. I'd told my mother I'd be home and to fix me a real good meal. I didn't see home for six months."

Ransom kept requesting assignment to the 92nd or 93rd Divisions.

"They said, 'No! You will not go to the infantry. You will stay right here and do what we tell you to do.' " Ransom was told not to be disappointed because the 92nd and 93rd were being used to harvest crops in Arizona.

Ransom was shipped by troop train to an Alabama training base with other black recruits. On the journey south there was no kitchen car and the men had to detrain in a town along the way and walk to a black restaurant. As MPs escorted the recruits to dinner, one of the townsfolk attempted to run their column down with his automobile. Only armed intervention by the MPs prevented serious injury to the startled men. Northern blacks were learning the ways of the South.

Every black who served in World War II remembers the sense of despair upon learning that he was heading to the American South for training. Bruce Wright recalled boarding a troop train in New York and assuming he was heading west to a training base. When he awoke from a nap and learned that the train had passed through Washington, D.C., heading south, his heart sank.

One black inductee wrote President Roosevelt about his fears of being trained and stationed in the South. "I have an unholy fear, not of the enemy, but strangely enough of my own fellow Americans. . . . I pray that I will not hear on the morrow that one of my relations or friends has been killed by a fellow citizen because his face is black."

General Davis remarked that training black recruits in Dixie seriously affected their proficiency as soldiers, and noted that "training Negroes in the South is two strikes against them already; they would rather train in forty degree below zero weather anywhere else."

Life for blacks in southern army camps during World War II was a horror, and as the army expanded to include millions of men, conflict between white and black GIs exploded. Black troops no longer passively accepted segregation and discrimination. The summer of 1943 brought severe strain between the races on and off military bases in the country. Army historian Ulysses Lee in his history, *The Employment of Negro Troops,* noted:

> By early summer, the harvest of racial antagonism was beginning to assume bumper proportions. Serious disorders occurred at Camp Van Dorn, Mississippi; Camp Stewart, Georgia; Lake Charles, Louisiana; March Field and Camp San Luis Obispo, California; Fort Bliss, Texas: Camp Phillips, Kansas; Camp Breckinridge, Kentucky; and Camp Shenango, Pennsylvania. Other camps had lesser disorders and rumors of unrest.
>
> The disorders of 1943 differed from those of preceeding years. They involved, for the most part, a larger number of troops. They occurred more frequently in the camps themselves where the possibility of mass conflict between men of Negro and white units was greater. . . . Two of

the disorders, those at Camps Van Dorn and Stewart, were especially serious, both for their potentialities and for their effects on the revision of plans for the employment of Negro troops.

The disturbances at Camp Van Dorn still reverberate. Rumors persist that the army covered up a massacre of some 1,200 black troops of the 364th Infantry Regiment at Van Dorn in 1943. The 364th was transferred to the Centreville, Mississippi, base, where the troops immediately tangled with local residents. There were beatings, even alleged killings, of black troops when the blacks ventured into the community. The soldiers retaliated and the violence escalated.

According to one investigative report, conducted nearly a half century later, MPs were called in one night to quell disturbances involving the 364th in the late fall of 1943. According to Carrol Case in his 1998 book, *The Slaughter: An American Atrocity,*

> A special riot squad armed with .45 caliber pistols and machine guns took charge. They shot everything that moved, until nothing did; not one defenseless soldier got away. When the shooting stopped, over 1,200 members of the 364th were slaughtered. Their bodies were loaded on boxcars and stacked inside like pulpwood. They were hauled off by train to the south gate of the base where they were buried and limed in long trenches dug by bulldozers.
>
> Following this bloodbath, records were not only altered but destroyed. The Army notified next-of-kin of the victims, saying that the soldiers were killed in the line of duty. It was easy to explain that the bodies were not recoverable, and no further explanation was necessary. Foul play was never suspected during wartime.

The rumors persisted for a half century, and in 1999 Mississippi congressman Bennie Thompson and the NAACP revisited the issue. The army committed thousands of hours and hundreds of thousands of dollars to answer the allegations of a massacre and issued its report on December 23, 1999. "There is no documentary evidence whatsoever that any unusual or inexplicable loss of personnel occurred," the army stated. Bogus or true, the issue is that the treatment of black troops during World War II was often so horrendous that blacks believed that an event like a massacre at Van Dorn could easily have occurred.

At Camp Stewart resentful black troops from the 264th Infantry Regiment rampaged through a nearby town following rumors that a black woman had been raped and her husband murdered by white troops and white MPs. Several MPs were wounded and one was killed in the ensuing melee.

Historian Lee reported: "In the aftermath of the riot . . . a board of officers appointed at Camp Stewart to investigate determined that the disturbance was essentially an outgrowth of long pent-up emotions and resentments. The majority of the Negro soldiers were convinced that justice and fair treatment were not to be had by them in neighboring communities and that the influence of these communities was strongly reflected in the racial policies of the command at Camp Stewart."

Much of the trouble at southern military camps can be traced to the army's disregard for the rights of blacks in the military. One army memo openly stated: "It is essential that there be a clear understanding that the army has no authority or intention to participate in social reform." The military left the control of southern military bases in the hands of local commanders who had no interest in equal and fair treatment for blacks.

The army's policies toward blacks were also based on outdated demographics and a lack of understanding of the social changes that had occurred in the United States since World War I. In the First World War one in five blacks came from the North. In World War II, one in three blacks came from the North. During World War I only 33 percent of blacks had attended high school. In World War II 63 percent of blacks had gone to high school.

One report made by the Research Division in 1942 noted these vast social changes that had taken place within the black population of the United States since World War I. "Only careful research would demonstrate the extent to which the northward shift of the Negro population . . . and vast improvements in school has created new problems for the army." The report added that a better-educated black population, unused to the crippling discriminatory environment of the South, was "facing patterns of life new to them."

One black soldier wrote from a Florida camp: "When the average man of color leaves his home, he leaves it with the feeling that he and his country are in serious danger. Although he is denied the full benefits of democracy, he resolves to make the best of the situation and to crush the common foe. But before the first week of his service ends he finds himself in almost the position as the enemies of the land. He is told that he cannot fight and is in the Army to labor. They look upon him as a second class citizen and he often feels he is not wanted. He is hounded, tormented and humiliated. His camp becomes his prison and his fellow Americans his tormentors."

Similar experiences and observations about the raw discrimination on southern army bases changed Arthur Holmes's attitude toward segregation, as it altered the attitude of many young blacks of that era. Holmes had never paid much attention to segregation, but, "they were doing things in the army during World War II that were outrageous."

Holmes was shipped in 1943 to Camp Shelby, Mississippi, where he was unprepared for the racial climate, which differed from that in his hometown of Los Angeles. Holmes recalled boarding a bus in Mississippi while in uniform and standing in the front with the whites. In Los Angeles, blacks sat wherever they wanted on public transportation and Holmes was ignorant of the mores of the South. Not only was he standing in the "whites only" front of the bus, he was flirting with a white girl. Suddenly a black man approached from the rear.

"Boy, you come on with me."

"I said, 'What's the matter?' "

"You'll get us all killed if you mess with that white girl."

"She was making eyes at me, I didn't do anything."

"Boy, it don't make no difference. Come back to the rear and sit your butt down."

Holmes recalled another humiliating experience. "Our barracks were across from a place where white soldiers were housed and I recognized one of the white guys. He had been the piano player at one of the clubs where I had worked in Los Angeles. We ran over to each other and were hugging each other and this white noncom comes up and separated us and says to me, 'You get over there with your people,' and he said to my buddy, 'You get over there with your people.' "

Segregation came as a shock to Clayton Des Journette, a member of the 5th of K. Raised in Seattle, he attended integrated schools where the races mixed and blacks were included in school functions. "In the army he couldn't understand segregation because he wasn't used to it," said Hattie Des Journette, his widow.

The pervasiveness of segregation was new even to some white soldiers. "I was surprised at first to find that the camp [Fort Knox, Kentucky] was segregated," remembered Joe Carcaterra, a white soldier in the 20th Armored Division. "But I soon stopped noticing, assuming that it was just that way in the South. Blacks were billeted in tents, while we were in barracks—barracks that had been built for World War I. Even in marching we were segregated by color. I never saw the colors mixed."

Holmes was sufficiently light skinned that when he joined the army he was listed as Caucasian on his army papers.

"Are you a black or a white boy?" a doctor asked Holmes during an army physical exam.

"Why do you ask?" Holmes responded with curiosity.

"Because it says here on your papers that you are white."

"I'm black," Holmes replied.

The doctor offered to send him to a white outfit but Holmes refused. "I said I've always been black and I think I'll stay black. People were very prejudiced in those days. I didn't want to go to some white outfit where somebody would pick on me. I could have been killed."

Military buses connected Camp Shelby with the nearby town, but white drivers often refused to stop for blacks. Holmes remembers one driver stopping and contemptuously informing a group of waiting black troops that he didn't pick up "niggers." The black GIs nearly overturned the bus.

Willfred Strange, a volunteer who served in the 69th Division in Germany, recalled a similar incident at Camp Claiborne, Louisiana. Blacks became so angry at post buses refusing to stop for them that they stormed and overturned a bus and set it afire. They then attacked the white troops exiting through the windows.

Camp Claiborne was the scene of a "disturbance" that was reported in the *Washington Times Herald* in which as many as sixteen thousand black troops armed themselves, mutinied, beat up their white officers, broke into arms lockers, and "shot up the works." At a press conference on September 14, 1944, Secretary of War Henry H. Stimson acknowledged that "there was a disturbance at Camp Claiborne" and that the matter was being investigated.

One constant source of anger among black troops was the respect with which the army treated German prisoners of war compared to its treatment of African-American soldiers. Holmes recalled black troops rampaging through a railroad dining car after they had been denied service while German POWs were seated for a meal.

Ransom's unit was detailed to guard a group of German prisoners being shipped by train to an internment camp in Indiana. "The blacks came back smokin' because when they passed through Kentucky and West Virginia the locals made no bones about their distaste at seeing whites guarded by blacks regardless of whether they were the enemy. At one stop the Germans were allowed to use the station bathrooms while the blacks were sent to the woods."

Ransom bitterly remembered a two-day train trip from Alabama to Camp Pickett, Virginia, on which he and his black comrades were never fed. "We left Alabama on a train that didn't have a chow car," Ransom said. "They gave us a bagged lunch of two sandwiches and a piece of fruit, but we didn't get on the train until late at night and then we didn't get anything to eat for two days. We stopped in the Atlanta railroad station, where the officers went to buy the troops some candy bars. But when the white girls saw whom it was for they refused to sell the officers anything.

And we weren't even allowed to stand in the main train depot."

One group of African-American recruits from the 514th Quartermaster Truck Regiment got a taste of "southern hospitality" when their unit was transferred in 1943 to Camp Pickett. Pickett was located in Blackstone, not far from Appomattox Court House, where Gen. Robert E. Lee surrendered his Army of Northern Virginia in 1865, and the base was named after Confederate general George E. Pickett, who led the disastrous Pickett's Charge at the Battle of Gettysburg.

Townspeople and white soldiers made life miserable for the 514th. There were confrontations and fights. "I knew better than to go into town," said James Chappelle, a soldier in C Company, 514th. "I was a hothead at that time and I knew I'd probably get hurt or hurt somebody." Sgt. James Blackwell, also a member of C Company, had to hire a cab to go on leave because white soldiers would not allow him on the bus that took the troops to the train station.

Clayton Des Journette was involved in an incident while stationed in Virginia in which blacks ransacked the lunch counter of a local store when they were refused service for a cup of coffee. The army confined the blacks to base until they were shipped overseas. "They did all that damage because they were being sent to fight to protect people who wouldn't even serve them a cup of coffee," Hattie Des Journette said.

Blacks also lived with the grotesque insult that the nation and the military refused to intermingle the blood of blacks and whites. In November 1941, the Red Cross established racially segregated blood banks even as it admitted that there was no scientific justification for the racial separation of blood. Red Cross administrators blamed the armed services for the decision.

The army's surgeon general defended the controversial practice as necessary to ensure the acceptance of a potentially unpopular program. Ignoring constant criticism from the NAACP and elements of the black press, the armed forces continued to demand segregated blood banks throughout the war. Negroes could appreciate the irony of the situation because it was a black doctor, Charles R. Drew, who had pioneered the plasma-extraction process and had directed the first Red Cross blood bank.

"We were bitter, very bitter about the things that were happening to us in the army," Holmes recalled. Even blacks raised in the South found their treatment in army camps intolerable. "With my being born in the South I knew the score," recalled Fred Watt, who served as a volunteer infantryman with the 2nd Division. "But the way we were treated in those camps was pretty horrible."

6

•

SHOW ME YOUR TAIL

"OH, IT WAS A lovely time," said Bradford Tatum, a black volunteer infantryman with the 12th Armored Division, describing his military service in England, where his unit, the 390th Engineer Battalion, was shipped in 1944. But he added, "It was a lovely time except when we ran into our own whites."

Black troops got some relief from segregation and the constant discrimination on U.S. training bases when they were assigned to England. Most went gladly. Arthur Holmes sailed on the *Queen Elizabeth,* and as the stately ship slipped out of New York Harbor, his main concern was surviving the war.

In prewar days up to three thousand passengers sailed on the luxury liner to and from Europe. Now the *Queen* was transformed into a troopship carrying sixteen thousand Americans to war. Big liners like the *Queen* made the transatlantic crossing alone, without antisubmarine escorts, because they cruised with such speed that German subs were unable to track and stalk them.

The troops aboard slept in shifts, with as many as three soldiers assigned to a bunk. The blacks were quartered in a separate section of the vessel but were allowed to wander around the ship. The *Queen* was under British control, and once beyond American shores the captain announced that henceforth there would be no color ban for black troops. The news was a blow to many whites aboard, and Holmes's company commander, a captain from Arkansas long steeped in segregation, reacted to the announcement by turning his back on his men and walking away in disgust.

Life aboard ship was pleasant. Cpl. Edwin L. Brice, a black soldier who had never been at sea before, described his impressions of one such voyage: "The sea was strange and new to these soldier landlubbers. Its vastness and ever-changing moods were sobering. Now, still and turquoise, later angry, gray and foaming, whipping up spray over the decks and causing the ship to dip and roll."

There were movies to attend, amateur theatrical productions, and the men could lose themselves in books and magazines. "In the evening, when open decks were cleared, the favorite pastime of many, was to stroll around the enclosed 'B' deck. Some of the boys formed impromptu vocal groups and gravitated to their chosen spot on the deck each evening to hold forth," Brice wrote.

England was seething with preparations for war, and more than a million American troops were stationed at bases and bivouac areas throughout the kingdom, many in isolated villages on the south coast. By D-Day the strength of American forces in Great Britain numbered more than 1,527,000, and to maintain this massive fighting force more than five million long tons of supplies had been landed. The blacks in the engineer, port, and truck battalions were at work, some building encampments, air bases, hardstands, and depots in preparation for the invasion, while others unloaded and distributed the supplies of war.

Holmes and Ransom were assigned to the 377th Engineer Battalion stationed in Cornwall with the task of building temporary bases for the infantry divisions training for the forthcoming invasion of France. Lawrence Boris drove a truck, while James Strawder dug drainage ditches around airfields and prepared graves in the American cemetery in Cambridge for U.S. airmen killed on missions over occupied Europe.

Willfred Strange's unit was shipped to England in June 1943 and was stationed in Derbyshire, not far from the city of Birmingham. "When we first got there the people were very gracious," Strange remembered. "We used to go to dances, socialize with them and play darts. They had never seen black people."

Strange was audacious enough to apply for a three-week seminar to be held at Oxford University that enabled soldiers of many nationalities to meet and discuss the war and the future peace.

"You got to be one crazy-ass nigger to think you're going to be accepted," his white platoon sergeant snorted. But Strange was admitted and befriended retired field marshal Lord Birdwood of the Indian army, who headed ANZAC forces (Australian and New Zealand Army Corps) during World War I and was later a corps commander on the western front. Birdwood lectured at Oxford. Strange also met with Harold Laski, the well-known British political scientist who was chairman of the British Labor Party. Laski introduced Strange to Una Marston, the Jamaican writer and poet, who was involved in the British League of Colored People. The experience was wonderfully uplifting for an American black for whom it would have been impossible to forge such friendships in the United States. Strange capped his Oxford experience with a three-week leave in London.

Bradford Tatum's unit was stationed near a Royal Air Force base where the men were sometimes invited by RAF pilots to hitch a ride in a bomber. "That would never have happened in the American air force," Tatum said.

Other companies of blacks experienced similar cordial treatment from the British. "We were invited everywhere; and considerable effort was made to keep us entertained. The facilities of practically every organization that could be of service, were made available to us," Brice recorded in his diary. The Central Methodist Church in the nearby village established a canteen, and the British Women's Volunteer Service provided a game room with table tennis, darts, a piano, radios, and magazines.

Many British women found nothing objectionable about dating black men. "Almost nightly dances were held and the girls came from all of the neighboring towns to attend them," Brice wrote. "Sometimes the band would play and things would really get gay in response to their torrid rhythms and harmonies. Things would really jump and the jitterbugging would do justice to Harlem's home of happy feet, the Savoy."

Blacks soon found their turf invaded by white American troops, who transplanted American racism overseas. For some blacks this created a paradox. While Great Britain was largely free of the discrimination and segregation of the United States, the attitudes of American whites became exaggerated in England. As a consequence the racial climate in England was sometimes worse than in the United States.

In particular, many American white troops could not tolerate the idea of blacks dating white English girls or drinking beer with whites in the same pubs. "When the air force guys came to our area they said, 'Oh my God, look at these goddamned niggers with these white girls,' " Willfred Strange said.

Relationships and romances between black troops and white English girls were common. Clayton Des Journette had an affair with a young English woman and lived with her whenever he had leave from the 366th Engineers. The affair ended, however, when Des Journette was shipped to France shortly after the Allies landed in France. He wrote often to her but his letters went unanswered and he never saw her again.

"If you were lucky enough to get a white lady, so be it," said James Rookard. "All the guys were doing it. African-Americans had to have women. They were away from home. But the white Americans couldn't stand for an African-American to be with a white lady. They were just that way."

In September 1942, General Eisenhower described the British attitude toward race relations in a letter to Maj. Gen. Alexander D. Surles, chief of the War Department Public Relations Branch:

Here we have a very thickly populated country that is devoid of racial consciousness. They know nothing at all about the conventions and

habits that have been developed in the U.S. in order to preserve segregation in social activity. . . . To most British people, including the village girls—even those of perfectly fine character—the Negro soldier is
just another man, rather fascinating because he is unique in their experience, a jolly fellow and with money to spend. Our own white soldiers,
seeing a girl walk down the street with a Negro, frequently see themselves as protectors of the weaker sex and believe it necessary to inter-
vene even to the extent of using force, to let her know what she's doing.

Ike issued orders that an official policy of segregation by American
forces in Britain would not be tolerated. But trying to do away with
centuries of prejudice could not be accomplished with the stroke of a pen.

An English woman who recalled meeting African-American troops
when she was a thirteen-year-old schoolgirl during the war summed up
the British fascination with black American troops. Norman Longmate
described the encounter in the book *The G.I.s: The Americans in Britain,
1942–1945.*

Huge vehicles dominated the lanes and quickly all of us children were
off to investigate. The only dark Americans I had seen were on films or
in history books, so it was shattering and fascinating to see not one darkie
soldier but hundreds . . . The thing which stood out most were the palms
of their hands . . . almost pink, the sparkling white teeth and glinting
eyes against the dark skin, the gentleness and big stature.

"They quickly made friends and we were happy to sit and listen.
We didn't need storybooks, here were people of a strange land, speaking
a different kind of English, a different colour; this was a storybook come
to life. Colour prejudice just didn't happen. We learnt they were just
like us underneath, same joys, fears, love and feelings.

The Brits sometimes had amusing encounters with American black
troops. Longmate wrote of one English girl who knew she was nearing
home at night because "the coloured troops provided a curious landmark
for her as she walked home in the black-out, as 'they had a watch-tower
from which they surveyed the main Evesham-Worcester road, situated
near the Fladbury crossroads. . . . I could see the whites of their eyes
gleaming in the dark, and . . . I knew I was nearing my destination.' "

Another remembered being frightened one night "at the sight of two
apparently disembodied 'white eyes' and a mouthful of 'white teeth' coming towards her after dark." Still another made a blind date with a Yank
in a blacked-out bus stop. "A week later the soldier showed up at her
doorstep, the biggest, blackest Negro she had ever seen."

Many British people found the blacks more courteous and correct than American white soldiers and were appalled by the whites' racial attitudes and prejudices. One racially motivated trick, played by American white soldiers on their black comrades, was to tell the British, children in particular, that blacks really were monkeys and had tails. "The Caucasian Americans were telling this to the British," Rookard remembered. "One time I got out of my truck and this little girl came up to me and started walking around me and she kept looking. I said, 'What's the matter,' and she said, 'I don't see it.' I said, 'Well what are you looking for?' She said, 'I don't see your tail?' That's the way they were, the Caucasians."

Arthur Holmes remembered being on a date with an English girl and when the clock struck midnight she said, "Art, it's past midnight, where's your tail?"

Stories of white prejudice and acts of violence against blacks were legion. "Hell, you know that every time black and white soldiers got together there would be fights," said James Chappelle, a truck driver and a comrade of Rookard's. Whites and blacks came to blows so often that the military imposed "black and white nights" in villages such as Newton Abbot in Devon.

Even then black troops often were permitted into towns and villages only when accompanied by one of their officers and "snowdrops" (MPs), who were present to ensure that whites and blacks did not mingle. "There had to be one officer and one snowdrop every time they [blacks] went on pass. If you had more then ten men you took two MPs," said Charles Stevenson, a white lieutenant who commanded a black unit. "You'd drop the men off and check in with the local police station to tell them where you were, how many men were in town, and then we could do what we wanted. But we usually stayed with the men."

Stevenson barely succeeded one night in dissuading a group of his black troops from arming themselves and returning to Plymouth, seeking revenge against white sailors with whom they had fought earlier in the evening:

"I heard a lot of noise in our arms tent and went in there and there's about ten or twelve of my guys, some of them half tanked. 'We're goin' down there and clean those whitey sons of bitches out,' they all said. I talked to them for half an hour and talked them out of it and made sure the arms stayed locked and put a guard on the rifles. We went downtown and reported the incident to the MPs and they went looking for these white guys, but this was just before the invasion and the town was filled with sailors and ships."

Another white officer interceded when groups of whites and blacks confronted each other in a Salisbury parking lot after one of the blacks had allegedly knifed a white soldier. The white troops were southerners and taunted the blacks with racial slurs. Officers and MPs were finally able to control the situation.

One white officer who commanded black troops during the war remembered that some of his men carried razor blades in the rims of their overseas caps with the blade end facing out. In a brawl with whites they would whip off the hat and swing it so that the blade slashed the victim. Holmes said blacks also became proficient at using the buckle of their garrison belts to thrash attacking whites. They would wrap the belt tightly around their fist with the buckle facing out and use it like a pair of brass knuckles.

Ransom recalled blacks carrying the biggest knives they could find to defend themselves against whites. "The first thing we did when we got to England was to go to a machine shop and sharpen our bayonets," Ransom said. "We used them in lieu of machetes, but we also used them for protection."

Despite the problems of race, the business of war was paramount, and the preparations for the invasion soon consumed everyone's attention. Arthur Betts, a volunteer infantryman in the 99th Division, wrote off the problems of race in Great Britain as a peculiarly American problem, a "southern custom" that was exported to England. Blacks tried to ignore it and enjoy their stay in the British Isles as best they could. "Somehow we lived through it," Betts said.

7

•

FRANCE

ISSUES OF SEX AND race followed the American armies to France after
D-Day, June 6, 1944, and white soldiers still could not tolerate the blacks
dating or mingling with French women, many of whom found African-
American soldiers intriguing. In one army survey some white officers listed
the principal recreation of black soldiers as "white women." It added, "In
fact, in many localities in this theater [the ETO] no other type of women
are available."

"French women were fascinated by those men," said Joe Carcaterra.
Black drivers on the Red Ball Express recalled the ease with which they
could rendezvous with French women who hailed them from the roadsides
as they sped along to deliver supplies to the front.

Chester Jones, a black Red Ball driver, experienced one harrowing
moment while with a black buddy and two prostitutes. They were the
only patrons in a Paris bar and his friend went upstairs with one of the
women while Jones had a drink with the other. Two drunken white soldiers entered and one took offense that Jones was with a white woman.

"You black sons of bitches don't sit with white women at home, and
I'll be damned if you'll do it here while I'm around." The soldier drew a
.45-caliber pistol and marched Jones outside with the gun shoved into his
back. Jones was surprised that he wasn't murdered. The white soldier only
warned him to stay away from white women.

While proximity to the front in France had a moderating effect on
racism in the army, it by no means ended it. Entertainment facilities,
including Red Cross centers, generally remained segregated. "Don't talk
to me about the Red Cross," said Harold Robinson. "For all the good
they did they weren't worth a damn to us blacks." In some places French
towns were off limits to black soldiers.

There were other humiliations. Many African-American soldiers were
bored and angry at being assigned menial work while the glory went to
whites. Most of the blacks in engineering units were little more than
laborers who used their brawn to repair roads, bridges, and railroad tracks.
"I wanted to get in there and get the war over with," Strawder said. "I'd
been digging ditches and doing all that crap for almost two years. The

army was just bullshitting around. I said if I get in there I'd kill all those MFs and get it over with."

Strawder still dreamed of becoming an infantryman but was again assigned to Graves Registration, this time in Normandy, burying the dead from D-Day whose bodies continued to wash ashore. The fighting among the hedgerows resulted in many more American killed. "There were thousands of dead," Strawder said. "We didn't bag them or anything, we'd just wrap them in a blanket or in whatever else we had, carry them up to the cemetery, and put them down there all lined up." Bulldozers dug trenches that served as mass graves.

The dead were all white, but Strawder and his black comrades saw that all had decent burials. "We were very honorable with those dead. You want to do the best job you can and you're feeling sorry for all these fellows, yet thankful because by the grace of God, it's not me."

The grave-digging details gave way to building holding pens for the thousands of German POWs captured in the battles for France in the late summer of 1944. Strawder recalled with amusement that the American guards were threatened with court-martial if they allowed prisoners to escape at night. But instead of missing prisoners, there were often more Germans in the pens the next morning than the night before. Demoralized enemy soldiers would sneak into the camps rather than fight on with the battered Wehrmacht that retreated in disarray to the German frontier.

Bill Windley, who served as a volunteer infantryman with the 1st Division, was equally frustrated with his work in the ETO. Windley graduated from high school in 1942 and enrolled in North Carolina A&T State University in Greensboro, where he joined Army ROTC. When the war began, Windley dropped out of college, expecting the army to make use of his education and military training. But the army had no use for his skills. Intelligence, education, training, strength of character, all the attributes the army sought in its white youths, were ignored in its black youths.

Windley was assigned to a Quartermaster Corps port battalion unloading ships on the Continent. It was critical work, but to Windley it was menial and demeaning. "I just felt my skills were beyond loading and unloading ships. I resented the work." When the call went out for black infantrymen, Windley was an eager volunteer. "I was gung ho."

Bradford Tatum had a college degree and was qualified to be an officer. "One of the things that disgruntled me most in the army was that I passed the test to go to OCS [Officer Candidate School], but they wouldn't let me go." Tatum became a company clerk in the 390th Engineers and was the first in his unit to see the orders from Generals Eisenhower and Lee asking for black volunteers. He signed up immediately.

A number of the infantrymen in the 5th of K, Arthur Holmes, Waymon Ransom, James Oliver, Bernard Bailey, Lester Boudreau, and Harry Lucky, served together in France in the 377th Engineers. Holmes was a platoon sergeant and Ransom was a sergeant and the regimental surveyor. The duty was good but humdrum.

When the 377th was shipped to France in July 1944, a month after D-Day, the men began mine-clearing operations around the invasion beaches. Later, they were assigned to assorted engineering duties with Gen. George S. Patton's Third Army. "We did whatever work was required until we got to Paris. From Paris on we did railroad repair until the Third Army stalled in front of Metz and then we transferred to the Seventh Army," Ransom said.

"We were like troubleshooters," Holmes added. "When there was roadwork to be done, the 377th was called in. When there were roadblocks to be destroyed or stumps to be cleared, the 377th got the job. We rebuilt bridges [and] railroad trestles and replaced or repaired miles of track that had been destroyed by both sides.

"We also did some combat work but never got credit for it," Holmes said. He led teams of men who occasionally found themselves operating behind enemy lines as they inspected the railroad network in northeastern France. As the Germans made a hasty retreat the Americans used every means available to haul tons of munitions, gasoline, and food forward to the front. At first trucks carried most of the matériel, but later the railroads became critical in keeping the combat forces supplied. Holmes and his team followed in the wake of the infantry and armor to check the tracks, bridges, and service roads for demolition charges and booby traps left by the retreating enemy. On several occasions they saw distant soldiers in gray-green uniforms going about their daily business and realized they had pushed through gaps in the front lines and followed the tracks into enemy-held territory.

"We were once walking down this railroad line and I got challenged by this white boy," Holmes remembered. "He said, 'Halt!'

"I said, 'What's wrong with you, boy?'

"He says, 'Hands up.'

"He's standing there and I say, 'Are you American?'

"He says, 'Yeah.'

"I says, 'What the hell do you think I am? You ever see any blacks in the German army?'

"The white boy broke up and started laughing and says, 'Do you know you're coming from German lines?'

"I told him we had been sent down the lines to inspect the track and he said he was waiting for his buddies who were coming to blow them up. I pleaded with him, 'Please don't blow that track. We're trying to clear it for supplies to come through.' We then sat around and had a few drinks and laughs, then he went his way and we went our way."

Those not assigned to work details often drove trucks, as did Lawrence Boris with the 366th Engineers, and Edward Jackson, also with the 366th, who later fought with E Company, 395th Regiment, 99th Division.

Leonard Rife, a volunteer infantryman with the 12th Armored Division, was involved in harbor and highway construction in England and France with the 1313th General Services Engineers. Before being assigned as a company clerk, Bradford Tatum drove a truck for the 390th Engineer Battalion, which was detailed to rebuild the bomb-damaged railroads across France.

Arthur Betts was assigned to an engineering outfit in North Africa in 1943 and served with the unit through Tunisia, Sicily, and Italy before making the invasion of southern France in August 1944. David Skeeters, who became platoon sergeant with the 5th of K, also served with the engineers in North Africa and Italy, where his most vivid memory was not of war but of the eruption of Mount Vesuvius near Naples in March 1944.

Fred Watt, a volunteer infantryman with the 12th Armored Division, was assigned as an instructor with the 1314th Engineers. "The army put me on cadre to train these guys," Watt said. "They figured they'd better give some of these colored boys ammunition and guns if they were going to war."

Being in a service unit was so much a part of the black experience in World War II that the historian Ulysses Lee wrote: "To many white troops and commanders, the sole Negro troops seen in overseas theaters were those in the ports and rear areas. This, coupled with rumors [of poor performance] about the two Negro divisions, left a strong impression that Negro troops were not only used for little else, but also that they were fitted for nothing else."

Most of the blacks in engineering and service units never got close enough to the front to fire a shot in anger. They toiled in virtual anonymity in rear-area bases throughout Europe and the world. Historian Lee best described their plight when he added: "There were few heroics and few chances for them. These units' employment careers, in general, were humdrum, their efficiency run-of-the-mine, their problems only ameliorated and not solved by their assignment to overseas duties."

For many of the black volunteers, the only way out of their wearisome existence was the infantry.

8

·

A SPECIAL APPEAL FROM IKE

AFTER TWO YEARS IN the engineers Arthur Holmes was ready for something new. "We'd been in the army too long and we were saying, 'There ain't nothing happening here, let's go up there to the front and see what's happening,' " Holmes said. "Now, the infantry was a challenge. We'd heard about it and all the good things they were doing, notwithstanding that people were getting killed. And we were young and stupid."

Edward Jackson had similar feelings. "I'd been overseas so long, through North Africa, Italy, and France, I didn't think they'd ever let me go home." Ransom too suffered from the same ennui: "A lot of the men wanted out of their chickenshit outfits."

None, however, ever imagined the army would finally offer them the opportunity to fight, since it had turned them away from the infantry in the first place. But in December 1944, infantry slots suddenly opened for African-Americans in integrated white combat divisions.

As in past wars, the color bar fell when America needed manpower, and in late 1944 the U.S. Army desperately sought men for its combat divisions. The nation's manpower reserves had dwindled as the pool of eligible young men declined and most of the infantrymen in the army's new divisions and in the replacement pipeline were eighteen-year-olds right out of high school. All were white.

By the end of 1944, the number of American casualties in the ETO since D-Day was staggering. Nearly 350,000 American troops had been killed or wounded or were missing. The Battle of the Bulge, which began on December 16, 1944, resulted in an estimated 80,000 American casualties with total casualties for December totaling 134,400. At the end of January 1945, an additional 69,119 American troops in the ETO were listed as battle casualties, along with 67,600 nonbattle casualties.

The casualties mounted until the end of the war. By V-E Day, May 6, 1945, total combat losses in the ETO were 586,628 men—135,576 dead—with 78 percent, or 456,799 of these casualties, inflicted in the infantry divisions. Of the sixty-one divisions that served in the ETO in 1944 and 1945, twenty had personnel turnover rates of 100 percent or higher. Five divisions had a turnover rate of more than 200 percent, with the 4th Division having a rate of 252.3 percent.

The army struggled to maintain a pool of about seventy thousand men to refill the ranks of the combat divisions thinned by casualties. The task, however, was impossible, as the demand for replacements was always greater than the supply. At the end of January 1945, the shortage of infantrymen in American divisions reached eighty-two thousand men. In February, the army estimated it would need ninety thousand replacements in each of the next three months. It was only in April 1945 that the pool exceeded its full complement when eighty thousand men were available for combat duty. By then, however, the war was nearly over.

The Battle of the Bulge forced the Americans to look for new sources of manpower. General Eisenhower, who even before the Ardennes attack had directed his rear-echelon headquarters to comb the ranks for men fit for combat, demanded redoubled efforts to find new infantrymen. He also indicated that the army would not "deny the Negro volunteers a chance to serve in battle."

One major source of new infantrymen was the hundreds of thousands of noncombatant service troops, many of them black, serving under Lt. Gen. John C. H. Lee, commander of the Communication Zone, which comprised the areas in Europe liberated by American forces. General Lee agreed to release twenty thousand men, including a number of blacks, from his command for infantry duty.

Noncombatant whites had no say when they were culled from their old units, handed a rifle, retrained for six weeks, and shipped to an infantry company. Air corps personnel also were being transferred to the army ground forces as the air war over Germany was being won and the need for replacement air and ground crews lessened. But blacks had to volunteer because of official army policies of segregation.

Unpopular among the American generals in the ETO, General Lee was somewhat forward thinking for the day when it came to race relations. He proposed that the army integrate blacks individually, "shoulder to shoulder" with white infantrymen when they went into the front lines. The Bible-quoting, deeply religious General Lee, whose nickname was "Jesus Christ," for his initials J. C., believed that blacks should have the same opportunities as whites and that the army's policy of segregation and its discriminatory practices were contrary to the teachings of the Bible.

In England, with Eisenhower's support, General Lee fought to offset efforts among whites to bar and contaminate black relations with the British. He urged Eisenhower to issue an order, which General Lee distributed to all bases in Great Britain, that any attempts to curtail normal associations between blacks and the British public were unjustified and illegal. General

Davis visited bases in England to see that the order was carried out.

Lee Nichols in his book, *Breakthrough on the Color Front*, states that General Lee sometimes accompanied Davis, and at one base he asked the commander why he was giving his white and black soldiers passes to town on different days.

"I asked if he had read Ike's directive," Davis asked. "He said, 'Oh, yes, we understand about those directives.'"

General Lee then asked, "You mean you're not taking the directives seriously?"

The commander replied by saying he believed General Lee had had to issue such orders with the assumption they would never be followed. General Lee then asked the commander how long it would take him to pack his bags. "He was promptly relieved, and so were many others who refused to obey," General Davis wrote.

General Lee considered black troops a large reservoir of "able-bodied, capable soldier material. . . . They could shoot," he said. "My chauffeur was a better shot than I. I have found them alert, willing, with good disciplinary and health records when under good leadership. And they knew how to handle weapons."

General Lee asked General Davis and Brig. Gen. Henry J. Matchett, commanding the Ground Forces Reinforcement Command, to devise a plan that called for the training of two thousand black infantry volunteers who would be individually integrated into rifle companies. After consulting with General Eisenhower, General Lee sent a letter to his base and section commanders in late December 1944, with instructions that it be disseminated to all troops in the Communication Zone (Com Z) within twenty-four hours:

> The Supreme Commander desires to destroy the enemy forces and end hostilities in this theater without delay. Every available weapon at our disposal must be brought to bear upon the enemy. To this end the Commanding General, Com Z, is happy to offer to a limited number of colored troops who have had infantry training, the privilege of joining our veteran units at the front to deliver the knockout blow. The men selected are to be in the grades of Private First Class and Private. Noncommissioned officers may accept reduction in order to take advantage of this opportunity. The men selected are to be given a refresher course with emphasis on weapons training.
>
> The Commanding General makes a special appeal to you. It is planned to assign you without regard to color or race to the units where assistance is most needed, and give you the opportunity of fighting shoulder to shoulder to bring about victory. Your comrades at the front

are anxious to share the glory of victory with you. The Supreme Commander, your Commanding General, and other veteran officers who have served with you are confident that many of you will take advantage of this opportunity and carry on in keeping with the glorious record of our colored troops in former wars.

The proposal was a bombshell. Historian Russell Weigley described the plan: "Nothing could have been more drastic than making combat soldiers of substantial numbers of black men." Ulysses Lee was more circumspect: "The plan itself represented a major break with traditional Army policy, for it proposed mixing Negro soldiers into otherwise white units neither on a quota nor a smaller unit basis but as individuals fitted in where needed." Under General Lee's plan the army would initially take two thousand volunteers, the largest number that could be trained at one time at the Ground Forces Reinforcement Center (GFRC) in northern France. No service unit would be allowed to send so many new recruits as to reduce its strength by more than 3.5 percent.

It was the radical concept of the integration of black troops into white combat divisions that caught the eye of Lt. Gen. Walter B. Smith, chief of staff at Supreme Headquarters Allied Forces Europe (SHAFE). Smith observed that the promise to assign black troops to combat units, shoulder to shoulder with whites without regard to race or color, would embarrass the War Department. He immediately took the issue to General Eisenhower.

According to Ulysses Lee, General Smith wrote to Eisenhower.

Although I am somewhat out of touch with the War Department's Negro policy, I did, as you know, handle this during the time I was with General Marshall. Unless there has been a radical change, the sentence which I have marked in the attached circular will place the War Department in very grave difficulties. It is inevitable that this statement will get out, and equally inevitable that the result will be that every Negro organization, pressure group and newspaper will take the attitude that, while the War Department segregates colored troops into organizations of their own against the desires and pleas of all the Negro race, the Army is perfectly willing to put them in the front lines mixed in units with white soldiers, and have them do battle when an emergency arises. Two years ago I would have considered the marked statement the most dangerous thing that I had ever seen in regard to Negro relations.

I have talked with [General] Lee about it, and he can't see this at all. He believes that it is right that colored and white soldiers should mix in the same company. With this belief I do not argue, but the War Department policy is different. Since I am convinced that this circular letter will have the most serious repercussions in the United States, I believe that it is our duty to draw the War Department's attention to the fact that this statement has been made, to give them warning as to what may happen and any facts which they may use to counter the pressure which will undoubtedly be placed on them.

While General Lee still persisted in promoting the idea that blacks be mixed in with white troops individually, the high command backtracked. According to historian Ulysses Lee:

> General Eisenhower personally rewrote the directive, changing all but the first two sentences and making dissemination permissive instead of mandatory. . . . The new directive, officially approved by both General Eisenhower and General Lee, appeared over General Lee's signature with the same date, file number and subject as the earlier directive, under a cover letter ordering return and destruction of all copies of the original version. The substitute letter read:
>
> "The Supreme Commander desires to destroy the enemy forces and end hostilities in this theater without delay. Every available weapon at our disposal must be brought to bear upon the enemy. To this end the Theater Commander has directed the Communications Zone Commander to make the greatest use of limited service men within service units and to survey our entire organization in an effort to produce able bodied men for the front lines. This process of selection has been going on for some time, but it is entirely possible that many men themselves, desiring to volunteer for front line service, may be able to point out methods in which they can be replaced in their present jobs. Consequently, Commanders of all grades will receive voluntary applications for transfer to the Infantry and forward them to higher authority with recommendations for appropriate type of replacement. This opportunity to volunteer will be extended to all soldiers without regard to color or race, but preference will normally be given to individuals who have had some basic training in Infantry. Normally, also, transfers will be limited to the grade of Private and Private First Class, unless a noncommissioned officer requests a reduction.
>
> "In the event that the number of suitable Negro volunteers exceeds the replacement needs of Negro combat units, these men will be suitably incorporated in other organizations so that their service and their fighting spirit may be efficiently utilized."

The army itself recognized that the new letter, issued by General Eisenhower, could be interpreted in a number of ways. It seemed to state most directly that any black volunteers would be used as replacements for existing black combat units, notably the 761st Tank and 333rd Field Artillery Battalions. Both of these units had suffered losses and had to train their own replacements.

But the revised letter could still be interpreted to mean that black volunteers in excess of those needed for existing black combat units could be placed in white combat units "in the same manner as white reinforcements," notably individually. SHAFE G-1, (personnel) therefore asked for further clarification of the directive. G-1 prepared a new directive which indicated that the black volunteers would be used to reinforce existing black combat units operating in the ETO and that any additional volunteers would be formed into separate infantry units for assignment to an army group. If these units constituted enough men, they could be formed into a battalion- or regimental-size unit.

This directive might have been carried out and would essentially have derailed the integration process except that the Ground Forces Reinforcement System (GFRS), in which the volunteers would be trained, was equipped to take individual replacements only and was unprepared to train battalion- or regimental-size units. Training for individual recruits concentrated almost exclusively on squads, with only a week's instruction given to platoon tactics.

In the meantime, overall command for the infantry replacement system became the responsibility of Lt. Gen. Ben Lear, the newly appointed deputy theater commander under Eisenhower. General Lee also received a new interpretation of General Eisenhower's wishes in January and sent them to General Lear. General Lee informed General Lear of Eisenhower's approval of the original plan, which proposed that individual black replacements were to be formed into all-black platoons and assigned to white infantry units.

According to historian Lee, "He [General Lee] informed General Lear that General Eisenhower 'now desires that these colored riflemen reinforcements have their training completed as members of Infantry rifle platoons familiar with the Infantry rifle platoon weapons.' These platoons would be made available to army commanders who would then provide platoon leaders, platoon sergeants, and, if necessary, squad leaders. 'It is my feeling,' General Lee said, 'that we should afford the volunteers the full opportunity for Infantry riflemen service. Therefore we should not assign them as Tank or Artillery reinforcements unless they express such preference. To do otherwise would be breaking faith, in my opinion.' "

In the end most of the credit for formation of the black platoons must go to General Lee. This was the opinion of General Davis. In a letter dated March 30, 1945, Davis explained the black volunteer replacement program to John J. McCloy, assistant secretary of war.

Here the most interesting development is the reinforcement training program. This is the plan set up in the directives issued by General Lee, which I showed you in February. General Lee started the program on an individual replacement basis. This would have meant the integration of individual Negroes into white rifle platoons. In this General Lee had the verbal concurrence of General Eisenhower. General Lee did not, however, show General Eisenhower the first directive at this time, nor did he show it to the Army commanders who had approved the original proposal. When the directive was received at SHAFE several persons became alarmed at the extent of its departure from previously existing War Department policy. Thereafter, General Eisenhower printed himself the second directive, which restricted the original proposal somewhat to provide for small unit inclusion on a platoon basis. This necessitated a change in the whole reinforcement-training program, which had previously been set up on an individual basis.

Recent developments here have been personally embarrassing to General Lee. An article appearing in the *Stars and Stripes* mentioned conflict between policy here and that of the War Department. Further, reference was made to the first directive, which was of course superseded by the one printed by General Eisenhower. Further, General Lear— among others—is not too sympathetic with the program even as it now exists. In this connection I want to emphasize again that the Army commanders, and particularly those in whose divisions the men are now being utilized, gave full approval of the original plan. General Patton in particular was very sympathetic.

Without the support of generals such as Walter B. Smith and Lear, how did the black replacement plan ever materialize? General Davis answered this question in a letter to his wife, Sadie, on March 19, 1945:

"I am sending a clipping from today's *Stars and Stripes*. This is the decision I secured December 26—use of colored troops in combat and their assignment to existing [white] units. Washington bucked it, disapproved it, but we had started it and gotten too far."

But if General Davis gave credit to General Lee he was also mindful of the part played by Eleanor Roosevelt. Bruce Wright, later a civil rights advocate on the New York bench, believed that Eleanor Roosevelt had great influence on the formation of the platoons. "I was told by General B. O. Davis that it [the plan for the black platoons] was Eleanor Roosevelt's idea," Wright said.

Lt. Richard Ralston, who commanded the 5th of K, also believed that Mrs. Roosevelt, because of her advocacy of civil rights, particularly in the military, played a major role in creating a climate in which generals such as J. C. Lee could advocate an integrated front line. She was directly credited with ending the use of racial quotas in the Army Nurse Corps and for being the catalyst for the integration of the Navy Nurse Corps in January 1945.

Others agreed. "Eleanor Roosevelt's stand on civil rights, her insistence that America could not fight racism abroad while tolerating it at home, remains one of the affirming moments in the history of the home front during the war," wrote Doris Kearns Goodwin in *No Ordinary Time*.

> She had insisted, against the advice of the White House staff, that the president meet with Negro leaders to discuss what could be done about discrimination and segregation in the armed forces. Progress was slow and incomplete, but these meetings, along with Eleanor's continuing intervention, eventually led to broadened opportunities for Negroes in both the army and the navy. Between 1940 and 1945, the Negro military force had increased in size from 5,000 to 920,000 and the number of Negro officers had grown from five to over 7,000.
>
> Moreover, whereas almost every Negro soldier in 1940 was confined to a service unit, by war's close Negroes held responsible jobs in almost every branch of the army as artillerymen, tankers, infantrymen, pilots, paratroopers, doctors and more.

Mrs. Roosevelt lobbied tirelessly for civil rights and was vilified by southern whites during Franklin Roosevelt's presidency for advocating integration and for attempting to destroy their "southern way of life." Mrs. Roosevelt made a point of meeting with black servicemen and -women both in the United States and overseas.

In the end, the vast majority of black volunteers were integrated by platoon into white infantry divisions because Generals Davis and Lee started a process that couldn't be stopped without the army's embarrassing itself. The indecisiveness of the high command and the efforts of some to sidetrack integration were things the black troops had come to expect. Promises of equality most often were false.

Enough black volunteers signed up to form fifty-three infantry platoons, thirty-seven of which were sent to the front in early March 1945 and integrated into all-white companies. The remainder were sent as additional black troops were trained. A number of platoons were formed into all-black company-size units with the 12th and 14th Armored Divisions.

By war's end the black platoons had served in ten infantry and armored divisions in the ETO: the 1st, 8th, 9th, 69th, 78th, 99th, 104th, and 106th Infantry Divisions and the 12th and 14th Armored Divisions. The volunteers assigned to the 106th were later reassigned to other divisions because the 106th had been badly mauled during the Battle of the Bulge. The platoons also had served variously in three different armies, the First, Third, and Seventh Armies.

"I never believed they would put us black boys up there with white boys," recalled Arthur Holmes. "And I didn't believe it until we were actually being shot at. I thought they would put us back with Quartermaster working in supply." They almost did; but for once, Holmes was wrong.

9

.

YOU'VE GOT YOUR TRANSFER

THE BLACKS WHO VOLUNTEERED for the infantry gave many reasons for their decision. Some, like Holmes and Ransom, were tired of the daily "chickenshit" of army life behind the lines. Others were encouraged to leave or were forced out of their old outfits and sent to the infantry because they were troublemakers and misfits. Many others expressed the desire to fight. Thousands volunteered and in some cases scores of men from the same unit signed up. In one engineer outfit, 171 out of 186 men volunteered, while 100 men volunteered from a Quartermaster laundry company of 260 men.

But when faced with the reality of combat and the choice between life and death, most discovered that they had volunteered to show the white boys that they were every bit as brave and were equally good as soldiers.

"We were going to make liars out of the whites," said Clayton Des Journette. "We knew what they were thinking all the time, that we weren't man enough."

"My thought was to prove ourselves," said John Hemsley, a "Black Timberwolf" with the 104th Infantry Division. "The volunteers I talked to wanted to prove that they would be good infantrymen. It was stupid for the whites to think otherwise."

"We had a point to make," said Willfred Strange. "We had been stereotyped and categorized. Blacks were supposed to be scared and wouldn't perform. We knew damned well we would perform. In fact we would show them how it's done. Eighty percent of us felt that way."

"There was this senator from Mississippi, Theodore Bilbo, who said black troops—he didn't say black troops, he used the N word—were good for nothing except loading ships and working as laborers. We wanted to show him otherwise," Holmes said. "And even when we were in combat he made some derogatory comments about blacks not measuring up because he didn't even know we were there."

Above all, the volunteers were aware that they were pioneers who were about to integrate the U.S. Army even if it was only on a small scale. They were to be a first.

"The black platoons offered an opening in the wall of segregation and I wanted to be a part of that more so than I can tell you," said Bruce Wright. He instinctively knew that by placing a black platoon in the midst of a white infantry company, the army had started a process of integration that it couldn't stop. "The dirty joke on the power structure was that once they included a black platoon in a white company, whether they liked it or not, it was integrated."

Wright knew that in combat there's no way to keep black troops segregated from whites. Men under fire don't stop to check the skin color of the man next to them racing for the same foxhole. Blacks and whites fight side by side.

To be sure, many thousands of black troops in the ETO wanted no part of the infantry, and appeals for volunteers had a hollow ring. The call to arms came from the same white command structure that enforced segregation and had relegated blacks to noncombatant roles in the first place. Their army and country believed they were not qualified to be infantrymen, and many blacks realized that it was the circumstances that had changed, not a fundamental attitude about race.

James Chappelle, a driver on the Red Ball Express, recalled being asked to volunteer for combat duty. "Davis [General Davis] wanted us to contribute to our country and came to entice us to join the infantry. Volunteer?! The infantry?! Are you crazy?!" Chappelle said. Chappelle's response reflected the feelings of many in his unit, C Company, 514th Quartermaster Truck Regiment.

"The way I felt about it was what's the use of going out and fighting when you're a second-class citizen. What good is that?" said James Rookard, a member of C Company, 514th.

Mary P. Motley, in her book *The Invisible Soldiers,* quotes Chester Jones: "Combat officers were coming around asking black truck drivers to volunteer for infantry duty at the Bulge. My opinion was: they said that I didn't have sense enough to be a combat soldier stateside—well if I didn't have it then I damned sure didn't have it in their emergency."

When assigned to infantry training in the winter of 1945, all the volunteers entered the army's controversial individual replacement system, which was established during World War I and continued into World War II. In contrast to the German army, which replenished its ranks by sending or rotating entire, fully trained units to the front, the American army refilled its combat ranks on an as-needed basis with individual riflemen. The vast majority of these men had no connection with their new units, had no allegiance to their new comrades, knew no one, and often died anonymously in the first hours of combat because they were so untested in the essentials of war.

While most troops during World War II were trained initially in the States, the army established special camps under the GFRS in France to retrain new troops as infantry replacements. While many of the volunteers were training in groups that stayed together and eventually wound up in combat divisions, the training was still focused on the individual rifleman, not the unit.

When the first 2,800 black volunteers arrived at the Ground Forces Reinforcement Command in Compiègne, France, in January 1945, many had only rudimentary combat instruction gained in basic training, and some had barely fired a shot with the standard army rifle, the M1. Few were proficient in breaking down a rifle and putting it back together again, a necessity for infantrymen. Rifles often jam in combat from grime and freezing weather, and riflemen have to know how to make them operational again as quickly as possible.

In some cases the army had been afraid to arm black troops or train them in rifle proficiency because of the race riots that had erupted at various military training camps in the United States in 1943. Some white commanders even believed that blacks would take up arms against whites, just as some American colonists were reluctant to arm blacks for fear of a slave rebellion. There were enough stories and rumors of rampaging black troops at military bases in the American South during the war to alarm many whites.

"I knew good and well there were people in the army who said it was a terrible thing to let blacks fight Germans because they would fight whites at home," Ransom said. "I had one officer who was transferred because he felt that way. He said we were going to have another war with blacks when we got home because they had learned to shoot whites."

"The army was skeptical about giving the colored troops live ammunition. It's a bad thing to say, but it's a fact," said Fred Watt. Other black former troops remembered an army policy that went beyond withholding ammunition. Several volunteers said that they were disarmed even when close to the front. In a letter to General Davis one black soldier quoted Senator James O. Eastland of Mississippi concerning military policy toward blacks. "It was necessary during the Normandy invasion to disarm a good many Negro soldiers. I was informed by a high ranking general in Paris," he (Eastland) said.

Willfred Strange stated that the men in his unit were stripped of their weapons once on the European continent. "We went up from France into Belgium at the same time the Battle of the Bulge started. We had been disarmed, and when we found ourselves surrounded by Germans we had no weapons to fight with," said Strange. "When I volunteered for the infantry at least they gave me a rifle."

Holmes and Ransom, and the others in the 377th Engineers, got their chance to fight one cold December morning before dawn in the 3rd Division rest area in France. "When the letter asking for volunteers came down they had a reveille formation and the company commander was out there reading it with a flashlight," Ransom remembered. "The CO told us that anybody who wanted to sign up was to see him in the orderly room. Then he ordered me to report in." Ransom wasn't thinking of signing up, but he approached his commanding officer nevertheless.

"Sergeant Ransom, you've got your transfer."

"Transfer to what?" Ransom asked.

"The transfer you asked for eighteen months ago at Fort Knox to the infantry."

"Yes sir," Ransom said, and went back to work. He knew he was being forced out of the unit. "Some people in the outfit didn't like me. The company commander wanted to see me elsewhere. The mess sergeant hated me worse than a possum hates an ax handle. The first sergeant, and several others as well, didn't have too much respect for me. I was a smart-ass all right and they wanted to get rid of me."

Ransom made no effort or plans to leave the company until several days later a young lieutenant approached him and notified him that he was scheduled to be on a truck the next morning that was taking volunteers to Compiègne.

"So the next morning I get on this deuce-and-a-half [truck] with a bunch of people who were drunk or raving about how they were going to fight. I said what is this; I ain't signed no paper to volunteer for anything. We trucked up to Dijon to catch a train there and just as we were about to pull out from the station I hear somebody calling my name and running up the platform. It was the regimental adjutant and he sticks a piece of paper in my face and says 'sign here.' That's how I volunteered for the infantry."

Ransom wasn't alone. Many black volunteers were misfits or trouble-makers and were "volunteered" for infantry duty by their officers and NCOs. Holmes was almost certain that Harry Lucky was shanghaied into the infantry.

James Strawder believes that "most of the volunteers were people the companies wanted to get rid of." He added: "The IQ ratings of the volunteers were much higher than the average. We were the smart alecks, the ones the company commander sent off. They put me down too as a smart aleck. I was always pulling heck on them and they could never prove me wrong because I knew my rights. They always had problems with me. I knew how to get out of trouble. We were half smart and half educated."

10

•

LT. RICHARD RALSTON

LT. RICHARD A. RALSTON was one of the most experienced junior officers in the U.S. Army. College educated and combat tested in the Battle of the Bulge, he had gone through Officer Candidate School in 1943 when OCS was far tougher and more demanding then it was in 1944 and 1945. "Only 46 percent of my OCS class graduated because the army didn't need company grade officers of captain or below," Ralston said. But after D-Day the army relaxed the standards for junior officers because it needed thousands of lieutenants and captains to replace those killed or wounded in the heavy fighting in the ETO. Many of these new junior officers did not measure up.

After OCS Lieutenant Ralston was placed in command of a weapons platoon in the 99th Division, which trained at Camp Van Dorn, Mississippi, and later at Camp Maxey, Louisiana. Capt. Charles Roland with 3rd Battalion, 394th Regiment, another OCS graduate who was assigned to the 99th, and who later led Lieutenant Ralston's 5th of K into the hills of the Remagen bridgehead, remembered that the training he and Lieutenant Ralston underwent on 99th Division maneuvers was brutally realistic.

I have read that the German high command deliberately made their maneuvers so hard their soldiers welcomed the relief of going into battle," Roland wrote. "I would not go so far as to say this was true of our maneuvers, but in some ways they were, in fact, more taxing than combat. When the maneuvers ended we had not slept on a bed, inside walls, or under a roof in four months, except for an occasional 24-hour pass during a break between tactical problems. We had become inured to the sweltering heat of the Mississippi summer and the bone-chilling cold of the late fall in north Louisiana, where the thermometer often dropped into the twenties at night and films of ice stood on the puddles in the morning, with no fires or lights allowed except during breaks.

We encountered nature pointblank, from myriads of redbugs and ticks to sting-tailed scorpions and cottonmouth moccasins and coral snakes. At first we were extremely careful about where we lay down to sleep, for fear of challenging some critter's territorial imperative. Fatigue and a certain feeling of indifference to danger that comes from this kind of life soon enabled us to drop to the ground at midnight in the midst of the densest woods and underbrush, and fall asleep instantly without the slightest regard for any of the denizens that might be lurking there. We had become so conditioned to living out of doors and sleeping on the ground that beds seemed somewhat uncomfortably soft and walls and roofs too confining when we had those rare opportunities to use them.

By September 1944, the division was deemed fit for duty overseas and was shipped to England. Six weeks later the 99th moved by landing ship tanks (LSTs) to France and was transported over the Red Ball Express Highway to Belgium. The company made the final run to the front lines in the cargo bays of the two-and-a-half-ton trucks, "standing up and stacked like cordwood," Ralston remembered. V-1 buzz bombs flew low and noisily above the vehicles as they drove on the rough roads. "The V-1s sounded like motorcycles with no mufflers going over just above tree-top level," Ralston said.

The troops knew that as long as they could hear the roar of the ramjet engines they were safe; it was when the engine quit and the V-1 plummeted to earth to explode a 1,800-pound warhead that those nearby had to worry. And a V-1 quit just above Lieutenant Ralston's convoy as the trucks entered a thick fog in the Ardennes Forest. Everyone heard the roar of the approaching buzz bomb, then silence just above the convoy. The men waited anxiously and braced for the massive explosion, that detonated about a mile back and out of harm's way.

Lieutenant Ralston's weapons platoon went into the line November 10, 1944, between the villages of Losheim and Losheimergraben about twenty-five miles southeast of Malmédy, where they dug in and faced supposedly understrength German divisions only yards away. Little did they suspect that in a few weeks they would be at dead center of the German attack during the Battle of the Bulge. The Ardennes was a rest and training area for U.S. and German divisions where the rule was "Live and let live." Veteran divisions on both sides came to refit and take in replacements, and newly arrived, green divisions experienced limited fighting as they prepared for heavy combat somewhere else on the front. Artillery units on both sides dueled from time to time, and skirmishes between opposing forces were generally limited to firefights between patrols sent out by each army to probe for weaknesses in the defenses. But generally the two enemies left each other alone.

Eisenhower and Gen. Omar Bradley, commander of Twelfth Army

Group, were aware that the Ardennes area was the weak link in the front lines that stretched from Holland to Switzerland and that the divisions assigned there were vulnerable. The Ardennes had been the avenue for German attacks into Belgium and France three times in past wars. But in late 1944, as long as the enemy showed no sign of aggressiveness, the Americans believed they were safe from serious assault in the region. Bradley also believed the highly mobile and mechanized American army could handle any threat coming through the Ardennes. In the end he was right, but the Americans paid a terrible price.

The greatest excitement for Lieutenant Ralston and his men at the front remained the continuing parade of V-1s that passed over their foxholes and dugouts. They were aimed at the port of Antwerp, where the Germans hoped to disrupt the unloading of supplies for the Allied armies. The enemy had launching sites in the Eifel, the forested uplands on the German-Belgian border, just behind their lines, and Lieutenant Ralston and his men became expert at identifying which site had just launched a buzz bomb. "If it were sunset it was a pretty sight to watch the V-1s as they flew down a corridor of exploding American antiaircraft shells farther and farther into Belgium," Ralston said.

The men of the weapons platoon turned their section of the front line into a relatively habitable area with well-appointed dugouts and deep trenches and spacious foxholes. On December 14, however, the platoon was relieved, and Lieutenant Ralston was displeased by the transfer because he expected the company's new quarters to have none of the luxuries his men had fashioned for themselves.

But Lieutenant Ralston was pleasantly surprised to find his platoon's new quarters consisted of well-built huts. "These were much better accommodations then the ones we had left," he said. But their stay would be short-lived. Two nights later, in the predawn hours of December 16, 1944, the men were awakened by the sounds of explosions erupting in the rear. "We thought the noise was from our artillery and we were really giving the Germans hell."

The explosions moved closer and closer, and it became apparent that the shells were coming from German artillery aimed at American targets. The enemy was marching its shells from areas behind the American lines forward to the front. When one area was saturated by artillery the enemy gunners moved on to another. The targets had all been reconnoitered by the German patrols that had daily infiltrated American lines.

It wasn't long before German artillery began falling on the foxholes and dugouts in the front line. The Battle of the Bulge had begun, and the initial German assaults struck heavily in the 99th Division sector. Lieutenant Ralston and many of his men survived only by a quirk of fate. They had been pulled out of the line just two days before the attack.

The Bulge tested Lieutenant Ralston's mettle and turned him into an experienced platoon leader. As dawn broke on the sixteenth the weapons platoon was sent to the nearby Buchholz railroad station with orders to hold against a German attack. "We had two jeeps, two light machine guns and three 60 mm mortars," Ralston said. The men started digging in and had just finished carving shallow holes out of the shaley ground when the order came to fall back to the company command post. Once again the weapons platoon was saved. Not long after the men withdrew, the Germans overran the station and killed or captured most of the Americans manning the defenses.

For the next several weeks Lieutenant Ralston and his men fought back and forth though the dense pine forests of the Ardennes. They had little sleep and scavenged for rations. One of Lieutenant Ralston's recollections during the monthlong battle was a chance encounter with a 99th Division kitchen train where the platoon had their first hot meal in days. "Dried beef and gravy. God it was good!" he remembered. When the German offensive was blunted and the front stabilized, the weapons platoon dug in on Elsenborn Ridge in the northern sector of the Bulge. Its job was to hold and let no Germans penetrate beyond their position. "We were on that ridge for several weeks. We had machine guns and a 57-mm anti-tank gun and a telephone in every foxhole for firing orders." The division also started getting replacements to fill the ranks of the killed and wounded. More than half the weapons platoon had become casualties during the fighting in the Bulge.

In February 1945, as the 99th and other divisions in Belgium licked their wounds and took in replacements, Lieutenant Ralston received new orders from K Company's CO, Capt. Wesley J. Simmons, "to report to a location far to the rear for the purpose of training some service troops for combat duty."

Simmons, a highly respected captain who was a graduate of the ROTC program at Western Maryland College in Westminster, Maryland, was looking for a platoon leader and a platoon sergeant to travel to France to pick up the new contingent of troops training at the army's replacement center in Compiègne. Lieutenant Ralston and Platoon Sgt. Oliver Sacco were to return with the new troops, who would be attached to K Company, 394th Regiment. Lieutenant Ralston would remain with them as their platoon leader and Sgt. Sacco would be their platoon sergeant.

Lieutenant Ralston was one of the few officers who had never been on furlough to France, and he looked forward to his new assignment. He might even get in a few days' leave in Paris. "We boarded a narrow gauge '40 × 8' freight car train and headed for France," Ralston said. "I'm guessing there were at least forty pairs of us lieutenants and platoon sergeants aboard, perhaps more." As the train approached Compiègne the officers and noncoms began noticing a curious sight. All the soldiers in the area were black. "We thought, 'Oh my goodness, Captain Simmons had said nothing about picking up black troops.' "

Lieutenant Ralston, however, was unperturbed by his new assignment. "I remember being surprised and kinda wishing that I could go back to the front. But I soon got into that enterprise and into the interesting things and qualities of these guys. Their attitude was so enthusiastic."

As the officers and sergeants took stock they learned that each pair was to command around forty-five black volunteers who would be formed into a "reinforced" infantry platoon. The platoon was classified as reinforced because it was 10 percent or more overstrength to include its own replacements, at least until additional black troops were trained. Because of the army's policy of segregation there was no plan to insert white replacements into black platoons as casualties mounted.

Each platoon was to be attached as a "5th Platoon" to an existing white company. They were called 5th Platoons because each infantry company comprised four platoons: three rifle platoons and one weapons platoon, which carried mortars and machine guns. There would be one 5th Platoon in each of a division's three regiments. Lieutenant Ralston and Sergeant Sacco's platoon was assigned to K Company, 394th Regiment, a 5th Platoon was assigned to the division's E Company, 393rd Regiment, and to E Company, 395th Regiment.

Many among the arriving officers and sergeants were deeply upset by the prospect of leading black troops into combat. "A lot of these cocky white officers and sergeants said they'd take a court-martial before they'd bring these black guys up to the front. I don't think any carried out their threats," Ralston said.

In the 5th of E, 393rd Regiment, the platoon in which James Strawder would serve, the unit's new company commander, a captain, was displeased with his new assignment. According to Harry Arnold, a white infantryman with E Company, "it was determined that the Second Battalion would get the black platoon and that the company commanders would 'draw straws' to determine who would get the added rifle platoon. One captain lost when he drew the 'shortest straw.' A Mississippian and in many ways the best company commander that we had, the captain was not happy about the 'dubious honor' of commanding a platoon of Black soldiers. He possessed all the hang-ups of a redneck southerner on this matter. Fate intervened for him. He never had to command this group of volunteers. In the initial action to take Ginsterhahn, he was wounded and evacuated."

In time, most of the whites selected to command moderated their views. "I think we were as much surprised by the fact that these guys had volunteered," Ralston said. "This was 180 degrees opposite of the normal black unit's attitude."

11

•

MEN FROM THE KILLING FLOOR

THERE COULDN'T HAVE BEEN a greater divide between men than the one between the black volunteers of the 5th of K and Lt. Richard Ralston. Lieutenant Ralston had grown up white in Long Beach, California, in relative privilege compared to the new men under his command. California in the 1930s was a sparsely populated realm of sun and surf that offered good living despite the Depression. "It was a wonderful world," Ralston remembered. "We went to the beach six months of the year. And we had a great school system that was financed by city owned oil wells."

After graduating from high school Ralston worked for two years before entering the University of Oregon. He had planned a career in engineering but there were few jobs available for engineers, so when a friend told him that Oregon had a well-established accounting school he decided to study there instead. Besides, there was great skiing only fifty miles from the campus in Eugene. In California he had to drive at least one hundred miles into the Sierras to ski.

Ralston's college days were pleasant and fruitful. He met his future wife, Marianne, and the couple were married in the summer of 1943 just before Ralston shipped out to the army. When he returned from war, provided he survived, he would pursue the American dream.

Most of the black volunteers whom Lieutenant Ralston commanded came from big-city ghettos or pockets of rural poverty and "were kids who grew up with knife fights and gun fights," Ralston said. They had no plans to pursue the American dream. Lieutenant Ralston immediately noticed a tough, raw quality about his men that he knew would make them superb combat soldiers. "They weren't scared of anything." It was Lieutenant Ralston's job to turn these eager recruits into an efficient group of riflemen.

But who were these men of the 5th Platoon who had volunteered to fight and die for a country that held them in contempt? To begin with, their disadvantaged upbringing had made them different, if not outcasts, in a white society. Waymon Ransom believed that whites, and even many blacks, perceived the men in the black platoons as "bad actors." Ransom himself was so regarded. He, and many of the others, were unwilling to accept the status quo of segregation and they fought back, sometimes violently, against racial prejudice and the white military establishment.

The lowly circumstances of the men of the 5th Platoons in civilian life had been even more extreme than those of the most economically depressed whites in the World War II army. These blacks had grown up in a different culture and in a parallel world of exclusion, deprivation, and separation. The life expectancy for blacks at the beginning of the war was 54 compared with 65 for whites. The death rate for blacks in infancy was 40 in 1,000 compared with 27 in 1,000 for whites. In the first year of life the death rate for blacks climbed to 73 in 1,000 compared with 43 for whites. By age 21 the death rate for blacks was 120 per 1,000 compared with 70 for whites. Blacks were subject to more disabling illnesses than whites. Nevertheless, there were only 20,000 hospital beds for the entire black population of the United States.

Waymon Ransom and Arthur Holmes were typical examples of the infantry volunteers. Both were on the street and on their own by the time they were fourteen, when they dropped out of the ninth grade. Lawrence Boris also dropped out of school in the ninth grade and survived by taking odd jobs. Herbert Pugh, from Louisiana, who served with 5th Platoon, 38th Regiment, 2nd Infantry Division, quit school in the fourth grade to work on his mother's truck farm and help raise a family of five boys and three girls. It was a struggle that paid off. Eventually all the Pugh children went to college. Pugh was fourteen when he joined the army and sixteen when he went into combat. James Strawder and Clayton Des Journette were among the few in the black platoons who had finished high school.

Many of the volunteers had had run-ins with the law, and one rationale for accepting blacks into the infantry was the army's notion that, being more accustomed to violence and bloodshed, they would acclimate quickly to battle. Several had actually been wounded in ghetto shoot-outs, and the sight of dead and maimed bodies lying in the streets was not new to them.

Holmes believed a number of men had done time on chain gangs in the South or had been incarcerated but kept their arrests secret. Time on the gang was common for blacks in the pre–World War II South, where African-American men were arrested on any pretext and used to collect garbage and repair roads. Holmes knew of one platoon member who was proud of his heritage on the chain gang.

Lester Boudreau from Louisiana, the "Ragin' Cajun," was celebrated in the 5th of K for his wild ways. But Boudreau put his energies to use against the enemy and became so proficient at killing Germans that admiring whites in K Company nicknamed him "Blitz."

Ransom summed up the life of many of the men in the black platoons:

"We lived on the killing floor," alluding to an old blues song that depicted a way of life among blacks that was raw and alien to most whites. The "killing floor" was the first floor of a slaughterhouse, where the animals were killed and only the less fortunate workers stayed for any length of time.

But even those who had not come from the killing floor were often regarded as bad actors, particularly if they agitated for equal treatment in the military. Bruce Wright was constantly on report in the army for his outspoken views on race and equality. Arriving at Camp Rucker, Alabama, Private Wright testily demanded to know what the major meant when he ordered Wright's black outfit to "make those mess kits shine like a nigger's heel."

Willfred Strange, who had taken several years of college courses before being drafted into the army, was equally militant. He scored so well on an army intelligence exam that his testers believed he had cheated. Roused from bed early one morning, Strange was made to retake the test. He scored even better the second time around.

Strange's philosophy was that if he had to serve in a segregated army led by white officers whom he believed were his intellectual inferiors, he was going to make life as difficult as possible for his commanders. For his recalcitrance, "I was assigned the most arduous, difficult jobs they could find and I took them all on with glee. I did everything I could to make their lives miserable." Strange reveled in the idea that the army couldn't figure out what to do with its black troops. "The question the army had was 'What are we going to do with all these niggers?' "

Few of the volunteers were college educated, most had not graduated from high school. In this regard Waymon Ransom was typical. Ransom was born in Ypsilanti, Michigan, in 1922, before the great migration of blacks to the North, where they sought better employment opportunities and escape from the more virulent forms of racial prejudice and segregation in the South. Ransom's father, Ray, had fled Oklahoma for Detroit one step ahead of a lynch mob. By World War II some three hundred thousand blacks had poured into the city to work in the war factories.

Ray Ransom had graduated from high school and took a job with the railroad. Because he was better educated than most blacks, and many whites, he was offered a job managing a water and coal stop on a stretch of track near Parsons, Kansas. When local whites discovered a black man was in charge of a contingent of Mexicans, they came looking for him. The Mexicans warned Ray Ransom and he hid in the bushes while the mob vainly searched for him. He jumped on the first train that came along and made his way north.

Ray Ransom was versatile and learned the plumbing and electrical trades and even a little bit of dentistry. Later he became an ordained minister and preached to black congregations in Canada, just across the border from Detroit in Windsor.

Waymon Ransom's life changed in 1936, when his father died suddenly of a heart attack. Without the patriarch, the family fell apart. The fourteen-year-old Waymon left school and lived parentless in a Detroit ghetto with his kid brother, who was five years younger. Their mother lived elsewhere in Detroit and Ransom seldom saw her.

"I was hustling as best I could," Ransom remembered. "I'd take a day's work with anybody, loading and unloading trucks in Detroit's produce district, taking out garbage, playing the numbers—things like that. My brother ran with kids who picked out things from the trash."

Living off trash became a way of life for the numerous black urchins of Detroit in the 1930s, and it got Ransom into trouble. There were licensed "ragpickers" who sold to junk dealers, many of whom operated gangs of thieves. The junk dealers sent their young thieves to break into various shops in Detroit, load a truck full of stolen wares, and drive it to a predetermined spot where it was parked for later delivery to the junkyard.

Some of these kids ran with Ransom's younger brother and were picked up by the police. They fingered a ragpicker, who fingered a junk dealer. Ransom was mentioned somewhere in the hierarchy and the police became interested in his activities. He grabbed his kid brother and the two fled by train to Kansas, where they spent the summer with relatives and waited out the storm.

Ransom lived this life for nearly five years, until 1941, when his mother remarried and the family was reunited. He worked in a print shop and as a janitor before joining the army in 1942.

Arthur Holmes was born five years before Ransom in Detroit in 1917, and the two knew of each other before they became squadmates in 5th Platoon. Holmes's father died when he was seven and his mother died a year later, Holmes believes, out of grief for his father. Orphaned, he went to live with two aunts who abused him unmercifully until he was fourteen. He was regularly beaten with a metal-tipped razor strap until the day he grabbed his aunt's hand and wrenched the strap from her hand. She never beat him again, and not long afterward Holmes went out on his own.

"I got a room and supported myself by selling papers, shining shoes, and doing little odd jobs here and there." Holmes moved briefly to Chicago and then to California, where he lived in West Los Angeles and worked in nightclubs in Hollywood.

For most of his young life Holmes was aware of discrimination but ignored it. He could work in Hollywood nightclubs but never patronize them, just as he had worked in but never patronized the Chicago club where Count Basie was a regular.

"I didn't experience much discrimination. I was aware of it, but I knew there were certain things you couldn't do and I didn't bother thinking about them. I learned to live within the confines of the segregated world," Holmes said. "I wasn't angry about it because I wasn't bothering it and it wasn't bothering me."

Ransom held similar attitudes about segregation. "It was like rain or snow. They were a part of life and you accepted them. Some people got bent out of shape by it. I didn't. I was prepared to duck and weave if I ran into it."

James Strawder believed as a boy that once blacks fought for their country the nation would be grateful and finally treat them with respect as human beings. He and fellow classmates discussed how whites would someday accept blacks, who would be assimilated into an integrated world. A high school teacher, who was also an officer in a black National Guard unit, assured them that once we put "our blood on the line we would gain our dignity." No doubt the teacher remembered the words of Frederick Douglass during the Civil War. "Once let the black man get upon his person the brass letters, U.S., let him get an eagle on his button, and a musket on his shoulder and bullets in his pockets, and there is no power on earth which can deny that he has earned the right to citizenship in the United States." Strawder wasn't looking for citizenship. He wanted respect.

Strawder was well educated for his day, particularly among blacks. He had the equivalent of a high school diploma. After high school he journeyed to Texas in hopes of attaining a college education. He had heard that if a black youth appeared at Prairie View College, an all-black institution in Prairie View, Texas, he could apply for a scholarship. Strawder set off with two comrades; none of them had any money so they hitchhiked all the way. When they finally reached Texas they were arrested and jailed for vagrancy. Rather than allow Strawder to continue on to Prairie View, the police told him to leave the state. He had to make his way through the Deep South on his way back home. He survived, "but I caught the devil getting back home."

Like Holmes and Ransom, Strawder survived on odd jobs around his hometown of Washington, D.C. He had a good job as a mechanic for a Lincoln-Mercury dealership but quit in a dispute over pay. "The man paid me one price and paid the white fellow another. I said why can't you pay me the same and he said because you're colored. You don't need as much money to live on as white people. I said to hell with the job. I'll be damned if I'm going to work for 25 percent less because I'm black."

"I was very arrogant and very angry at whites all my life," Strawder said. "I just couldn't conform because of all my anger." A District of Columbia police officer once taunted the young Strawder and picked a fight. "I understand you are a good boxer," the officer sneered. "I was good and fast with my hands," Strawder said. He took on the officer, won the fight, and wound up in jail.

In the army Strawder took the tests and qualified for pilot training but never got the call because he was black. He couldn't even join the infantry. When the opportunity came to volunteer Strawder grabbed it. "I always wanted to be in combat; from the time I was a teenager all I wanted to do was fight."

"Just about all of us in the black platoons were misfits," Strawder said. "The ones they picked for the infantry were the ones they wanted to get rid of. We were arrogant and difficult, but most of us were a little above average in intelligence."

Bruce Wright was one of the few volunteers who did not come from the killing floor. But a better upbringing did not protect him from the same wounding discrimination that had affected his less affluent comrades.

Wright was born in Princeton, New Jersey, and learned about discrimination one day as a youth when he was turned away from a community swimming pool because he was black. He found American attitudes about race confounding and outrageous, and he carried his anger through his adult life. It became particularly evident many years after the war, on the New York Supreme Court bench, where Wright was known for his leniency toward black defendants because he believed they were victims of racism. For his views he earned the moniker "Turn-'em-loose Bruce." His persona became the basis for the television program *100 Centre Street,* starring Alan Arkin as the liberal New York judge who is nicknamed "Let-'em-go Joe."

Wright learned as a teenager that America's racial attitudes infected the highest realms. As a senior in high school he applied to and was accepted at Princeton University in the late 1930s. The acceptance was later rescinded however, when the university discovered he was black. Admissions officials explained that they had not known about the color of his skin and a dean suggested that he would not be a good fit among this elite group of Ivy Leaguers.

Wright received a letter from the dean that provocatively demonstrates the insidious and profound discrimination that gripped the United States even in "enlightened circles."

With the salutation of "Dear Mr. Wright," the dean stated that Princeton did not discriminate against "any race, color or creed," and pointed out that this benevolent tradition had been maintained since the university's founding in the eighteenth century. The dean reinforced his comments by stating that he had "very pleasant relations with your race, both in civilian life and in the army." He added however, "I cannot conscientiously advise a colored student to apply for admission to Princeton simply because I do not think that he would be happy in the University and a member of your race might feel very much alone." He gave as a reason the fact that there were many southern students at Princeton who would not tolerate a black student being a member of the student body. He concluded that a colored student would be more suited to a college or university in New England where there was greater tolerance for blacks or in an all-Negro college.

"I write these personal reactions simply because I would wish you the greatest success in your college course both as a student and as a member of a university family."

Wright recalled attending, as a child, a concert featuring Paul Robeson, "that heroic giant," in Princeton's Witherspoon Hall. "Little did I dream that one day Princeton would give me the same distinction of rejection it had given Robeson," Wright wrote in a memoir, *Black Robes, White Justice*. "That quiet little Central Jersey academic retreat was a bitter paradox. Its university boasted of service to the world and pointed with pride to Woodrow Wilson, a Southerner who had taught Constitutional Law. His first executive order after becoming President was to segregate Washington's public facilities."

Wright recalled Robeson's description of Princeton as a "Georgia plantation town, and it fully justified that comparison. . . . It was indeed a curious place. The town, dominated by the university, differed in no large degree from that institution. Blacks were huddled behind Princeton's main street, and their enclave continued on down to the unpaved avenues next to the trolley tracks that ran to Trenton, past the adjacent dump."

After his rejection by Princeton, Wright went on to graduate from Lincoln University in Pennsylvania and spent one year in law school before going into the military. In the army this future New York judge wrote and recited poetry as he agitated for equality both in civilian life and in the army. Men such as Wright challenged all white authority and demanded that blacks be treated with the same respect as white troops. When the opportunity came to form the black platoons, Wright signed on knowing it was a half measure, but a step in the right direction.

12

•

COMPIÈGNE, FRANCE

WHEN LIEUTENANT RALSTON ARRIVED in Compiègne the men who would constitute the 5th of K had been in infantry training for six weeks. In their combat ODs and potlike helmets they all appeared alike, but they were a diverse lot, coming from all over the ETO and the Mediterranean theater as well.

Thirty-eight percent of all volunteers came from the engineers, 29 percent arrived from Quartermaster Corps units, 26 percent were from transportation units, 3 percent came from the Signal Corps, 2 percent had been in Ordnance units, and the remaining 2 percent came from other branches, according to historian Lee. "Sixty-three percent had formerly had one of the six following occupational specialties, in order of frequency: truck driver, duty soldier, longshoreman, basic construction foreman, and cargo checker."

On average the black volunteers were younger than the rest of the army. Ten percent, however, were thirty years old or older, compared to 20 percent of white infantrymen. The volunteers had better educational backgrounds and test scores than the average black soldier, but their scores were lower than those of the average white soldier. Forty-one percent of white riflemen were high school graduates compared with 22 percent of the blacks. The army noted that a major difference between the volunteers and the majority of African-American troops in the ETO was their motivation and "call to duty."

To Lieutenant Ralston's and Sergeant Sacco's combat-tested eyes, their men weren't ready for the front and the still-formidable, battle-hardened German army. The new platoon leader and platoon sergeant would deal with these deficiencies, but first they had to gain the confidence of their new troops.

"There was a learning process on both sides. They were pretty ginger about me and Sgt. Sacco because we were white," Ralston said. "But once they were convinced that we were talking serious stuff and we weren't racially prejudiced they got down in the dirt and did what they had to do. They knew then we were talking survival."

Being thrown in with blacks for the first time was a totally new experience for the young lieutenant, and he learned quickly to adjust his stereotyped thinking. In some ways his men were different from whites, yet it many ways they were alike. Other white officers who commanded African-Americans in World War II came to realize that there was little difference between whites and blacks except the color of their skin. Lt. Col. John H. Sherman, who commanded black troops during the war, wrote of his experiences: "Any officer who lives their life with them, eating in the same mess, sleeping in the same area, attending their chapel, visiting their dayrooms, buying in their exchanges, and showing interest in their sports and social activities, soon finds that these men are passionately eager for pride, self-respect and friends to whom they can give trust and loyalty. Those are the things Negroes will work for, eagerly fight for, gladly die for. I know. I have seen them do all three."

To Lieutenant Ralston his black volunteers were both innocent and artful. "I saw them get in fights and bite each other and cry," Ralston said. Off duty they could be wild, carousing, laughing, joking, and telling stories, and their black patois had a melodious flow that Lieutenant Ransom called "black platoon talk." But he was most surprised, and impressed, by their sharp, innate intelligence.

Lieutenant Ralston's surprise would not have been unusual in a society that segregated blacks. African-Americans of that era were stereotyped, and the army made a point of instructing white officers in command of blacks not to perceive them in these roles. An officers' manual warned that blacks were generally portrayed in movies as "lazy, shiftless, no-good, slew-footed, happy-go-lucky, razor-toting, tap-dancing vagrants." Other racial and cultural stereotypes had disappeared, the army noted—the monocled Englishman and the brogue-accented Irish immigrant—and the negative perception of the African-American also would vanish.

The white perception of blacks was also influenced by scores on the Army General Classification Test (AGCT) in which blacks generally performed poorly and consistently scored lower than whites. The AGCT results were unfairly seen as a measure of intelligence. But the test classified men by how well they performed at certain skills and not by their innate abilities and intelligence.

Historian Lee quotes Dr. Benjamin V. Bingham, an army psychologist: "There is nothing in the title of the Army test that says anything about native intelligence. . . . Performance in such a test reflects very definitely the educational opportunities the individual has had." In the AGCT vocabulary test, for example, many blacks did not understand such words as *chevron, discipline,* and *cadre.* Thirty-five percent of blacks scored in the lowest test category compared with 4.1 percent of whites. While 6.4 percent of whites scored in the top category, only .02 percent of blacks were in this category.

Despite their educational and cultural handicaps, his men impressed Lieutenant Ralston. "They were oddly superior to whites in some respects," Ralston recalled. He wouldn't have called them book smart, because reading was not their habit and some were close to being illiterate. Less than a quarter of them had finished high school. Rather, Ralston described them as street smart. He also noticed their wonderful flair for language that most whites lacked and how easily they picked up French and German from the people around them.

Boris recalled an incident involving Lester Boudreau that relates to Ralston's observations. Boudreau was from the French-speaking bayou country of Louisiana and spoke French, albeit with a North American accent. But U.S. MPs weren't aware of the finer points of language. Once, they caught him in a restricted zone and were prepared to arrest him and throw him in the stockade. Boudreau immediately began gesticulating like a Frenchman and playing the part of a French soldier, all the while claiming that there was nothing illegal about a French poilu's being where he was. Since the French troops in World War II wore lend-lease American uniforms, the MPs had difficulty determining if Boudreau really was French. But the Ragin' Cajun's jabberings in French hoodwinked the MPs and they released him.

"The blacks also had a cunning that the whites didn't have," Ralston said. He noticed it particularly in areas relating to discipline. "You'd accuse them of something and bang, they'd have an answer. It was a half-assed answer, but plausible enough that you couldn't do anything to them except slap them on the wrist."

Ralston could have been describing Private Strawder, who learned quickly that he could outwit his white superiors, particularly young, arrogant lieutenants, by memorizing the FM 100, the army field manual. "We blacks were smart enough to outsmart most white officers. They just didn't have enough on the ball, so as long as you stayed within the rules you could get by with a lot. The FM 100—that was my bible and I learned it by heart, just like a lawyer," Strawder said.

Strawder used the FM 100 for good measure once in England while serving with the 561st Quartermaster Service Battalion. A young, inexperienced "shavetail" lieutenant ordered Strawder and his detail of men to clean a batch of "honey buckets" left by a departing unit. Honey buckets were pans that slid underneath outhouses and filled with sewage that had to be regularly emptied. The job was odious.

"The lieutenant said he wanted the honey buckets to be spotless,"

Strawder remembered. "I was a corporal and I had about twenty men in my detail and I said, 'Sir, please give a demonstration of what you mean by spotless.' The lieutenant said, 'What do you mean, give a demonstration!' I stood my ground and said, 'Sir, a demonstration, please.' He didn't act like an officer. He was acting like a child. I wanted him to lose control and he did, hollering and hooping and saying you're gonna do this and do that. I called my men to attention and marched them back to the company area. The officer followed us and told my company commander that I had refused to obey an order.

"Now my CO knew my strategy—he'd faced it with me before—so he right away said to the lieutenant, 'This man asked for a demonstration and did you give him a demonstration?' The lieutenant said, 'Hell no! Do you think I'm gonna do that?' And my CO told him that I was perfectly within my rights. If an officer asks an enlisted man or noncommissioned officer to do something outside his military specialty and if it's not described in the FM 100 the soldier has the right to ask the officer to demonstrate how it must be done. That lieutenant never did demonstrate how to make honey buckets spotless. He left me alone."

On another occasion in Germany when Strawder was an infantryman with the 5th Platoon, E Company, his commanding officer asked him to jump into a stream to see how deep it was. Strawder recited chapter and verse from the field manual. It stated that the officer leads and the enlisted man follows. "We were on patrol and I said, 'You lead and I'll follow. You're the platoon leader.'

"There are a lot of things in the FM 100 and if a soldier sat down and really studied it he can beat out the average court-martial. The officers like they were making back then, those ninety-day wonders, weren't smart enough. I had fun with them." But Strawder admitted he never would have tried the same thing with a West Point–educated officer, who would have known how to handle his men. "Those West Pointers were real officers."

Willfred Strange had a similar flair for frustrating his superiors. He also learned to grab any opportunity that knocked, particularly when it came from the white world. Just after V-E Day the regimental colonel asked if anyone could open a riding school in his occupation zone. Strange jumped at the chance: he portrayed himself as a former polo player, found some old German army workhorses, and opened the school for the colonel. He was neither a polo player nor an accomplished rider; in fact, he could barely mount a horse. "It took BS to get along in the army," Strange said. "I can be the king of Prussia if you give me time enough."

Lieutenant Ralston would learn to deal with this type of artifice in his men, but he first had to gain their confidence. The fact that he and

Sergeant Sacco were combat veterans helped immeasurably. Sergeant Sacco had the distinction of having been wounded during the Bulge, and when he spoke he knew what he was talking about.

Lieutenant Ralston requested, and received from the 16th Reinforcement Depot, Ground Forces Reinforcement System, two weeks of additional training with the men to get them ready for the rigors of combat. To start with they needed to familiarize themselves with the BAR, the Browning automatic rifle, a magazine-loaded submachine gun. It had been developed at the end of World War I and would survive through the Korean War. Every squad was built around the BAR man, and the men had to know how to use the weapon because it was likely they would be called on to fire it in combat. It was big and bulky, weighing sixteen pounds, but it did the job.

Lieutenant Ralston was applying the hard-won lessons of war. In one wartime survey of men in infantry divisions, the army discovered that its troops wanted more instruction on the "weapons and tools" of combat and less on drill and bivouac. In particular, the army noted, "we need more practice for men on crew served weapons."

The instruction for the men of 5th of K also focused on knowledge of German weapons and how to defend against them. Prime examples were the German MG-34 and MG-42, the standard enemy machine guns, which had an extremely high rate of fire that sounded to military historian Charles MacDonald like "the voice of an angry cougar." Many inexperienced troops who heard these guns ripping away on the battlefield froze in their tracks. They had to understand that the machine guns sometimes fired high and were often ineffective unless handled by experienced soldiers. The men also learned about standard German infantry tactics and how to defend against them, and how to attack various types of German bunkers and other defensive positions.

They also studied American small-unit tactics used in attacking villages and built-up areas where enemy troops would be holed up waiting for a chance to take out a few "Amis," as the Germans called their American enemy.

The 5th of K went on field exercises and made river crossings. The men studied and practiced the use of tactical formations to attack through deep woods and across open fields, and how to employ marching fire. This tactic was a critical element of the instruction, and many infantrymen, and even some officers, were new to it. Marching fire involved entire units moving across a battlefield in skirmish-line with all soldiers rapidly firing their weapons from the hip to keep the enemy down in their foxholes and trenches. The American semiautomatic M1 rifle was ideal for this kind of tactic because it did not need to be constantly reloaded and could fire eight shots in succession by simply pulling the trigger. The average German soldier carried a bolt-action rifle that did not lend itself to such volumes of fire.

Many of the volunteers had had no intense infantry training in the army before they went through the course, and they found conditions rugged and tough at Compiègne. To begin with, the men were housed in barracks that had no heat and 1944–45 was one of the coldest European winters on record. Ransom's group was in buildings dating back to the Napoleonic era. They had fireplaces, but the fuel allocation was so skimpy—several logs each night—that lighting a fire was hardly worth the effort.

Willfred Strange was quartered in a building in which the roof had been blown off. To sleep, the men wrapped themselves in as much clothing as possible, slid into sleeping bags, and braved it through the night. They often awoke covered with snow and ice.

The men got up for breakfast outdoors in the predawn darkness, sometimes in snow. Then they were marched out to the hinterlands of forests and fields for training. Each man carried his rifle and equipment along with a full field pack, his head topped by a steel helmet. In the freezing temperatures the men's overheated heads steamed like boiling pots of water whenever they removed their helmets.

On the rifle ranges they smelled the acrid odor of gunpowder and heard the ripping, cracking sounds of continuous M1 fire. In their old service companies, no one had paid much attention to a rifle. The enemy was too far away for that to be a worry. But now the rifle could save their life or the life of a comrade, and they learned to strip the M1 down in minutes and slap it back together again.

The men also learned the art of loading the M1, and those who didn't pick it up fast enough were guaranteed a badly bruised or broken thumb. The weapon loaded from the top with the clip of eight rounds pressed into the breech by the thumb. When the clip was seated it tripped a lever that forced the bolt to slam shut, and if a soldier didn't get his thumb out fast enough it was smashed into the breech with the bullet casing. This sometimes brought the mocking cries of drill instructors on the rifle ranges of American training bases as they ranged up and down the line announcing the latest case of what some called "M1 finger." Every neck strained to see the suffering GI doubled over in pain and gripping his throbbing thumb.

The men were taught to hurl hand grenades from special sandbagged cubicles that contained small pits at the center. If a man dropped a grenade in the act of throwing, the instructor kicked it into the pit and everybody dove for cover. Cadre, positioned nearby, carefully observed as each grenade was thrown, and if it wasn't thrown far enough they yelled "Short" over a bullhorn and everybody ducked as dirt, rocks, and steel fragments cut through the air. Men who had never heard the blast of a grenade were aghast at the deafening roar from such a small bomb and the hail of debris that crashed into protective metal and earthen barriers.

Every man was made to crawl and squirm through an infiltration course as explosions were set off in nearby pits to simulate artillery fire, and bolted-down machine guns sent streams of tracer bullets zipping just inches above his head.

There were forced marches that started with five-mile jaunts and worked their way to twenty-five-mile hikes that tested the men's physical and emotional stamina. On numerous occasions the training didn't stop when the sun went down. Night combat training was an important component of the course, and the men learned infiltration tactics and took night firing drills, blasting away at invisible targets by sighting over the barrel of their M1s.

Each man had his own impressions of the infantry training. "It was a lot of run, run and jump, jump in small-unit tactics out there in the mud and snow," Ransom recalled. "But it wasn't any worse than doing construction work in the mud and snow back in the engineers."

If the volunteers were at first wary of the all-white instructors, they quickly overcame their reservations. The instructors, to a man, were required to be combat veterans, and many had been wounded in previous fighting in the ETO. They were teaching survival, and all hands listened intently. "No one objected to the white instructors because these guys had been there. They had been in combat," recalled Leonard Rife. "Nobody cared what color they were. They had come to teach us. That was their objective."

Lawrence Boris remembered the admonitions of Sergeant Sacco during the training. Sacco warned that when a man was being shelled he would do anything to get deeper in the ground. "If all you had in your pocket was a pen, you'd use it to dig a deeper hole," Sacco said. He had survived the Battle of the Bulge, and Boris would soon understand what he meant.

Some of the volunteers thought they detected racial bias among the instructors, although it was never overt. "The cadre were good," Willfred Strange said. "But they were still white and had basic prejudices about blacks. They kept calling us 'you people.' I said what is this 'you people'?" Holmes noted also that the cadre stuck to themselves during off-duty time. They had separate quarters from the volunteers.

"We kept training in earnest," Ralston remembered. "I exaggerated considerably about how many of them were going to die to try and scare them out of the unit. I only wanted the best and bravest. But nobody quit. They were pretty darned good."

Not only did the volunteers not easily scare, they were determined to get into combat. Clayton Des Journette was a gung ho volunteer who breezed through training camp but was struck on the head by grenade fragments in a training mishap a few days before the men were to move out to the 99th. He was confined to the base hospital when the platoon finished training and set off for the front.

Des Journette was not to be denied the right to fight. He rose from his bed, dressed in his combat outfit, and sneaked back into the platoon even though he wasn't listed on the roster. "I was going to the front AWOL from the hospital," Des Journette said. "Lieutenant Ralston didn't notice until we were on the line."

In late February the 5th of K Company finally moved out. The training had ended for some two thousand black volunteers and they now embarked on a mission to prove themselves.

General Davis visited the training camp several times and addressed the men prior to their departure for the front. He knew the real issue for these troops was not their own mortality; they also had a much larger issue, to defend in the dignity of the black race.

Your presence here justifies my faith in you. It also justifies the faith of the high command in this theater as well as the veteran officers who served with your fathers and grandfathers. Before the letter offering you the privilege of volunteering for this training went out, I was asked if I thought many of you would want to take advantage of it. I stated . . . that you would come forward and be happy to serve in the way that you could make the largest contribution toward winning victory.

The letter went out and you are here which is the best answer as to your attitude. It may be of interest to you to know that after the surrender of the Spanish forces at Santiago in Cuba in 1898 a large part of the Army was stricken with Yellow Fever. The 24th U.S. Infantry [all-black] was invited to send a few volunteers to assist in caring for the Yellow Fever patients. Some folks back in those days had the idea that Yellow Fever wouldn't attack us. Instead of some men volunteering, the entire regiment volunteered and fought Yellow Fever with the same valor that they had fought the Spanish enemies. I also remember a story of old Sgt. Carney. It is said that when the colors were presented to the 54th Massachusetts Infantry on Boston Commons during the Civil War, that upon receiving the colors Sgt. Carney said: "I shall carry these colors aloft or report to God above." In the assault on Fort Wagoner, Sgt. Carney was shot down but still waved his colors aloft, and when they were taken from him by another he said, "Tell the Colonel the old flag never touched ground." As many of you know, that has been immortalized in the song, "The Old Flag Never Touched the Ground."

So you see, you have a tradition to live up to. I want at this time also to remind you that the going will not always be easy. In addition to being outstanding soldiers, you must at the same time be diplomatic. You are going to run into some who will doubt your ability to carry on and do a job as well as they think they are doing it. I hope that you are going to be as mentally strong and as mentally efficient as ambassadors of good will, as you are going to be reinforcements for military purposes. I hope that you are going to be sufficiently strong and broad-minded so that when things do not go to your liking, that you will not feel that the hard going or any unpleasantness that may arise, has been inflicted upon you on account of your color or race. I hope that you will think of the following extract editorially mentioned in *Stars and Stripes* as the Eisenhower ideal:

We of the United Nations must live and work together, regardless of race or nationality, creed or service, uniform or rank. Supported by our homelands, we must fight on relentlessly, side-by-side, at sea, on land, and in the air, so that we will win together a better world, secure and free for all men everywhere. Your presence here in response to the invitation of the high command to volunteer for retraining as reinforcements indicates that you and the race you represent wish to "live and work together regardless of race or nationality, creed or service, uniform or rank, so that we will win together a better world, secure and free for all men everywhere" at home as well as abroad.

The men of the black platoons were on their way.

13

•

ON THEIR WAY

THE 5TH OF K, 394th Regiment, crossed the Rhine River at Remagen March 12, 1945, after a two-day ride from Compiègne. They first rode in antique French 40 & 8 railway box cars, so called because they carried forty men and eight horses, and later in trucks that transported the platoon into the Rhineland.

The platoon was joining the Allies' drive in late February 1945 through France, Belgium, and the Netherlands into Germany with the objective of reaching the Rhine River. According to General Bradley some eighty-five German divisions were massed west of the river, and if the Allies destroyed or reduced these enemy units before they fell back behind this strategic waterway, the drive into the heart of Germany would be more rapid.

The American advance was arrayed from north to south in Lt. Gen. William Simpson's Ninth Army, Lt. Gen. Courtney Hodges's First Army, and Lt. Gen. George Patton's Third Army. Lt. Gen. Alexander Patch's Seventh Army, farther south, was flanked by the First French Army under Gen. Jean de Lattre de Tassigny.

After two months of intensive training the black volunteers of the 5th of K were becoming a cohesive unit, but they were still green and had much to discover about warfare and themselves in the days ahead. They hailed from all over America and a good many had served together in the same units before infantry training and so knew one another well. Holmes and Ransom came from the 377th Engineers along with Lester Boudreau from Louisiana, James Oliver from New York, Harry Lucky from North Carolina, and Raymond Day and Bernard Bailey from Maryland.

Lester Boudreau was the most celebrated of the group. He loved combat and would soon inherit the nicknames "Ragin' Cajun" and "Blitz" because he took no prisoners and sometimes had to be restrained from killing Germans. He proved to be expert with the BAR, and platoon buddies rationalized Boudreau's ways by thanking God he was on their side. He was light skinned, with a thin mustache. His reputation grew until he was something of a legend in the 99th Division, even among some high-ranking officers. Five years later during the Korean War, Ransom ran into American soldiers who knew of Boudreau and his love of combat. Boudreau was also known for his antics off the battlefield, carousing and ever in search of wine and whiskey.

James Oliver was nicknamed "Sakie" by his buddies. He was a happy-go-lucky New Yorker who turned into a trusted infantryman and scout. Boris remembers him always singing a jingle, "Tippie, Tippie Tay, Tippie, Tippie Tay," as he patrolled ahead of the platoon. Oliver won the Silver Star for heroism during the 5th's first action in the Remagen bridgehead. He also served, for a time, as Boudreau's BAR assistant, carrying his ammunition and backing him up whenever necessary, but the two argued and feuded so often that the team was broken up.

Harry Lucky was considered an exuberant, amusing character and Holmes still laughs at his antics. "If you listened to Lucky, he was the baddest person who ever grew bread," Ransom said. Holmes remembers when Lucky had one too many drinks and tried to make a German dog stand at attention and salute. Lucky claimed to be part black and part Cherokee Indian and was proud of his heritage.

Lawrence Boris came from the 366th Engineers, which worked its way across northern France repairing bombed-out railroads and highways. A solidly built man and a reliable soldier, Boris became squad leader of 2nd Squad in Germany.

Harold Robinson, Sam Wade, and Willie Cope came from the 487th Quartermaster Battalion, which had served in the Mediterranean theater. The 487th accompanied the army through North Africa, Sicily, and Italy and participated in the invasion of southern France near Saint-Tropez in August 1944. When the three volunteered for the infantry the 487th was in northeastern France near the German frontier.

Sam Wade, a tall, good-looking country boy from Tennessee, inherited the nickname of "Subway Sam" not from any association with a big city, but from his service in Italy, where the girls had difficulty pronouncing his name. Sam Wade came out "Subway," and the nickname stuck. Because of his size he could tote the heavy BAR, so he often anchored his squad with his weapon throughout their days in combat. Wade was also something of a wisecracking comedian who once refused a direct order from regimental commander Col. John Jeter to get out of bed one morning. Wade pleaded, with a sheepish grin, that he couldn't get up because he had the "shits." Jeter told him to stop eating from contaminated mess tins and to get the hell out of the rack!

Willie Cope grew up in Detroit with Ransom and Holmes and was nicknamed "King Kong" by comrades because of his muscular build. "He was solid and bowlegged and walked on the outside of his feet and referred to himself as King Cope, so everybody took to calling him King Kong

Cope," Ransom remembered. "But don't say that to his face when he's not feeling good."

Ransom, Holmes, and Cope had attended the same school and lived near one another. "Out the back door, across the alley, and up their stairs and there was Cope's house," Ransom said. The two had been in eighth and ninth grades together. Holmes and Cope had been rivals as youths, often feuding and fighting. "We used to fight like cats and dogs when we were growing up and he still thought he could beat me in the army, but he couldn't," Holmes remembered.

Harold Robinson was associated with Oliver in a roundabout way, since Robinson's future wife, Sherry, had gone to school with Oliver in a suburb of New York City. Robinson had been in a quartermaster unit before joining the infantry.

Clayton Des Journette came from Seattle, Washington. "D.J." to the men in the platoon, he had been a chauffeur before the war, and became the soft-spoken radio operator shadowing Lieutenant Ralston in combat. He came from the 366th Engineers as well. Holmes remembered D.J. for his wry sense of humor and from an amusing incident during the fighting around the city of Giessen. The various platoons in K Company had call signs of "Bug One," "Bug Two," and so on, and one day in combat D.J. tried to contact one of the platoons on the radio.

"Come in, Bug One," D.J. said into the mike. There was no response.

"Come in, Bug Two," he repeated. Again there was no response.

In desperation, D.J. yelled into the mike: "Come in any goddamned Bug!"

David Skeeters, later the platoon sergeant, came from the Baltimore area and had been in the 385th Engineers in North Africa, Italy, and Sicily. After he made the invasion of southern France, Skeeters volunteered for the infantry. Bernard Bailey also hailed from Maryland, where he lived on the Eastern Shore.

Eddy Hunter was one of the youngest members of the 5th and was given the nickname "the Deacon" because he was religious and was involved in his church in Plant City, Florida. Ransom remembered Hunter as a kid with a talent for drawing who sketched naked women on the barracks walls in Compiègne. Ransom gave Hunter the additional nickname "Judo Crouch" because he was always practicing judo moves. "There wasn't nobody talking about judo back then and he was always doing his judo moves," Ransom said. "I told him, 'Don't you worry about that judo crouch, because those Germans aren't going to judo you. They're going to take a burp gun and shoot you full of holes.'" It was a prophetic comment. Hunter planned to return to an agricultural school in Florida if he survived the war.

Private First Class Shaw was an introvert from California who became a schoolteacher after the war. He was tall and "very serious." Holmes remembered him because he coveted Shaw's captured binoculars, which came in handy when Holmes wanted a better look at the battlefield.

Private First Class Francis was a quiet type who trained at Compiègne at the same time as the 5th of K, but joined the platoon after it had arrived in the bridgehead. Francis had originally been assigned to the 106th Division, but the 106th wasn't ready for a black platoon because it had been so badly mauled during the fighting in the Bulge, so the African-Americans assigned to the 106th were shipped to other divisions.

Charles Robinson, a pipe-smoking lawyer from Baltimore, was the wise man of the unit. He was levelheaded and sometimes offered himself as a spokesman for the 5th around high-ranking officers. He occasionally accompanied Skeeters when the platoon sergeant met with company-grade officers to make sure that the commands were properly understood. "He was older and didn't do a lot of talking," Ransom remembered. "He had a lot of education when the rest of us didn't and he was very persuasive when he spoke." After the war Robinson returned to the Baltimore area to continue his practice.

Private First Class Gibson was a New Yorker of Jamaican descent who earned Holmes's lasting enmity for taking a cigarette break while the German lurked about. Thomas Branch, a good man who turned out to be very reliable in combat, by Ransom's account, was often used as Lieutenant Ralston's runner. "He did what he was supposed to and didn't give anybody any trouble," Ransom said.

Earl Jones, from Chicago, the old man of the outfit at thirty-eight could always find schnapps and wine whenever the platoon bivouacked for the night. Ransom remembered him claiming to have been a bootlegger during Prohibition and to be a relative of well-known black racketeers in Chicago. Jones survived by making his age a joke, and the men tried to make life as easy as possible for "the old man," but he refused any special treatment.

Ransom remembers Pfc. Richards as a tough guy who used his image to become a squad leader in the 5th of K. Ransom never got on with Richards. "I was a little skinny kid, and Richards thought I wasn't big enough, bad enough, and loud enough to be a good infantryman," Ransom said. Richards expressed his reservations about Ransom to Lieutenant Ralston as the 5th prepared to leave Compiègne, but Ransom had the support of his mates from Detroit, Holmes and Cope. "They both had a word for me," Ransom said. It was good enough for Lieutenant Ralston, and Ransom marched out with the 5th Platoon to fight in three wars. Richard's fighting career ended two months later.

Ray Dexter, whom Ransom nicknamed "Peter Rabbit" because of

his youth, was a country boy proud of his rural heritage, particularly around the city boys in the 5th. "Dexter was a lot of fun but would run his mouth," Ransom said. "He was going back to being a country boy in the Carolinas when the war was over."

Preston Williams also liked to appear to be tough, and after a fight with Boudreau he nearly burned down a house where part of the 5th bivouacked during the advance through southern Germany. But in reality he was a quiet young man who kept to himself. "He kind of said, 'Don't mess with me,' " Ransom remembered.

Private First Class Edwards was known as "Jinx" to Ransom. He was a short, light-complected black with freckles. Cloyce Blassingame, from Indiana, was quiet and thoughtful, and Holmes remembered him as a boy with whom one could have a good and interesting conversation.

Sampson Jones, from Florida, was another kid under the age of eighteen. The men teased him because of his youth but they also took him under their wing. Holmes worried about Jones's maturity as an infantryman. Jones sometimes didn't demonstrate good sense in tough situations.

By Holmes's account Private First Class Baker was the best infantryman in the 5th of K. He was unafraid in combat and took on the most dangerous assignments. Memories of Pfc. Brandon Williams from Kentucky quickly faded. He would be the first of the 5th of K killed in action in the bridgehead as the platoon set out to find K Company.

T. C. Williams was the rock of 5th Platoon and the one man whom everyone remembers. He was steady and reliable and the best of NCOs. "He kept us in line. He was maybe a little older than the rest of us and he knew what he was doing," Ransom recalled.

"T.C. and Skeeters stand out the most in my memory," Ralston said. "T.C. had intelligence. He was a good soldier and [had] a sort of bouncy bonvivance about him." T.C. started off as a squad leader and later became platoon guide when Skeeters was wounded.

14

•

THE GERMANS ARE THAT CLOSE!

THE 5TH OF K'S objective was to link up with the 99th south of Dusseldorf, where the division had gone into corps reserve, but before the platoon arrived, the 99th was hurriedly shipped upriver to reinforce the Remagen bridgehead. Five American divisions, the 99th among them, were rushed to the east bank of the Rhine immediately after Lieutenant Karl Timmermann's company of armored infantrymen captured the Ludendorff Bridge on March 7.

The American advance over the Rhine in 1945 marked the first time since Napoleon's army crossed the river in 1805 that a modern invading army had breached this natural defensive barrier. The Romans had done it near Remagen almost exactly two thousand years before, when legions under Caesar's command traversed the river to drive back hostile Germanic tribes. The Romans built their bridge near Neuwied, some twelve miles south of Remagen, and campaigned for eighteen days on the east bank subduing their enemies before pulling back. As they withdrew, the Romans destroyed their bridge to prevent the tribes from following.

With the Americans across the Rhine in 1945, the German high command knew that the road to Berlin was wide open and they had to destroy the invading force or be destroyed themselves. Hitler demanded the summary execution of Maj. Hans Scheller, commandant of the Remagen Bridge, for his failure to destroy the span. Hitler also dismissed the long-standing dean of German generals, Generalfeldmarschall Gerd von Rundstedt, and replaced him as commander in the west with Generalfeldmarschall Albert Kesselring, "Smiling Albert," an expert on defense who had used his skills to blunt Allied advances in Italy.

All German soldiers retreating back over the Rhine were ordered to join the nearest combat unit, and those who refused were subject to execution. The collection of enemy troops grew until the bridgehead was ringed by an estimated nine German divisions in three corps facing five American divisions east of the Rhine.

No one had expected the capture of the Ludendorff, because the Germans were destroying all the bridges spanning the Rhine in the vain hope of preventing an Allied drive into the heart of Germany. But when Lt.

Emmet J. Burrows, commanding the lead infantry platoon in Lieutenant Timmermann's company, scanned the river with his binoculars he couldn't believe his eyes. Through the morning haze the old railroad bridge was still standing. Timmermann immediately ordered his men across. Ironically, Karl Timmermann's father, John, crossed the span in 1919 as a member of the American army that occupied the Rhineland after World War I, three years before his son was born.

The news of the bridge's capture electrified the American command. "Hot dog!" exclaimed Gen. Omar N. Bradley, commanding Twelfth Army Group, of which the 99th was a part. Bradley ordered First Army commander Lt. Gen. Courtney Hodges to get as much "stuff" across the Rhine as quickly as possible. "This will bust him wide open," Bradley said. The Rhine had been the Allied objective for months, and Bradley knew that once the Allies were across, Germany's defeat was sealed.

The drive to reach the Rhine had started on D-Day, June 6, 1944, with the invasion of France. The Allies struggled for six weeks to break the Germans' grip in Normandy, and in late July they finally smashed their way out and pushed rapidly across northern France to the German frontier. The Rhine was within reach, a few days' thrust in some places, but German resistance stiffened at the Siegfried Line, the fortifications and barriers guarding the borders of the Reich. The Allies found themselves stalled short of the river at places such as Arnhem in the Netherlands, the Heurtgen Forest in Germany, and Metz in France.

At Arnhem, the British 1st Airborne Division, supported by an overland drive through Holland that included parachute drops by the American 82nd and 101st Airborne Divisions, failed to capture the Arnhem Bridge over the Lower Rhine. German resistance proved too strong and most of the shattered remnants of the 1st Airborne were captured.

In the Heurtgen the U.S. 9th, 28th, and 1st Divisions advanced into these darkened forests that guarded the German frontier just south of the city of Aachen in an effort to break through to the Rhine. The Heurtgen turned into an epic and futile struggle, in which the Germans prevailed, that lasted from September to November 1944 and cost the Americans thousands of casualties.

Even Patton's rampaging tank forces couldn't crack the German defenses around Metz and Nancy in eastern France before winter's onset in 1944. Then in December 1944, the Germans counterattacked in the Ardennes to drive the Americans back during the Battle of the Bulge. K Company and the 99th had been involved in the Bulge, and the division and the company suffered heavy losses. Only in February 1945 had the Allied armies once again resumed the offensive; now in the waning winter months of 1945 they advanced through the Heurtgen, beyond Metz and

Nancy in France, and through the Rhineland, the region bordering the Rhine. By early March the Allies controlled most of the west bank and prepared for an attack across the river.

The main Allied thrust over the Rhine was to be commanded by British field marshal Bernard Montgomery, and the focus of the attack was north of Cologne, where the terrain was deemed more suitable for a drive to Berlin. But once the Ludendorff Bridge was in American hands Montgomery's plan became redundant, so Eisenhower ordered the U.S. divisions to converge immediately on the Remagen area to establish a bridgehead on the river's east bank.

When the Ludendorff was built in 1916 engineers had considered the possibility that someday the bridge would have to be defended and even destroyed in the defense of the Fatherland. The 1,069-foot span had four towers, two at each end, from which guards had full view of the surrounding countryside, and each tower had small apertures through which soldiers could fire. The four towers together had enough space to house a full battalion of soldiers. Passageways connected the towers, enabling defending troops to go from one to the other under cover.

German engineers had also constructed the massive stone supporting piers to house large demolition chambers that could be packed with TNT to destroy the bridge and prevent its capture by an enemy. French forces occupying the Rhineland after World War I filled the chambers with concrete, thus helping to thwart destruction of the bridge in 1945. When the Americans advanced on the Ludendorff many of the TNT charges attached to the superstructure failed to detonate, so although the bridge was damaged, it remained strong enough for several days to carry tanks and military vehicles.

The 5th of K followed the 99th across the Rhine four days after the division arrived in the bridgehead. As the platoon neared Remagen the thump of artillery echoed downriver like a distant kettledrum providing percussion for the sharp crack of American antiaircraft guns. Streams of red tracer bullets swarmed around the German aircraft dodging up and down the Rhine to bomb the Ludendorff Bridge. The planes came at regular intervals, ME-109s, FW-190s, Heinkel twin-engine bombers, and the old workhorses of the Luftwaffe, Stuka dive bombers, coming in low from the south or plummeting down from on high with the sirens in their wheel pods screaming death and vengeance. The enemy was determined to destroy the span and choke off the expanding bridgehead.

In Remagen the men of the 5th of K were silent as they viewed the streets of this two-thousand-year-old town, which were littered with the rubble of blasted buildings and the occasional corpse of an American soldier left where he had fallen because of the constant and accurate German artillery fire. No one wanted to die picking up the dead.

"We paused here and there to extract K Rations and D Bars from the packs of the dead," remembered one American soldier from E Company, 393rd Regiment, 99th Division, as it moved through Remagen several days before. "The combat soldier who survives is, first of all, a realist. There was nothing callous in the act. Combat infantrymen have a reverence for the dead unequaled and unspoken, for death and the dead are constant companions."

The men of the 5th of K were new to war in a town that had seen conflicts come and go through the ages. Remagen was originally a Celtic town that was later fortified by the Romans, who named it Ricomagus, and vestiges of the Roman occupation were still evident. Before World War II Remagen had been a tourist destination of hotels and restaurants, with visitors attracted by the scenic river and the mountains and valleys that stretched out beyond the Rhine.

By the time the 5th of K arrived Remagen had nearly been destroyed by artillery fire and bombings by both Germans and Americans. Once it was captured by the Americans, the Germans intensified their bombardment of the town in the vain hope of stopping the U.S. advance. The importance of the Remagen bridgehead to the Allied cause was immense: journalist Hal Boyle, who covered the ETO, wrote that American military analysts estimated that the bridge's capture saved the U.S. fifteen thousand casualties that would have been inflicted on American forces attempting Rhine crossings at other locations.

The trucks transporting the 5th of K joined a vast convoy of U.S. military vehicles waiting to cross into the bridgehead on a newly erected pontoon bridge spanning the river just north of the Ludendorff. War correspondent Andy Rooney remembered the pontoon bridge being distorted by the rapid current "into a long, graceful loop." Several other bridges had been hurriedly erected under constant German artillery fire to carry the thousands of American soldiers and vehicles to the east bank of the Rhine.

The men of the 5th felt vulnerable and naked as their vehicles approached the river and drove slowly over the narrow span. When they reached the middle of the surging Rhine the trucks halted, and the men had a harrowing seat dead center on the stage of war. In front of them were the German-infested hills of the Erpeler Ley.

Lieutenant Ralston watched warily as the battle raged around his men on land and on water as they waited to proceed to the east bank of the Rhine. Enemy artillery bursts sent up geysers of water or exploded in ugly black puffs on the west bank amid the welter of American troops and vehicles. In the army newspaper, *Stars and Stripes,* Rooney described the artillery and mortar shells as falling "like huge raindrops into still water, exploding . . . as they struck the water."

Behind the 5th, on the west bank, winding its way toward the Ludendorff, was a massive array of American military vehicles and men that stretched from the river's edge back into the hills above Remagen. This was the tip of the hastily formed spearhead making the final push into Germany. Backing up the spearhead was a force of 4 million Allied soldiers, 3 million of them American, advancing into Germany in seventy-three combat divisions, twenty-one corps, eight armies, and three army groups.

"We didn't even know where we were or where we were going," Ransom recalled. All he knew was that the 5th of K was crossing a river somewhere near the front and had left its artillery support behind on the west bank. "When you start passing your artillery you know things are going to get hairy," Ransom said.

"Hey, what's the name of this river?" one black GI yelled out from Ransom's truck to a sailor manning a nearby landing craft. The last time the men of the 5th had known their location they were in Belgium. The seaman laughed. "This is the Rhine, buddy." The men in the truck looked ill at ease.

The line of GMC Jimmies finally lurched forward and the 5th rolled on to the opposite bank under the shadow of steep bluffs, colored mauve and charcoal in their winter cast. The convoy rolled through a railroad tunnel carved through rock, and finally moved into the open in the village of Erpel, which flanked the river. First impressions in the bridgehead quickly extinguished any sense of relief at reaching dry ground. "The first thing I saw was a row of eight dead Germans," Ransom said. He recognized another terrifying portent: "There was this sawed-off 105-mm gun with the trail spades sitting in the water along the bank and the barrel cranked up to maximum elevation." Ransom knew that the cannon company troops were using their artillery piece more like a mortar and lobbing shells with as high a trajectory as possible to bring them down on German positions in the hills and ridges only a few hundred yards away. "Oh my God, I thought. The Germans are that close." Ransom didn't notice that the day was springlike after the long winter.

Lieutenant Ralston's sense of relief also was to be short-lived once on the east bank. "We had just gotten onto land and made a turn and again traffic had stopped but now we had a wonderful view of the bridges and really hundreds of American vehicles on the west bank hills," Ralston recalled. "Most of them had machine guns. It was a hazy sunny morning and we suddenly heard all these machine guns firing. Three German planes, flying under 1,000 feet, came weaving up the river to bomb the bridge. It must have been some of the most intense antiaircraft firing of the war. The tracer bullets, as they converged on one plane at a time, were so profuse there was an actual pink glow around the planes. None seemed bothered by the firing; however, none of their bombs hit the bridge either. The interesting thing about these planes was each had no propeller. We all exclaimed about it—none of us had heard of the jet engine we had just seen for the first time."

These were the new ME-262s and Arado twin-engine jets that the Germans had been employing in combat since late 1944. Their speed was astonishing, and they came in with a high-pitched whine. Pfc. Lawrence Boris remembered an incident later in the bridgehead when he and his squadmates dove for cover when an ME-262 whined down the river. It sounded to them exactly like artillery.

The enemy planes flew on and powerful explosions from their bombs blasted plumes of water higher than the superstructure of the Ludendorff and unsettled these young men who had eagerly volunteered for the infantry. They were new to the violence of combat.

As the trucks rolled into the village of Erpel the men dismounted and formed up in front of a shattered building. "Welcome to the 394th," came a distant salutation. The startled men turned to see a high-ranking officer whose helmeted head protruded from a basement window, Col. John J. Jeter, commander of the 394th Regiment. "He stuck his head out of a cellar and welcomed us and gave a little speech, reminding us about this being the first time foreign troops had crossed the Rhine since Napoleon," Ransom remembered. "He was interrupted a couple of times by the jets but told us not to worry, they usually miss."

Boris also recalled Jeter's remarks. "He told us to take off our galoshes and 'those heavy overcoats.' He said we wouldn't need them, that they just added weight. Jeter said the equipment would follow along and then he wished us well and told us there was no going back across the Rhine."

Jeter waved the men on and they moved up the river road at the base of the steep face of the Erpeler Ley. Their objective was K Company, 3rd Battalion, 394th Regiment, somewhere in the hills above.

15

•

NO COLOR LINE–JUST THE FRONT LINE

FIFTH PLATOON SET OFF upstream single file and separated by several feet in combat intervals. The face of the Erpeler Ley rose some five hundred feet almost vertically from the east bank of the Rhine and the men marched at its base along a road that paralleled the river and railroad tracks. The day was mild and the afternoon sun had burned off the chill of the previous night. Spring was arriving slowly along the Rhine, but only on sunny days; the deep chill of winter descended on the front each night.

The troops barely spoke as they moved forward through a strange and threatening landscape, absorbing the crackle and rumble of war in the hills above them. This same landscape, a mile or so upriver, was the setting for Wagner's opera *Das Rheingold*. That was in a more peaceful time when the Rhinemaidens swam gracefully in the depths of the river. Charles MacDonald described the region as a "fabled domain of legend, romance and history—of Siegfried and Brunhild, of Vercingetorix, of Charlemagne." Now, however, it was the scene of war, and the tension mounted as the men approached their objective and mechanically checked and fidgeted with equipment—rifles, ammunition belts slung across their upper bodies, and grenades that dangled from chest harnesses. Yet there was a soothing familiarity in the soft clinkings of equipment as canteens bumped against bayonet scabbards and mess gear rattled loosely in their packs. An occasional shell landed in the river and rifle bullets zipped by overhead fired by German troops and snipers from territory on the west bank still in enemy hands.

In 1919 the 2nd Infantry Division had made its way along the Rhine at Erpel and Remagen as it began occupation duties after World War I. "The battalion came into a town with paved streets and trolley-cars and tall factory chimneys. . . . Platoon commanders said it was Remagen: those towers on the right would be the bridge. There was a ridge, a great steel structure of high black arches. The battalion filed upon it. Under it black water flowed swiftly, with surges and eddies dimpled by the rain. High rocky hills came down out of the mist on the farther side. . . . The battalion turned right on the eastern bank and went up the river, on a broad road between a cliff and the swift black river. There were many houses, a continuous town," wrote John Thomason Jr. in his book, *Fix Bayonets,* which recounts his experiences in World War I. This was the same road on which the 5th of K now marched.

A few hundred yards beyond the bridge the platoon cut upward into the forested ridges, passing a U.S. mortar section located in a draw where a weapons platoon was firing 4.2 mortars almost straight up into the hills. These mortars were sometimes used to lob smoke projectiles at the enemy. They were light and easily carried around a battlefield. After an hour's march the formation reached 3rd Battalion headquarters in the village of Ariendorf, where it halted for the night.

"It was just about dark and we were ordered to man an outpost line in front of the battalion headquarters," Ransom remembered. "German patrols had penetrated to the line the night before and we were commanded to go out and find ourselves a rock or a tree, anything, and wait for the Germans."

Ransom moved out just beyond the battalion perimeter with his squad—Holmes, Bailey, Oliver, Lucky, and Gibson—and all hastily piled up makeshift earthworks and burrowed as deeply into the earth as they could. Night descended and became filled with ominous sounds to their front and rear. Every sound was magnified; every shadow became the enemy. Ransom was startled to hear Germans conversing not far away in the woods.

Occasionally the impenetrable darkness was shattered by the ripping sound of an enemy machine gun and the return response from American M1s. The rattle and thump of distant skirmishes somewhere up the line reminded each volunteer that the war could instantly become real with sudden and deadly violence. Everywhere there seemed to be German grenadiers slinking and crawling toward the outpost line. No one slept that night as the men of the 5th of K kept their first combat vigil among the demons, real and imagined, in the hills above the Rhine.

Dawn arrived and the men of the 5th congratulated themselves for surviving their first night in the front lines. They were like freshmen subs in their inaugural varsity football game who untangled themselves from a pile of grunting, cursing athletes to find their bodies still intact. They were joyous and smiling at their good fortune.

By midmorning on what was becoming a warm, sunny day, the 5th of K saddled up and began the march to K Company, which desperately needed reinforcements. It would be an uphill climb. The ground on the east bank of the Rhine above Erpel consists of deep valleys running perpendicular to the river. Most of the villages are in the valleys and separated from one another by steep, wooded ridges that rise to heights of several hundred feet. The Americans already fighting in the area loathed the terrain. One member of nearby F Company, which had been in combat in the bridgehead for two days, noted: "The men were disgusted with this hill fighting, some hills being like mountains and almost straight up." The 5th of K began the march knowing that this was where the Germans were dug in and where they would meet the enemy sooner or later.

The 5th of K was accompanied to its destination by Captain Roland, operations officer (S-3) for 3rd Battalion, 394th Infantry. Years later Roland, who became a professor of history at the University of Kentucky and lecturer at the Army War College in Carlisle, Pennsylvania, recalled the importance of his role:

> At Remagen my battalion began to play a small role in a development of great future significance. We received a platoon of black troops [Lt. Ralston's platoon]. This represented a move by the army to obtain more front-line Infantrymen by accepting black volunteers from such rear-echelon services as Quartermaster, Ordnance, or Transportation. The decision also grew out of an effort to give black troops an opportunity to prove themselves as fighting men after adverse reports had come from the performance of a black division [the 92nd Infantry Division] in Italy, and from certain other black units. The battalion commander delegated me to place the platoon in a gap that had formed in our line.
>
> On the way to the line we came under sporadic artillery fire. A shell burst some distance behind us, and we instinctively dropped to the ground for protection. Then another shell struck ahead of us. Fearing we were being targeted for bombardment, I told the black sergeant [probably Sergeant Skeeters] we must move forward at once, otherwise, we were likely to be killed.
>
> 'Get it moving,' he roared to his men. 'You ain't in the Quartermaster no more. You're in the Army now.'
>
> Obviously with any troops coming under fire for the first time there was going to be some nervousness—they wouldn't be human. But I saw no hesitation on their part—no panic—they kept moving. Indeed, they soon proved themselves to be excellent soldiers.

Ralston vividly recalled the events of that morning as the platoon set out to locate K Company. "Now began the initiation of the black platoon," he said. The men passed through the outskirts of Ariendorf, which was filled with men and equipment from a mechanized unit taking a temporary breather from the fighting. Lieutenant Ralston was struck by the incongruity of the moment, the scores of tanks, tank destroyers, and half-tracks on which tired white infantrymen relaxed as though the war were some benign abstraction. The day was warm enough that the troops were lounging and eating in their shirtsleeves. The sight of the 5th aroused their interest, and Lieutenant Ralston was suddenly self-conscious for his men. They were untested and green, while the men of the mechanized unit wore the mantle of veterans, unperturbed by the sights and sounds of war. As the 5th reached the outskirts of the village and was about to cross an open field before entering the woods on the march to K Company, Lieutenant Ralston ordered his men into a combat formation. This was as good a time as any, he figured, to practice the tactics of an advance even if they weren't going to run into Germans.

"Spread out. Diamond formation. Scouts out," Lieutenant Ralston ordered, and the men maneuvered into position. The white infantrymen on the vehicles loved the drill and the catcalls came like hailstones. "Hey Sambo!" "You guys would be better at night fightin'. What you doin' up here during the day?"

Lieutenant Ralston kept the men moving toward the woods as the chorus of provocative insults from the whites rose to such a crescendo that he had to use hand signals to communicate with his men and keep them advancing. The gibes seemed innocent enough to Lieutenant Ralston, but the men of the 5th were experienced in the world of epithets. Boris remembers wanting to turn his M1 on these whites lounging on their vehicles. He had volunteered for the infantry to help win the war and he was being insulted for the color of his skin.

As an assistant squad leader, Holmes tried to ignore the catcalls as he and his comrades moved forward into the forested area. Oliver had gone ahead of the platoon to reconnoiter for enemy troops.

"The scouts entered the woods at the far side, came back out and signaled OK, and we moved forward. I was relieved to be out of the crowd's sight," Ralston remembered. The lead elements of the platoon had just entered the tree line when the troops were suddenly stunned by the sharp crack of a German flak gun. A machine gun opened fire and instantly the lead elements of the platoon hit the ground and returned fire. Boris looked in vain for some depression in the earth and crawled as fast as he could to a nearby ditch. Bullets hissed in the air above the men. Deafening explosions signaled that the platoon was under mortar fire from some unseen position. Germans had infiltrated into the heights behind K Company and knew exactly where 5th Platoon was located, but the Americans were blind.

"Keep moving, keep moving!" Lieutenant Ralston exhorted his men as he sprinted forward. Combat in the Battle of the Bulge had taught him that remaining in one spot and digging in was more dangerous than advancing. The enemy could not register artillery and mortar fire on moving men, so the projectiles would explode behind them. Lieutenant Ralston also knew that shells exploded when they hit the tops of trees and blasted shrapnel downward over a wide area. A standing soldier presented a smaller surface area to hit then one who was prone.

Lieutenant Ralston left one squad behind at the edge of the wooded area to provide covering fire and took off through the forest with the other two squads to take out the machine-gun and flak-gun nests. His ear had become attuned during the Bulge to the various sounds of German fire. Bullets snapped as they went by while a 20-mm shell whined through the air. Ahead the sounds of American M1 rifles began to drown out the German fire. The men were dashing through the woods seemingly fearless, yelping like veterans on a rampage. A mortar shell exploded in the treetops above Lieutenant Ralston's position, and one of his men went down.

Oliver led a group around the machine gun and came in from behind to fling grenades at the position that slammed the enemy gunners with killing force. Other men from the 5th of K converged on the flak gun, their M1s firing in unison with the rapidity of a machine gun.

The fighting fell off to a few rifle shots and the blast of grenade explosions muffled by the woods. Then a strange silence descended as the members of the 5th slowly regrouped, many of them leading prisoners through the trees. Others had time to study the dead enemy soldiers, unnaturally still, their field gray uniforms and sharply angled helmets oddly incongruous and unthreatening now.

"We blew the breeches of the AA guns, and kept accumulating prisoners, sending them back in groups of four or five with two of our men," Ralston recalled. "Seems like we had only half a platoon when we reached the company, what with our casualties and before our prisoner details returned. I was told by the prisoner details that the crowd in town was stunned by all the shooting in the woods and the sight of these black soldiers bringing out all of their prisoners. It was very gratifying."

Lieutenant Ralston took stock of his platoon; four men had been wounded, and mortar shell fragments had killed Pfc. Brandon Williams, Lieutenant Ralston's runner. The sight of one of their own dead stunned some of the men.

"I looked to my left and saw one of my buddies lying dead, shot through the brain. That really shook me," Holmes remembered. "I had to sit down and the guy next to me gave me a cigarette and told me to pull myself together."

Ransom was unfazed even though the mortar fragment had taken off the top of Williams's head and his brains lay in a bloody, grayish mass on the ground near his body. To Ransom they appeared like a clump of "bloody oatmeal."

Each man had weathered the terror of combat in his own way during the first encounter. Boris remembered Sergeant Sacco's warning that if a man had only a pen he would use it to dig deeper in the ground.

Ransom and three comrades carried Williams's body back to a collection station. There were no litters, so the men rolled the body onto Williams's field jacket and carried him down the steep slope toward the river. Ransom noted that all the way down the dead man's head bobbed limply as it hung below the jacket.

Slowly, in squads and half squads, the men of the 5th moved upward toward K Company, emerging in small groups from the woods and moving into the company perimeter. They were veterans now and had proved themselves in their first combat. Lieutenant Ralston was proud. His men had performed "without fear and carried out instructions with zest and efficiency." And he had to admit, these men were as good as any white infantrymen in their first encounter with the enemy.

To the K Company troops on the hill, these dusky soldiers were saviors, and they treated them as brothers. The men of the 5th Platoon had learned that in combat there was no color line—just the front line.

16

•

5TH PLATOON, E COMPANY

IF THE 5TH OF K had a brother unit in the 99th it was 5th Platoon, E Company, 393rd Regiment, which fought in the same sector of the Remagen bridgehead. E Company moved across the Ludendorff Bridge on March 11 under desultory fire from German artillery and snipers hidden in the rugged hills above Erpel. The men were also treated to the spectacle of German ME-262 jet fighters and twin-engine Arado jet bombers taking aim at the slowly sagging bridge as the warplanes dodged American antiaircraft fire.

Once across the Rhine, on March 12, E Company immediately advanced toward the hamlet of Ginsterhahn situated atop a ridge that provided the Germans with a natural defense line. From these heights enemy observers had a clear view of the bridgehead from the Rhine to the Wied River, no more than five miles distant in some areas. Advancing with marching fire E Company stormed into the town and fought the enemy house to house until the main body of Germans fled into the nearby woods. The cost to E Company was four killed and seven wounded. Total casualties for the day, however, had mounted, and the company's effectiveness was seriously diminished.

The Germans were determined to retake the lost ground and counterattacked on the morning of the thirteenth with armor and infantry. The men of E Company returned fire and killed or drove off most of the enemy troops. But the tanks continued and took up positions all around the town.

"The place was taking a pasting," recalled Harry Arnold. "We had to dodge mortars, artillery and machine gun fire to reach the town. We had to run across to a draw near the edge of town. The draw was a mess—it had been hit by mortars and shellfire, and a couple of mortarmen were lying half-covered with dirt beside their overturned mortar. On the edge of the draw crouched a number of black soldiers, obviously shaken. Their first time under fire, they had just arrived as the 5th Platoon of Company E."

James Strawder was one of the newly arrived black infantrymen, having just crossed the Ludendorff Bridge with 5th Platoon. Strawder recalled the short march from the bridge a mile or so up the river road in the shadow of the overhanging bluffs as the men went in search of E Company headquarters. The men then cut into the rugged hills, straining under weapons and equipment as they climbed toward the forested uplands. The rattle of small-arms fire sounded in the distance, broken now and then by the sharp and distinct crack of tank fire. They began to distinguish between the steady popping of the Americans' weapons and the chatter of German Schmeisser machine pistols and the sharp report of enemy Mauser rifles.

The noise of battle intensified as the 5th plodded upward over the hills that deflected the sounds of battle, and the men went into instinctive crouches as they approached a railroad embankment near Ginsterhahn. The Germans were no more than a few hundred yards away but they were as unseen as ghosts. There was a strange emptiness to this rugged battlefield, no enemy in sight and hardly a comrade visible as friend and foe ducked and dug in as deep as they could.

"Dig in," came the bellowed command from the platoon leader, a lieutenant from Texas, who ranged up and down the line along the embankment. Strawder and his buddy, Lloyd George, pulled out their entrenching tools and began clanking away at the rocky, shaley earth, ducking down low and working from their knees. They were getting nowhere and Strawder threw away his shovel in frustration.

"There were a couple of white GIs that had gotten their heads blown off. I'm basically lazy so I said there ain't no use for us digging a hole in this rock and shale, so we just pulled the bodies out of their hole, took a shovel and cleaned the blood and gore off the sides of the foxhole, and got in," Strawder remembered.

The lieutenant came running back down the line warning the troops to get as low as they could. Air strikes were coming in. The platoon leader came to Strawder's hole and saw the two dead white men pushed off to the side. His furious yell was heard clearly heard above the din on the battlefield. "Strawder, I told you to dig a hole not take one from the dead. I'm gonna have trouble with you."

Strawder raised his rifle and waved it in the general direction of his commanding officer as he shrieked epithets at the lieutenant: "I don't like no black man from Texas and I sure as hell ain't gonna like no white man from there!" Years of a black man's rage at discrimination, his recollections of being run out of Texas as a boy in search of a college education, and the terror of combat exploded in the lieutenant's face.

"I had anger in me then, plenty of it, because of the way we was treated, and I was just fit for killing—anybody, I was just right for it. I remember seeing German prisoners getting better treatment than we colored right in the States."

Strawder and George ducked into their hole as some five hundred yards up the hill German troops and tanks continued to pour fire on E Company's position. The regiment had called in fighter-bombers to dislodge the enemy, and armored troops from several supporting American tanks laid down bright orange panels to designate the U.S. positions.

The men waited. The noise of the battle drowned out the distant hum of the approaching P-47s. But the throaty roar of the planes' engines was soon heard and the rattle of fire diminished as Germans and Americans alike dove for cover. The planes circled like angry raptors before homing in on a point just in front of the 5th's position. The roar became a scream as the fighter-bombers dove and gained speed. Their wing 50s spit fire in an unearthly brittle clatter that sent up spouts of dust and blasted out shards of rock as the bullets worked their way into the German line. The bombs floated down to explode with a suctioning thunder that blasted out shock waves that took men's breath away. Clouds of dust and pulverized earth darkened the battlefield as it drifted toward the American lines. The men of the 5th Platoon were weathering their first combat and many shook with terror and gasped for air.

"I was pure scared," Strawder remembered. "I was 100 percent scared. It was a whole lot different than I expected it to be. You'd think you'd be on top of things, but you don't know what's happening. You want somebody to tell you what to do because you don't know what to do. You're lost and if it wasn't for your training you'd be messed up altogether. This was my first real experience in combat and it was hideous."

Silence enveloped the battlefield as the planes droned away. Strawder stuck his head up and noticed that medics had been summoned somewhere up the line. E Company's commander had been wounded and another man had been killed during the air strikes. The men of the 5th of E Company emerged from their holes and began moving forward toward the old German line, anticipating a resumption of the fighting. But the Germans had fled and the tanks had pulled out.

Pfc. Arthur Betts, a comrade of Strawder's in 5th Platoon, recalled the horror of that first combat experience. "There were German and American dead and they were just lying there in the middle of the battlefield. Back in a service outfit, fifty to one hundred miles behind the lines, you really don't realize what's going on at the front. You hear reports from time to time, but you really don't understand. Now I said to myself, 'What have I gotten myself into? What have I volunteered for?' "

The 5th of E moved on to make contact with E Company's command post in a nearby farmhouse. The milling white troops paid no attention to these rookie black soldiers. Their attention was focused on the bodies of three comrades who had been killed in the last action and lay in a row outside headquarters.

"They told us to help drag the bodies inside because it had started to rain," Strawder recalled. "They didn't want the dead to get wet even though they already were. So the first thing I had to do with the company was to help pull these dead fellows inside to keep from getting wet. I said that was foolish. We got to pull them in to keep them from getting wet? They're dead! But that's how they felt about one another, the closeness they felt, and it didn't take me long to see the love they held for one another. In a few days I was feeling the same way. We just had a love for one another." It was strange for Strawder to experience this camaraderie where survival brought men together and where the color of a man's skin made no difference.

Combat had brought a heavy dose of reality and tempered Strawder's bravado. Real war was far different from fictional accounts. His vulnerability became evident the following day when he and three buddies became lost while advancing against the enemy in the vicinity of Ginsterhahn. They moved through the dense forest where daylight was additionally obscured by fog that had descended to ground level.

"There we were and we didn't know whether to go this way or that way and you have no business staying where you're at. But you got to go somewhere. We knew the Germans were all around. That's when I realized: 'I'm not Mr. Big Shot.' I didn't know it all."

A strapping Irish sergeant whose booming voice broke through forest and fog like the voice of God saved Strawder and his comrades. "Follow me," the sergeant yelled out, and the four black men followed their white sergeant to safety.

Strawder was experiencing a new and electrifying phenomenon. The color line between whites and blacks had vanished as though it had never existed. "There was nary a bit of prejudice up there in combat. It was like there never had been no color. They forgot I was black."

Strawder was to find that combat, like politics, made strange bedfellows. He soon became a best buddy with a southern white boy who somehow was assigned to the platoon. Strawder affectionately nicknamed the man "Calvados" because of his penchant for the French apple brandy. The angry black man from Washington, D.C., was sharing a foxhole with a redneck from North Carolina. Years later Strawder reflected on the friendship: "I don't remember his name because we always called him Calvados. But I loved him dearly. We was hole buddies until the end of the war. We dug in together at night and worked point together. We got along like peas in a pod."

17

•

YOU, YOU, AND YOU-ON PATROL

THERE WAS NO TIME for celebration after 5th Platoon reinforced the beleaguered white infantrymen of K Company. Night was falling and enemy troops would infiltrate the American positions. The company was dug in on the heights above the Ludendorff Bridge, and the line of foxholes ran nearly to the bluff that dropped steeply to the Rhine five hundred feet below. A soldier could stand and see the top of the bridge, but it would be his last act. German snipers lay in wait for unsuspecting Americans. But snug in their holes the Americans on the Erpeler Ley could watch the never ending spectacle of German warplanes streaking downriver chased by streams of antiaircraft shells that flashed upward and swarmed about the planes like lighted insects.

The men of the 5th appropriated foxholes once occupied by the dead and wounded of K Company or they hastily carved new ones from the earth. The sounds of German infantry in the nearby woods lent urgency to their digging.

"We had a company member from the Midwest who spoke German and they kept him at company headquarters," Ransom remembered. "The Krauts were out there hooping and yelling and they would ask him what they were saying and he would translate."

Years later Ransom speculated that the Germans were so vocal because many of their troops in the bridgehead were a hodgepodge of units and men pulled together from the remnants of once solid formations that had been destroyed and scattered on the west bank of the Rhine. They were now makeshift combat units responding to verbal and shouted commands from noncoms and officers trying to keep morale high and their men fighting.

Ransom's preparations for the coming night were suddenly interrupted by the approach of a sergeant who ordered 1st Squad out of their holes. He pointed to the men and spoke tersely: "You, you, and you, patrol out that way and see if you can find B Company." Ransom was startled. "I remember thinking, 'Hey, that's a helluva way to run a railroad. We greenhorns have just arrived and they want us to go out and find B Company—with all those Germans out there.'"

Ransom saddled up with Holmes, Bailey, Oliver, T. C. Williams, and Gibson and slipped cautiously into the woods. They knew they would probably encounter enemy troops who were making their presence known all around. First Squad's point of reference was a water tower some two hundred yards out that was adjacent to a logging trail that ran along the top of the ridge and down the steep slope toward the Rhine. The incessant crackle of small-arms fire and the crump of artillery bursting in the distance covered the sounds of the patrol's movements.

The men reached the trail within minutes and Williams motioned half the men across to reconnoiter the woods beyond. While Holmes, Ransom, and Gibson prepared to offer covering fire, Bailey, Williams, and Oliver scurried over the trail into the underbrush. They had just gotten across when the penetrating crack of German rifle fire filled the woods. A hail of small-arms fire snapped overhead and thudded into tree trunks as squad members on both sides of the trail dropped and clung to the earth. Bailey screamed and crumpled as he dove for cover.

More ominous than the small-arms fire was the distinct bark of a flak gun, which the Germans had in abundance in the bridgehead. Across the trail T.C. tended to Bailey's wound as Holmes's group gave covering fire for their comrades and the woods filled with the sharp, rapid bursts from multiple M1s. T.C. grabbed Bailey under his arms and wrestled the wounded man back across the trail.

"Bailey was hollering and cussing that the damn Germans had shot him almost in the exact spot in the thigh where some guy back home had shot him in the street," Ransom remembered. Once in relative safety the men laid Bailey out and dressed his wound before Williams dragged and carried him back toward the company aid station, leaving the rest of 1st Squad to finish the mission with Holmes in charge.

Holmes ordered the men to dig in as he and Gibson deepened their hole. Ransom was farther back from the trail, hidden in dense underbrush. He yelled out to Holmes that the Germans were shooting with something larger than small arms. The men dug furiously and waited for Germans to materialize. It didn't take long, and Holmes swears that when the enemy appeared a guardian angel was at Holmes's side.

"It was like somebody tapped me on the shoulder and said, 'Turn around, there's a guy there.' I was looking to the front for Germans and Gibson was supposed to be covering our flank but he got scared or something because he was slumped in his foxhole smoking a cigarette. I remember I turned and saw this stream of smoke coming from the hole." Then as Holmes looked up, just beyond Gibson, on the left flank he saw a German staring straight at him. This was no ordinary enemy soldier. From the markings on his uniform Holmes figured him to be an officer.

The man was armed with a rifle and hand grenades. "This guy was trying to see what was out there in front of his position."

The enemy soldier moved first and ducked behind a tree as Holmes dove into his hole. He recovered quickly and popped up with his M1 ready to fire. "The German was looking at me, following me." Holmes raised his rifle and opened fire—eight shots in quick succession aimed at the tree with armor-piercing bullets. When his clip was expended Holmes looked out and saw the man sprawled dead a few yards in front of his position.

The sight of death this time did not upset Holmes as it had earlier in the day at the sight of Brandon Williams's blasted head. "There was no shock. It only takes a few hours in combat to become acclimated to war," he said. But Holmes was furious at Gibson for his lax behavior. Gibson's cigarette break had almost cost Holmes his life.

Holmes often wonders why the German did not open fire. He could easily have killed two Americans. Holmes believes the enemy was so bewildered by seeing blacks that he failed to react in time: "I'm sure he was thinking, 'What the hell are all these black guys doing up here? I'm supposed to be looking for white guys, Americans, not Africans.' " The men of the 5th of K were to discover that many Germans were unsettled and frightened at the prospect of fighting black troops.

The unseen firefight somewhere to the front alerted Ransom, and he began digging deeper and faster as the Germans seemed to be closing in from all directions. He laid his M1 against a nearby tree and flailed away at the ground with his entrenching tool, aware of occasional shots ripping through the trees and the bang of bigger-caliber guns. As Ransom dug he began hearing a peculiar sound, like distant sleigh bells on a wintry eve. The jingling continued and intensified as though the sleigh was nearing his position.

Ransom ceased his frantic digging and cocked his head to listen. The jingle of bells was very close through the trees. "What the hell is that?" he cursed under his breath. He dropped his entrenching tool and reached for his rifle. His hand was halfway to his weapon when he glanced up. A German soldier no more than ten feet away was looking Ransom in the eye. The enemy was as unprepared for the sudden encounter as Ransom.

"Here's this German walking through the woods. I reached for my M1 just as he sees me and we both go to throw up our piece, but I beat him to it and that was the end of him. He was dead and not moving anymore. I wasn't going to waste another round," Ransom recalled. He turned quickly back to his work. Night was falling fast and the squad needed the protection of the earth.

Years later, as an experienced infantrymen of three wars, Ransom would scold himself for his ignorance about what he had heard. "I should have known, but I didn't realize it then. We had web belts for our .30-caliber machine guns but the Germans had little link belts made of metal and they liked to play Pancho Villa and hang the belts around their necks. I heard those jingling belt links every time the German moved. I have never approved of hanging machine gun bullets around your neck. Dirt on the bullets can damage the projectile and jam a machine gun."

Coming face-to-face with death and killing a man had little impact on Ransom. "You see, back in the old peaceful, good life back home, down in the rough parts of town you saw people get killed all the time. I was used to seeing dead people and it didn't faze me. My main concern that day was to sit tight and hope the rest of the Germans didn't see me."

As darkness descended, the men of 1st Squad peered out from their holes and listened for the movement of Germans. They hunkered down, expecting to spend the night in the forest, but they were finally relieved by another patrol and told to return to company headquarters. They scampered back to K Company. But no sooner were they back than they received a new set of orders.

"Somebody says, 'Now you go back to where those dead guys are and bring them in for ID.' Shit, you got to be kidding," Ransom remembered thinking. First Squad set out once again into the forests above Erpel. But Ransom was consoled. "I lasted for a day on that hill. Some people didn't."

18

•

WAITING OUT THE NIGHT

A PATROL FROM 1ST Squad, 5th Platoon, climbed stealthily from their holes and low-crawled well beyond the company perimeter deep into the oppressive darkness of the enemy-held woods. They scanned the impenetrable night before rising to a crouch to scurry to the spot where the two Germans lay dead.

The bodies were still supple, and the men grabbed at lifeless limbs and dragged the dead men over the rugged ground back to the K Company perimeter. Having encountered no live Germans, the patrol stumbled through the outpost line with their quarry. G-2 (Intelligence) was curious to know the units to which these dead soldiers belonged.

To counter the American thrust over the Rhine the Germans were assembling a jumble of men and units that were falling back from the west bank of the Rhine and crossing the river by any means possible, on barges, ferries, pleasure craft, even rowboats. Enemy units were also being collected from any garrison that could spare men and machines in the shrinking Nazi empire. The 130th Infantry Regiment, with two thousand fresh troops, was rushed to the bridgehead area from the Netherlands.

Most units assembling to choke off the American advance had fallen back from the west bank of the Rhine and their ranks had been ravaged by constant combat; there were few veteran combat soldiers available to fight. Gen. Fritz Bayerline, designated by Generalfeldmarschall Model to coordinate the German counteraction against the expanding bridgehead, had mostly service troops to hold the line. The 11th Panzer Division and the once formidable Panzer Lehr Division, Bayerline's old unit, might be available, but Panzer Lehr could field only three hundred men and fifteen tanks. The 9th Panzer Division also was counted but could muster only six hundred men and another fifteen tanks, while the 106th Panzer Brigade had only five tanks. Also present were remnants of the 340th Volksgrenadier Division, which was stiffened by the 130th Infantry Regiment.

The quality of the German soldier facing the Americans in March 1945 was declining. K Company infantryman Ralph Treadup noted that the bulk of the veterans of the old Wehrmacht were gone, killed or wounded or transferred to the eastern front to stop the Russian onslaught.

But the new soldiers on the western front could be no less dangerous. While the Americans faced older men, they also faced "kids under twenty who were considered Hitler's children," Treadup stated. These "Hitler Youth," many barely in their teens, were determined to drive out the Allies, and many were prepared to give their lives for what they believed was inevitable victory. "Even after the war, when I talked to them they said: 'We'll win someday,' so naturally those kids thought the same way when we were still at war." Often these kids fought with deadly ferocity and refused to surrender.

When Holmes's squad returned from patrol the men were ordered back on the perimeter to await the inevitable German nighttime counterattacks. "Now began the long, drawn-out night," Treadup recalled. "Would we have an attack? Did the Germans see us, thereby shell us? Time would only tell." Ransom remembered the night well: "The Germans were all around hollering and screaming."

Holmes took a position on the platoon's left flank and prepared for attack by keeping his M1 at the ready. He checked the clips of ammo that were packaged in the pockets of a canvas bandolier that ran diagonally down and across his chest. He removed several clips of eight rounds each and slipped them onto the bandolier strap for quick removal in a fight. Each clip could then be slapped into the rifle's breech. "I was put in a foxhole with a white boy with a BAR. He stuck to one side of the hole and I was on the other and he wasn't too happy at first to see me because I was black," Holmes remembered. But before the night was out there would be no racial distinctions in Holmes's foxhole. "The fighting got real bad and we had our arms around each other trying to protect one another," Holmes remembered.

Des Journette took a hole down the line from Holmes on the company perimeter with Eddy Hunter, "the Deacon." Hunter set up his M1 and also readied his ammunition clips. Lawrence Boris was farther up the line as night shrouded the forest. Boudreau anchored the 5th's right flank with his BAR and extra clips at the ready. In just a day of fighting Boris was quickly learning the ways of combat. He, like many of his comrades, had to shake off death, and the recollection of Brandon Williams's battered head and oozing brains had been their first test. Those who witnessed Williams's body would remember the scene vividly for the rest of their lives.

Everyone in the 5th knew their mettle would be tested in the coming night. "There was firing going on all the time and screaming minnies, those German rockets, coming through," Boris remembered. "The echo when they exploded was deafening and they had the effect they were supposed to have on you. They made you want to jump out of your hole and run. But to where?" In their precarious position on the ridgeline above the Rhine, the men of the 5th could run into Germans even if they went backward. If they moved to the right they would go over the cliff into the Rhine below. It was the anxiety of waiting that bothered Boris. Once a fight began the tension lifted and he was in control. Boris would get his fill of fighting before the night was over.

The enemy had stepped up their shelling, and artillery rounds were falling in front of and behind the outpost line. An occasional white phosphorous round exploded in a brilliant cloud and sent out deadly streamers that seared men to the bone when the fragments found their mark. The 5th of K was also receiving shell bursts, some inadvertent, some requested, from its own artillery firing on the west bank of the Rhine. The American front lines were at right angles to U.S. artillery positions across the river, so it was difficult for the artillerymen to fire at the Germans on the ridges without sometimes placing shells in among the Americans.

The night was so black that seeing movement beyond the perimeter was difficult. The Americans sent up star shells that burst like giant Roman candles high above, turning the brown faces of the men an unearthly ashen color and casting stark shadows that made every bump and mound in the forest resemble a German infantryman. Once the light was extinguished the Germans continued to infiltrate up to and through the outpost line.

"We could tell the Germans were coming by the sounds they made," Boris remembered. "You'd be surprised what you can hear in war. It makes an animal out of you. I remember times when we'd get into a new position and it would be raining and the rain would be hitting the trees and the ground. I became so alert I could hear my wristwatch ticking. Your ears were waiting for the sound of Germans."

"The Germans were in amongst us that night," Ransom remembered. He was dug in near Boris and stayed low in his hole as firefights broke out along the perimeter. More ominous were the firing from behind and the explosions all around. The Americans could see the muzzle flashes of German weapons sparkling down the incline in front of their positions. An occasional grenade was hurled unseen to explode in a deafening, disorienting blast. "I'd jump up and fire a few rounds at muzzle flashes and duck back down again," Ransom said. "You don't fire in one position at night and stay there because the enemy's going to fire back at you aiming at your muzzle flash."

The Germans mounted small counterattacks all along the line that were sometimes preceded by the shrill commands of German officers and noncoms. K Company's German-speaking soldier translated the enemy commands that came from the woods. "I heard a lieutenant ask the fellow what they were saying," Ransom said. "The translator replied: 'They're saying, "Fix bayonets and charge for the Führer." ' The white lieutenant screamed, 'Oh my God,' and bolted down the hill."

The men of the 5th waited expectantly as Boudreau and the other BAR men along the line delivered measured bursts with their automatic weapons. Each member of the platoon fought his own isolated battle against real and imagined Germans and continued popping up to empty clips of M1 bullets at enemy muzzle flashes in the blackness. At times the shooting reached crescendos and fire poured into the night from each hole.

Des Journette and Hunter pumped bullets at anything that seemed to move and at German fire a few yards in front of them. Hunter stuck his head above the foxhole and jerked off several rounds. His M1 went silent with the ping of the ejected clip and Hunter reached for another.

"Get down," Des Journette yelled at the Deacon. Hunter fumbled to extract an eight-round clip from the bandolier strap and ram it into his weapon.

"Get down!" Des Journette yelled again as Hunter continued to work the clip into the breech. The bolt slammed shut as the Deacon succeeded in loading the rifle. He turned to take aim in the direction of the enemy and silently threw up his arms and collapsed in the hole. By the light of a star shell Des Journette saw a clean hole drilled through Hunter's head and ruby black blood staining the trampled earth at the bottom of the foxhole. A German sniper had found his mark. Des Journette was surprised. The Deacon hadn't made a sound.

The Germans had infiltrated into the company area, and the only way to dislodge them was to call for American artillery to rout them out. "Several times the FO [forward observer] called for artillery on our own positions," Ransom said. "You'd duck down and see the sky all light up on the other side of the Rhine and it looks like all the artillery in the world is going to fall right on top of you."

The warning went out for the men to brace for a barrage of American shells. On the left Holmes and his white hole mate were working together as they fired on suspected targets to the front. The white boy kept his distance for a while but slowly he inched closer to his black companion. The two had started a dialogue of sorts. "We talked," Holmes remembered, "about nothing in particular because the Germans were so close. But we were finally talking."

The men went deep into their holes as they awaited the artillery barrage. Boris too peered out to see the sky to the west flash orange and red as the gunners launched shells that whined and groaned into the company area a few instants later. Some roared in like clacking freight trains; others whistling like fireworks rockets to explode in a torrent of noise, debris, and shrapnel. Holmes threw himself to the bottom of the foxhole and found himself clinging to his white comrade, who was desperately clinging back. The barrage seemed to go on for hours as the batteries across the Rhine fired round after round. The artillerymen dispatched thousands of shells each day in support of the infantry in the hills of the bridgehead.

The firing lifted and the men cautiously poked their heads above their holes, whispering softly to their mates on either side. Holmes and his white companion quietly, but urgently, appealed for a white soldier nearby to get into his hole, but the man remained unmoving. An eerie silence had spread over the battlefield, broken only by the occasional sound of distant firing. Men began to stir and peer over the rough, smoking ground to check with comrades and to look for their dead and wounded. Hunter was the only KIA in the 5th, and the white soldier near Holmes's hole, from another platoon, had been killed. Holmes and his white hole mate had continued to call out for him to take cover from the artillery until they realized he was dead. The 5th had lost another man besides Hunter. Sergeant Sacco had been wounded and was out of action for the second time in his combat career.

The distant firing made the men wary, and they prepared for another German counterattack. As dawn began to light the eastern horizon and the landscape regained definition the Germans remained surprisingly bold. Dark figures, faintly silhouetted by the dawn, darted about and advanced toward the outpost line, some concentrating on the right flank in front of Boudreau's position. Like a hunter looking for the best shot Boudreau waited for his quarry to come closer. His comrades grew anxious as they watched.

"Get 'em now, get 'em now!" several whispered hoarsely.

"Wait till they get real close and then I'll let 'em have it," Boudreau whispered back impatiently.

"He waited almost until he could see the whites of their eyes," Holmes remembered. Boudreau was staring down the barrel of his BAR as a group of Germans rose in the gray light to attack his position. The eerie dawn was suddenly shattered by rapid bursts from Boudreau's BAR. The Ragin' Cajun cut them down.

Left to right: Arthur Holmes,
Harold Robinson, and
James Oliver in Germany,
June 1945.
RICHARD RALSTON

Six members of the 5th of K
in Germany at war's end.
Left to right: Waymon Ransom,
Lester Boudreau, and Sam
Wade are in the back row,
and in the front row are
Bernard Bailey, Arthur
Holmes, and Raymond Day.
RICHARD RALSTON

K Company in Germany, June 1945. RICHARD RALSTON

Clayton Des Journette in 1945.
HATTIE DES JOURNETTE

Richard Ralston, Aub, Germany, June
1945. RICHARD RALSTON

Lawrence Boris, *left,* and Thomas Branch, both of the 5th of K, in Germany at war's end. LAWRENCE BORIS

Staff Sgt. David Skeeters, recovering from wounds, Paris, 1945.
MRS. DAVID SKEETERS

Staff Sgt. Pete Bonavich, a combat veteran of the 2nd Division in the battles of Normandy and Northern France, instructs black volunteers during infantry training at Noyen, France, in the maintenance and use of the BAR (Browning Automatic Rifle). The men are disassembling and reassembling the weapon. The date is February 28, 1945. U.S. ARMY MILITARY HISTORY INSTITUTE

Smoke rises from Honningen, Germany, on the Rhine River, under artillery fire from 99th Division gun positions. The photo was taken on March 15, 1945, as the 5th of K advanced on the town from the smoke-shrouded hills in the background.
U.S. ARMY MILITARY HISTORY INSTITUTE

This aerial view of the town of Remagen, Germany, was taken March 14, 1945, as the 99th Division, including the 5th of K, advanced through the hills on the east side of the bridge toward the objective of Honningen. The 5th of K was in the hills just above the Rhine River to the far right of the photograph. Smoke rises from the far side of the bridge from the constant German artillery fire that rained down on American positions. The bridge collapsed three days later, on March 17.
U.S. ARMY MILITARY HISTORY INSTITUTE

Two unidentified members of the 5th Platoon, E Company, 393rd Regiment, 99th Division, on their first day at the Remagen Bridgehead. These men were comrades of James Strawder, also in the 5th of E.
U.S. ARMY MILITARY HISTORY INSTITUTE

Warrant Officer Arthur Holmes, circa 1966. ARTHUR HOLMES

"Blitz," after the war in Bamberg, Germany. RICHARD RALSTON

Sergeant Major Waymon Ransom, *left*, wearing the 99th Division patch on his right shoulder, receives the certificate of retirement from the army from Major General John D. McLaughlin at Fort Lee, Virginia, October 29, 1970, after three wars and nearly thirty years' service in the U.S. Army.
WAYMON RANSOM

Clayton Des Journette, *center,* with wife, Hattie, *second from right,* and daughter, Margaret Scobbie, *second from left,* at a reunion party in Las Vegas in 1993. Margaret's husband is at far right, and son, Mark, is at far left.
HATTIE DES JOURNETTE

Former black platoon members gathered at a reunion of the 99th Division in 2000 in Philadelphia. *Left to right:* James Strawder, 5th of E Company, 393rd; Harold Robinson, 5th of K, 394th; Arthur Betts, 5th of E, 393rd; Edward Jackson, 5th of E, 395th; and Lawrence Boris, 5th of K, 394th.
LAWRENCE BORIS

Bruce Wright, 2001.
ELIZABETH KEEGIN COLLEY

Arthur Holmes, 2001
ELIZABETH KEEGIN COLLEY

Willfred Strange, 2001.
ELIZABETH KEEGIN COLLEY

James Strawder, 2001.
ELIZABETH KEEGIN COLLEY

Richard Ralston, *right,* and his former runner during the Battle of the Bulge, Andrew Trulac, meet at a reunion of the 99th Division in the 1990s.
RICHARD RALSTON

19

•

PROMISE OF SALVATION

DAYLIGHT BROUGHT PROMISE OF salvation as the Germans withdrew into the forested ridges, leaving the dead they could not retrieve sprawled in misshapen heaps that sometimes resembled piles of rags. Intelligence reports noted the night's events: "Third Battalion reported a strong counterattack . . . 150–200 enemy in draw in front of K Company. Normal barrage fired."

Second Battalion also reported strong German counterattacks "which penetrated our lines. . . . Attack was supported by MGs [machine guns] and one AA [antiaircraft] automatic weapon, but was successfully repulsed and our front line reestablished."

The 5th of K had survived but the new day brought other perils. Snipers in both armies picked off the unwary and the Americans remained hunkered down in their holes. "Every time you moved some German in the bushes would put a round at you or they'd call in artillery fire," Ransom said.

Curtis Whiteway, a white infantryman with the 99th, helped train the blacks about the dangers of snipers in the bridgehead. "It took awhile to teach how the Germans would sucker you into a trap, especially with snipers." But the blacks "caught on fine."

The Americans also employed snipers to good effect. Boris admired the marksmanship of some of the southern white boys in K Company who stalked the enemy as though they were wild game back in the pines of Georgia. At home these same young men would have been regarded as armed and dangerous to any black man. "Some of those boys could really shoot," Boris recalled.

Prisoner interrogation confirmed that the enemy feared the marksmen of the 99th. A captured German officer spoke admiringly of the sharpshooters in the 99th because they had killed ten of his unsuspecting men.

Daylight also brought long-range German artillery that arrived intermittently on the American positions, each shell reminding the Americans of their vulnerability. Treadup recalled that the barrage began around 7 A.M. "Several of the shells landed close to our dugout and I thought to myself if we went through another shelling we would abandon the foxhole and run for the nearby house and take cover in the basement." On the Rhine below, the air war raged noisily from American antiaircraft guns. Once the shooting stopped, the men ducked down to await the rain of shrapnel from exploded and spent American antiaircraft shells.

Boris controlled his urge to stand up and peer down toward the river to watch the aerial combat. Treadup had the protection of the house and reveled in the spectacle. "At times the sky was red and black from our tracers and air artillery shooting at the German planes. I, like a darn fool, would run out of the house and watch the proceedings, even aware of the fact that I could have easily been hit by falling artillery and tracer bullets. But it was a grand sight to watch those German planes spin crazily out of the sky, spinning earthward leaving a trail of black smoke behind them."

The German warplanes were also trying to take out the pontoon bridges that the Americans had hastily constructed over the Rhine between Remagen and Erpel. Two had been completed and a third would soon be open to help carry the thousands of American troops and vehicles into the bridgehead. The Ludendorff no longer conveyed men and supplies; the engineers had closed it down because it was too unstable to handle the volume of traffic crossing the river. Scores of engineer troops labored around the clock in an effort to save the structure.

Occasionally the ridge shook from exploding V-2 rockets that the Germans aimed at the Ludendorff. The V-2s approached after penetrating the stratosphere from launching sites in Holland and took a supersonic dive to earth. They were unseen and unheard until the last seconds, when they announced their arrival with a sudden rush of air and a deafening explosion. Their 2,200-pound warheads exploded with a force that rocked the countryside for miles around, but none ever hit the bridge, although several landed in the Rhine not far from the Ludendorff and several others hit in and around the town of Remagen.

By March 14 the fighting in the bridgehead intensified as the Germans fought even more desperately to contain the U.S. foothold on the east bank of the Rhine. The Americans, in turn, were equally dogged in their attempts to push the Germans back and to capture the numerous German artillery and observation positions in the rugged landscape that stretched from the Rhine to the Wied River. As long as the enemy held these ridges his observers had a clear view of the Rhine and could direct artillery fire on most U.S. positions.

The Americans were pouring in reinforcements. Alongside the 99th in the bridgehead were the 9th Armored Division and the 1st, 9th, and 78th Infantry Divisions. The 99th held the southern flank of the bridgehead.

The Germans also continued to reinforce the bridgehead, and the Americans faced an estimated nine enemy divisions in three corps. The greatest concentration of enemy troops was along the northern edge of the bridgehead, where the Germans expected an American breakout north toward the heart of the Ruhr industrial area. Without the Ruhr providing the Wehrmacht with tanks and munitions, the German war machine would grind to a halt.

Because of the high concentration of German guns in the bridgehead, the 5th of K was subjected to constant artillery barrages and came to expect the nightly barrage or enemy counterattack. The struggle seesawed back and forth and up and down the ridges, with troops being pulled out of one line to advance or retreat to another set of foxholes that had been used before by soldiers of both armies. Time became obscured.

The Americans by now had perfected the use of fighter-bombers in support of ground troops. Whenever GIs were held up, frequently in towns and villages, Air Corps P-47s and P-51s were summoned to dislodge the enemy with strafing and bombing attacks. Holmes recalled an air support mission as the 5th of K slugged it out with die-hard Germans. The men of the 5th were ordered out of their foxholes and pulled back several hundred yards up a ridge to await air strikes. The men dispersed in the trees and began digging in against possible friendly fire and German snipers.

But the sky remained empty of planes, and after more than an hour the 5th of K was ordered back into their old holes. It was then that they heard the drone of approaching aircraft that suddenly shot over the hills with a collective, throaty roar. As the P-47s circled to get their bearing, the men prayed the aircraft were aware of K Company's position.

One by one the U.S. fighter-bombers peeled off and dropped from the sky, aiming directly at the enemy no more than fifty yards in front of 5th Platoon. Every man in the line went deep in his hole as the .50-caliber rounds struck German positions just beyond the perimeter. The rattle of the P-47 guns sounded above the roar of the powerful engines. One plane screamed by, then another was in line for a pass. The armor-piercing fifties splintered trees and kicked up the earth in front of K Company's position and marched forward into enemy-controlled ground. Mercifully, there were no bombs, and the strafing attacks ended within minutes.

The greatest threat came from constant enemy shellfire. The aim of the German artillerymen was excellent and the enemy had observation points on high ground, in the trees, and in isolated farm buildings that dotted the Erpeler Ley. On its third day in the bridgehead the 5th of K was ordered to take some farmhouses on K Company's right flank. The

company had taken fire from several of the buildings that were also suspected of serving as a German observation post and a flak-gun position.
To reach their objective the troops first had to cross an open field that was
in full view of the farm. If there were Germans in that observation post
the advancing men would be raked by machine-gun and rifle fire.

Lieutenant Ralston commanded the operation, and as the men reached
the open ground, he ordered the platoon into a diamond formation
"spread out so that we could all fire at once as we crossed at a fast walk."
The men moved quickly across the freshly cultivated land intent on reaching a snaking mound of earth that was twenty yards from the farmhouse.

"The mound was a trench silo," Ransom recalled. "The German
farmers dig a trench and put their sugar beets in it and cover it for silage."
It was high enough to provide cover for the platoon, and the men raced
to the protective barrier and ducked behind it.

Holmes and Ransom and several others moved to the end of the beet
pile and peered cautiously around the corner at the farmhouse. They had
seen no activity and taken no fire, and after quickly scanning the scene
Holmes ordered Ransom to rush the building. "We'll cover you," he said.
"Get to that door."

"What door?" Ransom asked.

"The door at the end of the house," Holmes replied.

Ransom gave Holmes a look of consternation and peered out at the
farmhouse, calculating that once against the front wall he would be safe
from German fire coming from within. He took a deep breath and dashed
off, expecting a hail of machine-gun fire. He reached the wall and slowly
began inching his way toward the back door. Once Ransom was in position, the bazooka man was to fire a rocket through a window into the
house to take out any Germans inside.

Ransom reached the back door and pressed himself against the side of
the house. He checked his M1 and gave Holmes the signal to fire as he
grabbed for the handle. He threw open the back door just as a rocket
explosion shook the structure and blew Ransom backward. Holmes and
1st Squad rushed forward and Ransom heard their heavy footsteps re-
sounding on the wooden floors as the squad noisily thumped through the
house, their voices echoing in the farmhouse as they yelled for anyone
inside to surrender.

Ransom picked himself up and peered through the open back door.
His shoulders sagged and he let out a frustrated sigh. He was staring down
the hole of an empty, stinking outhouse.

"We didn't know what the door at the end of German houses was
for," Ransom said. It was a cultural eye-opener. The door concealed the

privy, which was often built on the outside corner of a farmhouse with a separate entrance.

The mission was a success. The men uncovered a radio that had been used to direct artillery fire on K Company's position, and they also rounded up several civilians hiding in a cave behind the farmhouse who were sent back to battalion for interrogation. The troops shot the radio full of holes knowing that life in the K Company perimeter would be a little more comfortable.

20

•

HONNINGEN

THE GERMANS IN THE bridgehead gave ground grudgingly, falling back from hole to hole and from ridge to ridge as K Company pressed the attack. On March 15 the three regiments of the 99th launched a coordinated drive to enlarge the bridgehead and to capture the small industrial city of Honningen that lay directly in K Company's path.

Honningen was an important objective for the 99th and for the American First Army because of its location on the narrow floodplain along the east bank of the Rhine. Control of the town meant command of the road and rail lines that ran along the river. It was the last major urban complex in the southern part of the bridgehead, and once Honningen was captured the Americans could advance the few miles southeast to the Frankfurt-Ruhr Autobahn.

General Bradley had his eye on that autobahn. "Beyond the Remagen Bridge, the steep woodlands of the Westerwald posed a barrier to any rapid advance east. But from a point across the river from Coblenz, 25 miles to the south of Remagen, a river valley penetrated those mountains to Giessen where it intersected the path from Frankfurt that we had chosen for envelopment of the Ruhr. If Hodges could gain the autobahn that ran six miles beyond the Remagen Bridge, he could drive south to that river valley gap and then turn east toward Giessen. At Giessen he would join forces with Patton for encirclement of the Ruhr," Bradley wrote.

But first, Honningen had to be taken. The town was surrounded by high ground from which the Germans had a clear view of the city. In anticipation of an American attack the enemy had constructed a series of interconnected strong points that ran through the hills and into the city itself.

To capture Honningen American troops would have to advance across open ground that was dominated by the German-held heights. "Every time we attempted to cross the flat land adjacent to the outskirts of the town we had artillery, tank 88s, 20-mm antiaircraft guns, and small-arms fire upon us," Ralph Treadup remembered. The only solution was to take the high ground around Honningen before the city itself would fall.

Lt. Samuel Lombardo, a platoon leader in I Company, 394th, recalled the struggle in the hills above Honningen. He and his men fought their way to the crest of a ridge that overlooked the city: "One could see the town of Honningen straight down to the south of the hill, and the Rhine to the southwest. There were machine gun emplacements several hundred yards down the hill, as well as some snipers. Our men soon found out that they couldn't even peek over the edge of the ridge. Any peeking invited either a burst of machine gun fire or a shot from a sniper," Lombardo said.

On March 14 American patrols reported signs that the enemy was preparing to evacuate Honningen. One U.S. reconnaissance team penetrated to the city's edge and told of seeing scores of white flags flying from buildings. But the Americans had learned from bitter experience that "shirttail allies," as these towns were called, could be traps. The civilians had decided to surrender and were hanging out white flags of surrender, but the German army had not been consulted and planned to make a stand. In some cases in the last months of the war, German civilians had hung out white flags and were rounded up and executed by fanatical SS troops bent on fighting to the death.

The 5th of K moved out with the rest of the company at dawn on the fifteenth and attacked through the hills that rimmed Honningen. As the platoon moved forward it encountered artillery and constant small arms fire from determined bands of Germans who stopped the advance of other American units in the rugged hills.

By day's end casualties in some of the advancing U.S. units were heavy and the units were severely depleted. C Company, 394th, suffered forty casualties while barely establishing a toehold in the northern sector of Honningen, and one of C Company's platoons was down to fifteen men commanded by a sergeant. The Germans had decided to make a fight of the city and intelligence later learned that the night before the enemy had reinforced the garrison with an additional 150 to 200 troops "with orders to hold the town at all costs." The Germans wanted to keep Honningen as a launching site for frogmen who were attempting to destroy the Ludendorff Bridge by swimming downriver and placing explosive charges against the bridge's pilings. The Germans also wanted control of the roads heading south over which the Wehrmacht could conduct an organized retreat from the bridgehead.

With its spearheading companies badly mauled, 394th commanders revised plans for the capture of the city and assigned K Company to reinforce C Company in the attack the next day.

The battle for Honningen began at 7 A.M. on March 16 with the 5th of K assigned on C Company's left flank to sweep the eastern edge of the city. Three tanks, one with an external telephone link, supported the 5th so that the infantrymen could communicate with the tankers. When U.S. tanks first went into action in World War II none had telephones and infantrymen communicated with the tankers by banging on their steel sides and waiting for the commander to stick his head out of the turret. In the noise of heavy combat, however, it was often impossible to hear the calls for help, so the army began installing telephones, which greatly assisted cooperation between tankers and infantry.

Lieutenant Ralston led his men out of the woods and down into the outskirts of Honningen, dodging artillery and sniper fire. "We were given the left one-third of the town as our sector was mainly the industrial area of large buildings with colossal machinery and big storage tanks," Ralston recalled. The Germans in town were waiting and immediately opened fire with machine guns and the rapid-firing Schmeisser machine pistols commonly known as "burp guns" by the Americans. The din of battle was deafening and caused confusion among the advancing Americans. "Inside the factories the Jerry burp guns would echo so loudly you couldn't tell the direction of the firing," Ralston said. The reverberating gunfire inside and outside made it sound as though the Germans were everywhere, and along the streets the men inched forward, crouching behind the tanks and leapfrogging from one position to another. Des Journette remembered the 5th working down one side of a street while a white platoon from K Company worked the other side.

The black troops looked like hardened combat troops and won the admiration of accompanying white soldiers. Treadup recalled: "We had our gun set up not far from a TD, or tank destroyer, and two of the crew told us about the wonderful job K Company did moving into town, especially the black boys. Very rarely one heard of black infantry being in combat. These men who had little experience, joined us at Ariendorf four or five days ago, but they crossed the field like veterans. They were dispersed, while one man was up running and firing, the other next to him was lying on the ground, then was up doing the same while his buddy was down."

Snipers and fanatic Nazis were everywhere, firing at advancing members of the 5th from cellars, from sewer manholes, from windows, from side streets, and from behind stone walls. The men moved down the streets shooting at snipers' nests and summoned the Shermans to direct their 75-mm cannon fire just below the windows where snipers lay hidden. The blast collapsed the wall and brought the enemy tumbling down with the debris.

"We were shooting at anything we could see," Holmes remembered. He ducked out of the way of one sniper and as he fired back he saw a group of about twenty Germans running away in an open area of town.

"Put a burst on those guys," Holmes yelled to a tanker, who obligingly fired off a round. Holmes watched as the .75-mm round exploded in an air burst near the retreating Germans. When the smoke cleared, no enemy was in sight. Holmes stuck with the tankers and rode on the turret as the Americans swept through the city.

Army after-action reports characterized the fighting in Honningen as "stubborn and house-to-house." "It was mainly fighting from building to building or what was left of buildings, moving, shooting, and throwing grenades," Ransom said.

"It was my first experience in house-to-house combat and it was exciting and scary too," Harold Robinson remembered. "You're in one room and the next thing you know the Germans blow a hole in the walls and come out at you. They're in the room with you. We'd blow holes in the walls and there would be the Germans in the next apartment. You'd go down the entire block blowing holes in the walls to get from one apartment to the next with bazookas or grenades."

German mines and explosive charges were strewn everywhere and the Americans used them against the enemy. Ransom knew how to rig the igniter and began throwing the charges into basements along the path of the 5th's advance. "One guy would say, 'There's something in the cellar over there, can you get it.' Somebody else would say, 'Yeah,' and throw the charge in the cellar. *Bam!* Whatever was in the cellar ain't there no more."

"We went into one building that may have been a schoolhouse," Boris recalled. "There were signs that somebody had recently been there but we weren't sure if they were Americans or Germans. We threw grenades down into the basement and all these Germans came running up. We lined them up against the wall and they were crying and hollering, *'Nicht schiessen, nicht schiessen.'* I told them as best I could that we weren't going to kill them. We had to count them before sending them back to POW pens."

The number of Germans who were surrendering slowed the fight. Details of infantrymen were required to accompany bunches of POWs back to confinement areas, and by day's end the 5th was credited with as many as three hundred prisoners. But not all Germans surrendered.

T. C. Williams poked his head into a dark hallway and held his fire when he spotted a figure approaching with hands held high in surrender. Suddenly the German dropped down, raised a machine pistol, and opened fire. Several rounds went through Williams's field jacket, one slashing through his left sleeve and the other tearing off the left side pocket. As the bullets whizzed around him Williams squeezed off several rounds and the enemy fell dead. He approached the fallen German cautiously to discover this was no ordinary soldier, but the corpse of a "Flakwac," a woman member of an antiaircraft crew drafted in the defense of Honningen.

"T.C. came storming out of the building cussing: 'That bitch come out with her hands up and then pulls out a burp gun and shot my sleeve out. But I got her anyway,' " Ransom remembered.

John L. Kuhn, a white infantryman with K Company, recalled his surprise at fighting women. "Here, for the first time, we came up against women combat troops firing from windows and doorways with their 'Burp' guns. And that is where they died. We had not come to Germany to kill women. We had no alternative, they made the choice."

If Williams was lucky once, he was lucky twice. Just moments after his encounter with the Flakwac, well-aimed bullets ripped away his other pocket and a dark stain began spreading across Williams's chest. "It looked like blood," Ransom remembered. "Are you hit?" he yelled at T.C. "Naw, it's just gun oil," T.C. replied. The bullet had hit his can of lubricating oil and it leaked out over his jacket.

Treadup remembered that Boudreau advanced his reputation that day in Honningen.

The tank destroyer boys mentioned a certain black soldier who carried a BAR . . . and they told the story of him killing a German colonel, two majors, two other officers and seven privates in this factory which turned out to be a bottling plant. He had taken six pistols of theirs and carried them inside his shirt. That afternoon our 3rd Battalion commander congratulated him and swapped his own .45 for a Luger.

We called him Blitz. Anyway, when the town was taken, he got thirsty and went out to look for a bottle and while doing this he walked into a German hospital. The first ward he came to he asked one of the six Wehrmacht soldiers what was the matter with him. The soldier pulled his sheet down and pointed to the leg that was all bandaged up. Blitz told him to take the bandage off, he refused but was persuaded to when the BAR was pointed at him. He took the bandage off, Blitz examined it and found nothing wrong, not a mark nor was it swollen. Blitz pulled the trigger and killed the man.

It's what I heard. Later on we heard the story told several times more. I believe it because I had gotten acquainted with Blitz a week or so later and got to know him real well and heard stories of other exploits he did.

Other members of 5th Platoon would believe the story. "If Boudreau had any excuse to shoot somebody, he would," Ransom said. "Better that Boudreau was on our side than with the Germans," recalled James Oliver. "I didn't see anybody shoot prisoners that day," Boris said. But he could understand if it had happened. "You'd see buddies get mowed down and it left you with a bitter feeling."

A platoon member captured a sniper after the enemy had killed and wounded a number of men from K Company. "Take this bastard back and shoot him," he told Willie Pace. Pace looked at him, his eyes widening in disbelief, and marched the man off—to a POW pen. Years later one of the participants recalled that men in combat will do things they would never consider doing in civilian life.

One black volunteer in the 99th experienced wrenching remorse after the war because he was involved in the killing of several German POWs. Ordered to escort the prisoners to a holding pen, he and two 5th Platoon comrades learned that their destination was four miles in the rear. They balked at marching their prisoners that far; they had been fighting for days and were exhausted. As the Germans began their walk to captivity with their hands clasped over their heads the Americans opened fire and cut them down. To this day the man remembers the POWs lying on the ground in death, their hands still raised above their heads.

It took two days to drive the Germans out of Honningen. The division history recalled the fight: "Resistance was stubborn, and the fighting continued all during the day and night and late into the next afternoon. That second day the entire town was taken, including the main crossroads south of the town, and our troops also sat on the commanding hills looking down on the historic little town of Rheinbrohl on the bank of the Rhine."

Ralston expressed amazement that the platoon's casualties were so light. Many of his men were spared, he believed, because the town's commanding officer decided to quit midway through the fight. Lieutenant Ralston recalled the incongruous battlefield encounter with the commander.

As the battle raged Lieutenant Ralston and a contingent from the 5th came upon a large open field at the end of which was a grouping of factorylike buildings. "I said, 'Oh shit man, this looks bad,' and I had a very bad feeling about advancing across it, but we had to do it. There was no cover and it was too far to run across."

Lieutenant Ralston ordered tanks out in front of his men "with the phone tank in the center and back a couple of hundred feet. I told the tank operator to drive about as fast as we could walk and we spread out behind each tank—at least five feet apart and we walked like hell waiting for the firing to hit us. It was a beautiful late afternoon but we were too scared to notice. I don't recall receiving anything but desultory rifle fire and so we crossed safely.

"And what a sight did we behold!" Ralston remembered.

The first factory fronting the large field had a cobblestone courtyard about three feet lower than the field, with a stone wall up to the field level. Along part of the wall were some large bushes and a few small trees. The courtyard was empty of people, but hidden in the bushes with their snouts just above the dirt pointed at the field were three 88 guns, with loads of shells beside them all organized for instant firing. We would have been blown off the field—tanks and all!

We were amazed, and after mentally thanking God, we plunged into the first building. In one of the first large rooms a party was going on, with 30 or 40 enemy soldiers and four or five women eating and drinking wine and beer!! And they kept on eating when we came in too. It was the German colonel, the commanding officer of the town, and his staff, and they had simply quit the war sometime that afternoon, as our platoon advanced toward them. We disarmed them in little groups, interrogated some that spoke good English, and allowed them to continue eating until the prisoner detail help we had radioed for arrived shortly.

The fortunes of war—had the colonel decided to continue fighting that afternoon, probably few of us in the black platoon would have lived. I did get his beautiful big nine-power binoculars with fire-adjusting reticules too!

Honningen had been taken and the men of the 5th of K were lauded for their valor and aggressiveness. Lieutenant Brown of L Company was impressed with their fighting behavior. "A higher percentage of men in the 5th Platoon aimed and fired their weapons than the white soldiers. All of them were just shooting hell out of everything. They were quite a bit more aggressive than white soldiers."

Brown's observations alluded to the courage of the men in the 5th of K. They were less afraid to expose themselves and trade fire with the enemy than white troops. "The whites were just a cross section of the American people," Brown noted. "They didn't want to hurt anybody unless they had to."

Ninety-ninth Division commander Maj. Gen. Walter E. Lauer acknowledged the contribution of the 5th of K: "Driving through the eastern third of the town [Honningen] the Negro platoon of Company K, which had already distinguished itself in its few days in battle, accounted for the major portion of the 300 prisoners taken. Sweeping through the town, it bagged a colonel and his staff of four, and killed many others.

"Based on the fact that all these men had had much service and training as infantry, and that they had volunteered for infantry action, many of them giving up high ratings to become doughboy privates, I decided to use them immediately in combat. The first real fight they entered was this one in Honningen. They proved their worth. . . . These men went through the town like a scourge."

Others also expressed their admiration for the black volunteers. Lieutenant Lombardo noted: "Co. K's Colored Platoon accounted for the major portion of prisoners taken and capturing that portion of Honningen assigned to them. This was the first we heard of colored troops in our sector being assigned to front line combat duties, and they proved themselves with distinction."

In an after-action report made April 3, 1945, Lt. Col. Robert H. Douglas, commander of 1st Battalion, 394th, who led the attack on Honningen, praised the black platoon. "Of particular interest in this attack, is the fact that the left platoon from K Company was a platoon of Negroes. . . . Under the command of a white officer, Lt. Richard Ralston, this platoon proved very aggressive and businesslike. Their attitude was that they were there to fight—to take their objectives. Unlike some platoons of white infantry, these Negroes—upon the capture of an objective and prisoners—did not stand round gawking at the prisoners, but immediately reorganized and continued on to their next objective. As one of them remarked—'If you white boys just tell us where to go—we'll go dere [sic].' In the fighting that morning and afternoon, this platoon supported by the TD's, knocked out several machine gun nests, snipers armed with burp guns, 20 mm flak guns, and cleared the eastern part of the town."

Sgt. Jack Dufalla, with K Company's heavy-weapons platoon, which supported the infantrymen with mortars and machine guns in Honningen, had a similar take on the quality of the black volunteers in his company. "These guys were very gung ho. They always wanted to lead and be on the attack. They were very brave and very foolish."

21

•

CONSOLIDATING THE BRIDGEHEAD

BY ST. PATRICK'S DAY, March 17, 1945, German resistance in the bridgehead was crumbling and enemy troops surrendered in droves or retreated behind the Wied River to the east of Erpel. The 99th captured hundreds of POWs that day and Wehrmacht troops refusing to give up were targeted by division artillery. Airborne spotters stalked bands of enemy soldiers and radioed their positions to distant batteries that laid down box barrages of 105s and 155s to corner terrified Germans and herd them toward American lines, where they surrendered.

K Company and the 5th of K advanced beyond Honningen over the ridges and through the gullies on the east bank of the Rhine. Along with the 394th they took the towns of Rockenfeld, Rheinbrohl, and Hammerstein and pushed on another 2,500 yards to take a ridgeline overlooking the town of Neuwied on the Rhine.

"We were crowded between the river and the hills, moving through woods south of Honningen skirmishing all the way," Ransom recalled. "It wasn't like the first days in the line, the Germans were pretty well broken up, but we were taking fire all the time." When the 5th of K encountered pockets of resisting Germans they radioed for long-range artillery to dislodge the enemy and took cover from the occasional shell that fell short.

The 5th continued through Neuwied, where Caesar had crossed the Rhine, and advanced into the hills above the town. "Lieutenant Ralston took the platoon down the landward side of a crest into a draw and that's where we again ran into enemy," Ransom said. "We didn't know they were there and they didn't know we were approaching, but we were warned when a bunch of deer ran toward us. We knew instinctively that they had been frightened by German troops and we just managed to get organized before we got into a firefight."

The exchange was sharp and quick, as the startled Americans hit the ground and opened fire into the dense underbrush and trees at the unseen enemy. The air filled with rifle blasts but the Germans were in no mood to press the fight and disappeared into the forests.

As the Germans retreated they dropped leaflets on the 5th of K, ejected from artillery shells or dropped from planes, depicting the blacks as victims of American racism and calling on them to surrender. One batch of leaflets came with the headline "Way Down upon the Sewanee River" and asked, "What wouldn't you give to be at home with the old folks again?" Even the black press, which lobbied extensively throughout the war for equality in the armed forces and for an end to a segregated military, scoffed at the gauche manner in which the Germans tried to win over these black Americans. A reporter from the *Pittsburgh Press,* a black newspaper, noted in a dispatch from the European theater: "The Boche would change his tactics if he could see the reactions of colored boys when they do chance across this Hun literary masterpiece. As a rule the colored soldier laughs the leaflets off or else takes offense at the outmoded 'Mammy' approach, feeling Jerry should give the colored soldier more credit than falling for this ancient wheeze."

The Germans had long hoped that America's racial tensions would cripple her war effort, and Propaganda Minister Joseph Goebbels threatened to stir up trouble in the United States. "Nothing will be easier than to produce a bloody revolution in America," Goebbels said. "No other country has as many social and racial tensions. We shall be able to play on many strings there."

Resentful and angry as they were at their treatment both in the army and in civilian life, the blacks expected worse treatment in an ethnically pure Nazi Germany if they surrendered. In fact, blacks were treated like all ethnic, religious, and political outcasts in Nazi Germany. Petru Popescu in his memoir, *The Oasis,* recalls seeing black American soldiers executed in a prison camp. "The men had been hanged by their necks but also by their wrists tied behind their backs. The nooses around their necks hadn't broken their dog tags, which dangled on their chests, glinting in the sunlight. They were colored American soldiers."

Blacks also knew that POWs were more likely to be shot than taken prisoner and the color of their skin would not save their lives if they surrendered in the heat of battle. They gave enemy prisoners little quarter and they expected little in return.

As the whites remembered the Malmédy Massacre, in which SS troops gunned down some eighty-six American POWs during the Battle of the Bulge, black Americans remembered a little-known massacre of African-American soldiers during the Bulge. Enemy troops from the 1st SS Panzer Division shot eleven unarmed black POWs on December 17, 1944, near Wereth, Belgium.

Other leaflets that the 5th of K found strewn about were directed at German troops and civilians. One batch characterized black American troops as West Indian practitioners of voodoo and cannibalism whom the

Americans had recruited from the Caribbean as the United States reached the limits of its manpower resources. Others described the blacks as convicted murderers who had escaped the electric chair by joining the infantry. The Germans were trying to harness the population's fear of blacks to strengthen resistance to the American armies overrunning the Reich in 1945.

"I didn't want the enemy troops we were fighting to be too terrified of us because it might make him fight harder," Ransom said. "But if it scares him and he runs, hey, that's great."

For many Germans, soldiers and civilians alike, black soldiers had reputations as murderers and butchers. "The Germans had an unadulterated fear of black troops," Strawder said. "It came from World War I when black Senegalese troops in the French army cut off the heads of German soldiers they captured and the Germans were shocked when they again saw blacks in World War II. From the stories they had heard they thought we Americans were the same breed." The French used the Senegalese on the western front.

The stories of black savagery during World War I were legion. "Are there any Africans opposite?" was a familiar question from German soldiers entering the trenches in World War I. U.S. Marine Capt. John W. Thomason Jr., who served with the U.S. 2nd Division at the Battle of Soissons in 1918, recounted the cruelty of Senegalese troops who fought alongside the Americans in a memoir, *Fix Bayonets!*

"These wild Mohammedans from West Africa were enjoying themselves. Killing, which is at best an acquired taste with the civilized races, was only too palpably their mission in life. . . . They were deadly. . . . They carried also a broad-bladed knife, razor-sharp, which disemboweled a man at a stroke. . . . With reason the Boches feared them worse than anything living, and the lieutenant saw in those woods unwounded fighting Germans who flung down their rifles when the Senegalese rushed, and covered their faces, and stood screaming against the death they could not look upon. And—in a lull, a long, grinning sergeant . . . approached him with a brace of human ears, nicely fresh, strung upon a thong. . . . *Voilà! Beaucoup souvenir ici!* [here are many souvenirs]."

"The Germans had been taught that we were savages," said Willfred Strange. "They'd heard about the Senegalese troops and they didn't want to mess with these black guys." Strange, who spoke German, once demanded in the heat of battle that an enemy machine-gun crew surrender immediately or his men would eat them after they were captured. The enemy soldiers quickly gave up.

"The Germans were afraid of us because they'd heard some things about us. They'd run up and throw their hands up to surrender," William Windley said of his experiences in the 1st Division. "There's no question, we were quite aggressive."

Aggressive they could be. Strawder and five buddies were scouring the countryside in the hills of the Lenne Mountains on the advance to the Ruhr looking for wine or schnapps when they heard German voices near a wooded area. Stealthily approaching the sounds, they realized they had stumbled onto an enemy outpost manned by three German soldiers.

"We didn't have no business being out of our holes and lollygagging in that area anyhow so one of the boys whispered, 'Let's kill them bastards!' " If they were going to carouse, they might as well make themselves useful. Gunshots and grenade blasts would alert other Germans in the area, so Strawder and his comrades sneaked up behind the chatting Germans.

"We didn't make no noise or anything and they were talking so they didn't hear us. There were three of them and one was sitting on the side of the hole smoking a pipe. Each of us took one and we killed them very quickly and quietly. The one I killed, I just reached down with my trench knife and pulled it around his neck."

A German civilian recorded his countrymen's fears of the 5th of K when it passed through his Bavarian village near the war's end. "We noticed on the sleeves of at least some of the men . . . patches of a black shield with a white-and-blue checkerboard pattern, which (we learned later) was the badge of the 99th Infantry Division. We had never seen black people of African origin. According to our villagers, they were recklessly brave in battle and savage and cruel in their behavior. To our family, their most noticeable feature was the contrast of their white teeth flashing in their dark faces that appeared to be perpetually talking and laughing."

Bruce Wright quoted Shakespeare to describe how the Germans may have perceived the black troops: "Yond Cassius has a lean and hungry look. . . . Such men are dangerous." Wright noted that many of the volunteers came from a different world than most Germans and their dark skin made them seem inscrutable and frightening.

Boris recalled moving through a village and coming upon a German officer with his arm in a sling and his bag packed in readiness to surrender to the Americans. The German wasn't expecting black troops and mumbled about his fear of being slashed and stabbed by these black Americans. To oblige him Boris withdrew his bayonet and thrust it under the enemy soldier's chin. He didn't break the skin but Boris enjoyed terrifying the battered Nazi.

Even American commanders perceived blacks as more aggressive. The army's rationale for recruiting black infantrymen was the notion that they would not be affected by the carnage they would encounter on the battlefield. "These men's youth had been spent in neighborhoods where knife and gunfights were commonplace and this didn't scare them at all," Ralston said.

Certainly, many of the men in the black platoons were adept at using knives. K Company infantryman Ralph Treadup recalled how easily some of the men in the 5th of K took to knives. Warned on their first night in the line with K Company that the Germans would soon be swarming over the area, Treadup recalled one black saying: "Ah's feel lots safer if ah's had a razor." Treadup said he pointed to a pile of captured knives. "They picked up what was there."

As the German army disintegrated, face-to-face confrontations between black Americans and surrendering Germans were becoming commonplace. Sometimes these meetings were deadly and resulted in killings on both sides. At other times they turned into amusing episodes of war as Germans went to great lengths to surrender to the Americans.

Harry Arnold recalled an encounter in which German troops tried to surrender to an American patrol from E Company, 393rd, in dense woods near the Wied River. The patrol came to a clearing and the men were reluctant to expose themselves in the brilliant moonlight but cautiously moved forward expecting to receive fire at any moment.

Suddenly they were jolted by a voice piercing the darkness. "Hallo!" The men froze in their tracks at the sound of the German-accented salutation. "The scouts turned and tore past, heading west. The rest of us scattered to the sides as we ran. Behind us was the sound of thrashing feet punctuated by, 'Hallo, hallo.' But still no fire . . .

"What did 'Hallo' mean? Why hadn't the Germans fired? The scouts had seen them sitting behind a machine gun, coalscuttle helmets reflecting moonlight. And why had they followed us a short distance? Sheepishly, we began to suspect we knew the answer—the bastards were trying to surrender! But we had demonstrated our superiority—we had outrun them."

Holmes remembered jumping into an abandoned foxhole one pitch-black night as German shells began falling around his squad. He landed on something that moved and turned out to be a German soldier also trying to escape the barrage. The two soldiers were too concerned with their safety to harm each other and bolted off on their separate ways when the shelling ended.

Ransom spoke of an encounter with Germans near Neuwied while scavenging for provisions. The 5th had run out of food and the men were starving. "Somebody said there was a friendly outfit down at the bottom of the hill along the river with lots of wine and food. So a couple of us went down to an armored recon unit in a vineyard and we started wandering through this big building and went into the wine cellars." It was dark and chilly as the GIs rummaged for food. The pickings were slim; cans of preserved boar meat but plenty of wine. As they scavenged, the men were startled by movement in the gloom and instinctively unlocked their rifles. As they worked their way cautiously forward they came face-to-face with three shadowy figures hiding among the wine barrels.

"*Kameraden, Kameraden,*" the Germans yelled as they shuffled forward with their hands up. Ransom quickly disarmed the enemy soldiers, amazed that with a few more steps he would have walked over them.

Strawder's encounter with the enemy was more bizarre. He was walking point for the 5th of E through a patch of woods well ahead of the platoon when the ground suddenly gave way beneath his feet and he tumbled into a hole nearly as deep as he was tall. He lost his rifle as he fell into a slit trench and wound up on his back. As his vision adjusted in the trench he found himself eye to eye with a German infantryman. For an instant the two stared at each other; then, in an unexpected twist, the German thrust Strawder's rifle back into his hands, stood back, and threw up his hands. Behind him, in the well-camouflaged trench, was a squad of enemy soldiers all with their hands high.

Fear of his impending death suddenly vanished as Strawder, by now an experienced scout for the 5th of E, had to find a way to explain this encounter to his comrades. Not many men capture a squad of enemy troops by falling on their ass. Luckily the rest of 5th Platoon was thirty yards behind and the trench and the dense woods had camouflaged his misstep. Strawder bolted out leading his prisoners, whom he waved to the rear. He knew he was the goat, but to his comrades Strawder was the hero and still the best point man in the army.

22

·

DIVISION RESERVE

As the Germans retreated east over the Wied River, enemy resistance in the bridgehead ceased and the 5th of K was ordered to pack up and began an all-night march back to Erpel. The 394th was going into reserve in preparation for the offensive to encircle the Ruhr.

Dawn found the 5th dog-footing it into Erpel. The troops were struck by the void left by the collapse of the Ludendorff Bridge, which had crashed into the Rhine in a thunderclap of snapping steel girders on March 17. It had taken too many jolts from German artillery shells and bombs. As a last desperate gamble the Germans had sent the frogmen, "swimming saboteurs," floating down the Rhine, but their attacks were thwarted by the Americans and the enemy infiltrators were killed or captured. No American troops had been allowed to cross on the span after March 14, and the only personnel on the bridge when it collapsed were army engineers working to shore up the structure in a vain effort to keep it standing. Twenty-eight GIs were killed when it fell.

"The big center span appeared to buckle and then to swing to the south and pull the other smaller spans with it. The whole bridge then collapsed into the river," recalled Major General Lauer, who witnessed the bridge's final seconds. "There were men of the Corps engineers working on the bridge at the time, but no enemy fire was coming in. I think the old bridge simply had taken all it could, and wearily settled down in the river to rest. The thought struck me at the time, of old General Ludendorff of World War I fame, in whose honor the bridge had been named, bowing his head in deep gloom and collapsing because he could foresee what was to happen to the mighty Wehrmacht. Yes, the Wacht am Rhein [code name for the German defense of the Rhine] had failed."

Near Erpel K Company and the 394th settled in for several days of R and R while the division's other two regiments continued advancing toward the Wied. Ralph Treadup described the simple pleasures of the regiment's much needed rest. "Many of the soldiers got their hair cut for a quarter by an enterprising ex-barber. We all changed clothes, shaved and even took a few minutes to brush our teeth. I had picked up a portable Victrola and some German long-playing records so we took turns winding up the Victrola and changing records. I recall one afternoon we had a few bottles of liberated wine while playing our music alongside a steep embankment that was about a hundred feet to the creek bed. Whether the wine got to us or the music, perhaps both, we crazy soldiers started a game of rolling down this steep hill. Looking back on this event, we were a bunch of guys in our second childhood, getting our jollies before going back into combat."

Ransom caught up on his eating. "We finally got some food, too much food. I ate pretty near a half case of C rations that first day because I was so hungry," he recalled. The rest of the 5th of K relaxed, slept, and stocked up on supplies.

Lieutenant Ralston noticed the interesting interaction between his black troops and the rest of K Company while on R and R. The blacks were like magnets drawing white troops from all around. "They had a terrific sense of humor," Ralston remembered. "On the occasions that we were in reserve far enough back to have a campfire, I would observe white members of K Company gather round the black platoon members and listen to all the great comedy and good fun. The blacks were very funny. Their sense of humor was more agile, and alert, than the whites'. I'm guessing that's why the whites gathered around us, to hear their quick puns and wordplay jokes regarding whatever the conversation was about at the moment."

Lt. Frederick Gerdes, platoon leader for 5th Platoon, E Company, 395th Regiment, 99th Division, remembered the men of his black platoon for their ability to forget the strains of combat. "They would fight all day and play all night," Gerdes said. "They're always kidding back and forth—seems like the platoon is the life of the company."

"We blacks had a wonderful esprit and great camaraderie," recalled Bruce Wright. Ransom noted that the blacks' isolation was mainly responsible for this esprit de corps. "We were forced to be that way. There were just over forty of us in 5th Platoon and we'd been dropped in the middle of the briar patch with all these white guys in the 394th. We were a novelty to them." Army surveys also found that the blacks took greater pride in their units than whites.

Among themselves the blacks developed a kind of macabre levity that sustained them in their isolation and through the worst fighting. Strawder remembered a moment of dark humor when the 5th of E was pulled off line for three days of R and R. The men deserved a break after several weeks in combat, but no sooner had they drawn their pay than they were ordered back into the lines.

"Oh Lordy, I cussed and cussed that we were going back to the front," Strawder said. "I was so mad I even cussed out the chaplain. We were walking back up the road, back into action, and we knew somebody was going to get hit," Strawder said. "So the fellows got to bettin'. One guy says, 'Hey, I bet Strawder gets it before the sun goes down. The way he cussed out that chaplain, you know he's gonna get it.'

"All the guys started taking bets about when I was going to get it so I took all the bets. I liked to bet and I said I'll take all of them bets and I'll hold all the money too." Strawder won the bet and the cash.

Ransom recalled indulging in a bit of macabre humor while in the front lines. He and his Detroit buddy Willie Pace were hole mates when the platoon dug in above Neuwied after the battle for Honningen. The 5th had outrun its supplies and had to forage for food. "Pace and I were sitting in the hole having a discussion about how hungry we were and right outside the hole there is this dead German, freshly killed because we had just killed him. We said, 'If we cut off a slice of him to eat, do you think anyone would notice?' " No sooner were the words out of Ransom's mouth than the Germans launched a rocket attack of "screaming minnies" that sent everyone to the bottom of their holes.

While the fighting in the bridgehead was often intense and the casualties sometimes heavy, the bridgehead was a strategic sideshow for Eisenhower and the Allied command for two weeks following its capture. Even though the Americans were across the Rhine, Eisenhower limited their advances in the bridgehead, much to the consternation and anger of American generals.

The main attack across the Rhine was still in preparation, and for reasons of politics and long-planned strategy, it was to be made north of Cologne by Field Marshall Bernard Montgomery's 21st Army Group in a massive assault, code-named "Operation Plunder." Montgomery's British and Canadians, along with Lt. Gen. William H. Simpson's Ninth Army, were to make the Rhine crossing on the night of March 23–24.

The American generals, however, believed that Eisenhower should unleash the American troops in the Remagen bridgehead and break out into central Germany. But it wasn't until mid-March that General Eisenhower gave final approval to the five U.S. divisions for an all-out advance.

It was in deference to the mercurial Montgomery and to British political sensitivity that Eisenhower stuck with Operation Plunder as the main thrust over the Rhine. The British were politically bruised, by war's end, by their diminishing power, which was highlighted by the massive American presence in the ETO. The Americans clearly were the dominant power, and the appearance of making the main Rhine crossing would restore some prestige to the British army.

Eisenhower also had solid military reasons for waiting for Montgomery's massive blow over the Rhine. The Allies were still smarting from the German exploitation of Allied weakness in the Ardennes during the Bulge, and the supreme commander was concerned that the U.S. divisions in the bridgehead were vulnerable to being cut off and destroyed. With the main attack over the Rhine coming from Montgomery's forces, Eisenhower also had few reserves with which to reinforce the Americans in the bridgehead should they run into trouble or advance out of it. He could, however, use the bridgehead to draw German troops away from Montgomery's crossing. Therefore, Eisenhower kept the Americans in the bridgehead fighting but declined to give the go-ahead for a complete breakout.

Despite the high command's plan for Montgomery's Rhine crossing in the north, the Americans forced two more crossings of the river south of Remagen on March 22 and 26. On the night of the twenty-second the American 5th Infantry Division in General Patton's Third Army crossed the Rhine at Nierstein and at Oppenheim, with negligible losses, much to the chagrin of Montgomery, who once again had been preempted by the Americans.

Four days later on the twenty-sixth troops of the American Seventh Army, under General Patch, forced a Rhine crossing at Worms. Seventh Army quickly linked up with Third Army and captured the city of Mannheim. The French First Army, serving in General Devers's Sixth Army Group, crossed the Rhine on April 1 at Philippsbourg.

By March 23 the wraps were finally off in the Remagen bridgehead and the 99th, along with the 1st, 9th, and 78th Divisions, prepared for breakout. Their target: the Ruhr and the heart of Nazi Germany.

23

·

ACROSS THE WIED AND BREAKOUT

WAYMON RANSOM MADE A career of the army and fought in three wars before retiring in 1970. One of the most vivid recollections from his military career was the morning of March 23, 1945, when the 5th of K and the 99th Division broke out of the Remagen bridgehead and advanced toward the city of Giessen. It was dawn and morning mists obscured thousands of GIs lying prone along the west side of a stretch of the Ruhr-Frankfurt Autobahn that ran through a large forest clearing and formed the front line between the Americans and the Germans. The sun's rays were streaking the horizon when the order came down to move out. Almost as one, thousands of American troops rose to their feet, readied their weapons, and began to advance. Ransom remembers the sea of OD brown progressing like a wave to engulf the enemy.

"As far as the eye could see, in every direction, were GIs at five-foot intervals moving across the empty highway." The brisk morning air was suddenly split by three staccato bursts from a German machine gun. To Ransom it seemed as though the next movements of the American troops were carefully choreographed. On cue, they now flopped to the ground in unison at the sound of the firing. "That was the largest bunch of infantry in one place, at one time that I ever saw in all my twenty-five years in the army," Ransom said. "There must have been ten thousand guys hitting the dirt."

Immediately engines revved and several Sherman tanks moved up the empty autobahn in a clattering roar, their machine guns sputtering out streams of tracers aimed into a collection of farmhouses to the left of the American line. Intermittently the tanks stopped, aimed, and fired 75-mm high-explosive (HE) rounds into the buildings. Once the Shermans had neutralized the enemy the American infantry formations rose again and set off in pursuit of the retreating Germans.

Fifth Platoon was going back into action after five days of R and R with the 394th to join the 393rd and 395th Regiments, which had already crossed the Wied River and were pushing east toward Giessen.

The 99th joined the assault, involving three U.S. Army corps, aimed at trapping and destroying what Allied intelligence at first estimated to be some 150,000 German troops massed in the Ruhr, Germany's industrial heart. Once these enemy formations were eliminated, the Western Allies would turn their armies toward Berlin some three hundred miles to the east.

The enemy troops in the Ruhr were in Generalfeldmarschall Walter Model's Army Group B, which comprised the Fifth Panzer Army, the Fifteenth Army, and two corps from the First Parachute Army. The American high command had concluded that a head-on thrust directly north from the bridgehead over the Sieg River into the Ruhr area would involve a drive against still-formidable German formations. The enemy was expecting a northward attack and had positioned his best forces along this front, but the Americans refused to take the bait.

"Frontal assaults against the German Army, even at the decreased strength and efficiency available to it in early 1945, would have been a costly business," Eisenhower wrote in *Crusade in Europe*.

Consequently, Eisenhower and General Bradley, overall ground commander of the American forces moving against the Ruhr from the south in the Twelfth Army Group, decided on an end run around the stiffest German resistance. Their plan was to move the First Army southeast in the direction of Giessen away from the heaviest concentration of German troops to link up with Lt. Gen. George S. Patton's Third Army. The two armies would meet around Limburg and together would drive northeast to Kassel. The First Army would then wheel north toward a meeting with the Ninth Army, which was to advance south from the Cologne area, and the two forces would envelop the Ruhr in a giant pincer to contain and destroy the German forces caught in between. The coming battle would be known as the Battle for the Ruhr Pocket.

The Americans attacked out of the Remagen bridgehead over the Wied with a three-corps assault on March 25 against relatively light enemy opposition. Maj. Gen. Lawton Collins's VII Corps struck almost directly eastward toward Giessen with its northern flank protected by the Sieg River. Brig. Gen. James A. Van Fleet's III Corps, of which the 99th was a part, was in the center of the attack with the Dill River as its objective. Third Corps would also shield Maj. Gen. Clarence R. Huebner's V Corps, which held the right flank of the attack.

At this point in the war the Americans outnumbered and outgunned the Germans. The Allies fielded some ninety divisions and had thousands more tanks as well as vast quantities of supplies that poured to the front on a conveyer belt of truck and train transport. The Allied air forces pummeled the once formidable Wehrmacht whenever its troops and tanks ventured forth in futile attempts to stop the Americans. The Germans were reeling and their only defense was to retreat and make a stand when they believed they had local superiority to stall the American juggernaut.

General Lauer sent advance elements of the 393rd and 395th Regiments over the Wied River at carefully selected crossing points just after midnight on March 23. The move took the enemy by surprise as the American troops quickly climbed the hills on the east bank. The 395th moved forward against light opposition, but the 393rd ran into stiff fighting.

E Company, 393rd Regiment, crossed the Wied at dawn and engaged bypassed pockets of Germans who had had time to recover from the earlier nighttime assaults. As the men of E Company darted across on a bridge they were swept by machine-gun fire that was "thankfully high," Harry Arnold remembered. But the men were also greeted by "a burned and charred human form, almost unrecognizable," that lay on the bridge approach. Amid the confusion and noise of battle Arnold thought: "I wondered at the manner of his demise—informer, deserter, spy?"

Once across, the men of E Company found themselves trapped between the Wied and a steep bluff as machine-gun fire raked the small roadway between river and bluff. As long as the men hugged the bluff they were safe, but progress was slow. "You couldn't move and every time you stuck your head out the machine gun would go off," Strawder remembered. "It was getting cold and this one boy in 5th Platoon, A.B., who was later killed in Korea and had a real loud mouth, yells out, 'I ain't gonna stay here and freeze to death.' So he led the attack and we went on, white and black, about five hundred of us, and took the cliff with A.B. leading the attack. Somebody got that machine gun because it didn't do any more shooting." The company continued its advance.

On the following day, March 24, the division passed through innumerable small villages and gained some 5,500 yards against several Volksgrenadier divisions, augmented by a number of miscellaneous units, and bagged more than six hundred prisoners. For the veterans of the 99th who had slugged it out with some of the best enemy units in the Battle of the Bulge and engaged the Germans in the Remagen bridgehead, the fighting beyond the Wied River was a surprise. The once formidable German army seemed no longer willing to stand and fight.

"This was a new kind of warfare for our Checkerboarders," General Lauer wrote in *Battle Babies*. "Morale was high! They slogged and doubled-timed along, taking objective after objective with monotonous regularity. It got to be a joke! Urbach, Uberdorf, Dernbach, Gierhofen and on and on rolled the names of towns and villages passed through and secured. It was a sightseeing trip, afoot and in high gear. This was, however, not fast enough to keep up with the enemy who disappeared faster.

"As one tired foot-slogger put it, 'What the ——— kind of war is this, when we advance mile after mile through Germany without having to fire a shot or having a single casualty? Supermen? Fight to the last man? Bah!' " The ease with which the Americans advanced southeasterly was due in part to the fact that the Germans had concentrated the bulk of their forces along this axis, leaving the terrain to the southeast exposed and largely undefended.

"On the 27th of March our units somehow or other motorized themselves and sped down highways after the 7th Armored for an advance of 19,000 yards. Our men rode everything that could roll. Tanks and tank destroyers crawled with infantry. Jeep trailers carried six men and the Jeep six more. Soon every vehicle had a trailer, and many captured vehicles appeared in our columns, carrying our doughboys," General Lauer wrote.

Ransom noticed the change. "The Germans were pretty well scattered and were withdrawing," he said. "Once we were out of the bridgehead the Volkssturm [a hastily formed militia] was all over the place and their resistance was varied. You'd be walking along and nothing, then you'd go to the next village and you'd have a real firefight on your hands. It was our job as infantry to sweep the bushes while the armor stuck to the roads and when you ran into something they'd say to the infantry, 'Go get em.' "

Most of all the Americans feared the flak guns and the nights. The Germans would place the barrels of 20-mm, 37-mm, and 88-mm guns at ground level so that their shells exploded in the ranks of advancing infantry. The 5th lost a number of men to these guns before the war ended.

"Then at night they'd gather up and counterattack," Ransom said. Harold Robinson remembered one such encounter as dusk descended on the 5th of K's perimeter. "We were on top of a hill digging in for the night when this one guy hollers, 'Robby, watch it! Get him, get him!' My buddy had put his rifle down to take off his jacket and the rifle got stuck in the fork of a tree and he couldn't get it out. He was twisting it out instead of lifting it out.

"Here's this German officer standing there with two other guys and they had these doggone *panzerfausts* [shoulder-fired antitank rocket launchers]. They were right up on us, no more than ten yards away. I dropped what I had and grabbed my rifle. They started running back down the hill and I shot the officer in the back of the head. If my guy hadn't hollered I wouldn't have seen him.

"The thing that saved us was that the Germans didn't have any arms. They just had *panzerfausts* and I'm saying, 'Damn, I'm glad they only had those antitank weapons. If they had had burp guns or rifles we'd have been shot."

The Germans were delaying the Americans as long as they could in a desperate effort to buy time to regroup behind the Lahn River some twenty-five miles east of the Wied. Ninety-ninth Division intelligence assessed the enemy's battlefield situation: "From 26 March to 31 March, the enemy, after realizing the success of our break through, tried to withdraw with as many troops as possible by infiltrating in small groups through our lines with the intention of reassembling somewhere east of the Lahn River. For this purpose he used every ruse, including dressing entire units in civilian clothing and assigning them an assembly area to the East."

The 5th of K continued its advance with the rest of III Corps, cautious, yet thankful that the Germans were retreating so rapidly. The numbers of German prisoners being taken slowed the American advance. The 99th was also delayed by the thousands of allied POWs and slave laborers being liberated along the path of the advance. "They lined the roads and streets, and cheered and saluted the Americans as they sped by with hands raised and fingers spread in the sign of the victorious V," General Lauer wrote. "Russians with smiles as big as Russia itself stood smack in the middle of the road and shook hands with a G.I. in every passing vehicle. Laughing, hilarious Frenchmen grabbed surprised doughboys and planted humid kisses on their cheeks. Uncontrolled enthusiasm, joy, relief, gaiety, gladness and rejoicing were evidenced by these poor souls who had given up all hope of redemption."

By March 28, the 99th had moved out of mountainous terrain into more open country as it advanced rapidly on Giessen. Near the city the 7th Armored Division passed through the 99th and was now roaming wildly and freely through the German countryside, giving the Wehrmacht a taste of its own blitzkrieg tactics. The tanks would advance and take on the enemy and then the infantry moved in to mop up. From the commanding general's perspective it was a walkover. To the GIs it was still a war where men got killed.

On March 29 the 99th had reached Giessen, the limits of its objective set by the First Army, and elements of the 394th took the city. Then the men settled in to await a decision about the division's next move. When the order came down, the 99th would start advancing north toward the industrial heart of the German Reich—the Ruhr.

24

•

GIESSEN

As a veteran of the Battle of the Bulge, Lieutenant Ralston found the fighting beyond the Remagen bridgehead fluid and freewheeling compared to the combat in the Ardennes after the German breakthrough on December 16, 1944. "In the Bulge the warfare was stationary for the 99th. We were there to hold ground and the fighting was often more intense against masses of German troops. They outnumbered us in the Bulge." Now Lieutenant Ralston and his 5th Platoon were told to advance and take as much ground as possible.

The more mobile warfare beyond the bridgehead emphasized the need for good intelligence about the enemy's strength and whereabouts, so scouts became critical to the advance. White officers quickly discovered that the black volunteers were exceptionally good "on point" and as scouts for their platoons because they had an acute sense of impending trouble. "They were damn good soldiers . . . and could handle flank security real well, which was rough," remembered Lieutenant Gerdes.

The scouts moved out ahead of the platoon to prevent the Germans from setting up ambushes, or to detect mines along the roads as the 99th advanced through wooded hills, deep gullies, and quaint villages. When the 5th of E moved out Strawder was usually a scout for his squad, and he later bragged about his keen eyesight and ability to detect the enemy: "I could see a mosquito on a rooftop."

Strawder concluded that his chances of surviving combat were better at the head of the platoon than with the troops farther back. If the Germans were waiting in ambush, he surmised, they would let the scouts pass and open fire on the main body of the platoon. He also figured that artillery fire was the enemy's most dangerous weapon and it would most likely be aimed at the platoon, not the scout. "The Germans weren't as good shots with the rifle as the Americans, but they could put a mortar shell in your back pocket," Strawder said. There were other advantages to being a scout. They didn't have to carry extra clips of ammunition for the BAR man or rockets for the bazooka man. "I could travel light at point," Strawder said.

Like all good scouts Strawder learned where to position himself. It depended on the time of day, the terrain, and the likelihood of an encounter with enemy troops. Sometimes he placed himself on the right, at other times to the left, sometimes in the center. He developed his own system of signals to alert the men to impending action. "If you see me everything is OK," he told them. "If I disappear it means the enemy has been sighted. If I come hightailing back, take cover, and if I come running back and keep on going, start running yourselves."

When a new second lieutenant tried to establish a series of hand and rifle signals for the scouts, Strawder balked. "He said when you spot the enemy raise your rifle above your head three times." Strawder quickly put the officer in his place, knowing that if he followed the lieutenant's instructions he'd be shot before he got his rifle in the air.

The American advance toward Giessen was so rapid that the Germans were unable to prepare adequate defenses or even conceal their antitank mines. They would just lay them on the roads, hoping the Americans wouldn't see them in the dark. Strawder and a buddy, Dixon, walked along kicking them down embankments.

"Your better watch it," hollered Strawder's buddy, Lloyd George, from up ahead. "You'll get killed!"

Strawder hollered back, "Tank mines ain't gonna kill you. Antipersonnel mines, yeah, but not tank mines. Tank mines are set to detonate from the weight of a tank, not a man."

Suddenly a German machine gun opened fire and Strawder saw bullets ricocheting off the road all around him, even passing between his legs. George was hit and screamed. "He took five bullets right across the chest," Strawder said. "The aid man said there was nothing he could do. I was next to George crying and carrying on. Dixon jumped up on one of our tanks and I followed him and we grabbed the machine gun and opened up on the hill where the fire came from and the machine gun stopped."

The scouts in all outfits were doing a big business as the advance continued toward Giessen. "We were marching 10 to 15 miles a day and it became so enervating that they had to put us on trucks and cart us 20 miles to catch up with the armor," Ralston said. The men were close to exhaustion.

"We marched for miles and we were all sleepwalking," Clayton Des Journette recalled. "We would take a shelter half and tie it to the guy in front and walk along asleep until the next time we ran into Germans."

One encounter with the enemy, however, brought the men to a heightened state of alertness. Just the mention of "SS" could strike terror in the hearts of U.S. troops. Boris recalled the sweaty fear that overcame men when told their next objective was defended by SS troops. Holmes remembered the 5th of K being warned to gird for the fight of their lives because die-hard SS troops were just around the bend. On hearing the news one member of the platoon placed one foot over the other and pulled the trigger to blast a hole though both feet. After he was bundled off in an ambulance the platoon resumed its advance, moving cautiously up the road. They had gone a few hundred yards when they encountered a sign of impending danger. A wounded GI came walking down the road from the front holding his badly mangled arm. He asked for a light and walked on. Soon the men saw a band of helmeted Germans ahead. But as the enemy approached they waved white flags and had their hands in the air. They turned out to be a motley crew of Volkssturm soldiers surrendering to the Americans. These were the vaunted SS troops that intelligence had warned about.

Relief and rest for the advancing 5th of K generally came at night when the weary infantrymen stumbled into German villages and towns and commandeered private houses. Finding good lodging became a contest with obsessive proportions, and units competed to get into towns first to take the best houses. Infantry and armored units would then post guards around their accommodations to ensure that no one else could take them.

Harold Robinson recalled a pact between K Company and accompanying units of the 7th Armored Division. If the infantry got into a town first they got the best houses and the armored boys had to stand guard that night. If the armored units got into town first they got the best billets and the infantry stood guard. This arrangement led to such intense competition that it almost caused an accidental death.

The 5th of K was advancing into one of the many towns on the march to the Ruhr when a vehicle from 7th Armored came racing up the road with GIs hanging from the sides. Everyone had their eye on a nearby farmhouse and the men of the 5th were running hard to be there first. The truck driver had the same idea and turned sharply into the long access road that led to the farmhouse. As the truck lurched into the turn an infantryman was catapulted off the vehicle and fell under a wheel, and Robinson and his buddies watched horrified as the tire ran over the GI's head. They immediately ran to his aid expecting to find him dead with a crushed skull, but miraculously the man had survived. Spring rains had softened the ground and his helmeted head was cushioned by the soggy soil. The biggest problem came in getting the man's head out of the muck and prying the smashed helmet off his head. In the commotion soldiers from the 5th got to the farmhouse first and claimed it for K Company.

The men of the 5th of E incurred the wrath of their regimental commander by advancing beyond one objective just to get into warm and cozy-looking houses with smoke curling up from the chimneys. "Our lieutenant was trying to stop us because we had orders to stay on a hill and await further orders," Strawder remembered. "We were cold and wet and the houses looked warm, so we just kept on going to get warm. The major raised Cain and said he was going to find out who ordered us into that village. That didn't make any sense to me, staying up on that hill and freezing to death."

Once the men were billeted in private houses, the German occupants were usually sent packing, but sometimes they were allowed to remain in the cellar or attic while the GIs cooked their dinners and relaxed after the day's march. German civilians could only pray that these conquerors would respect their houses and belongings. One German remembered the arrival of troops from the 99th Division in the vicinity of Bitz in Bavaria. "That night, American soldiers were quartered in most farmhouses. They came to the Holzapfel house with great noise and without any courtesy took it over. Victor was in bed when a soldier entered his room above the stable, ordered him out and fell into the vacated bed fully clothed and booted and holding on to his rifle. My brother joined the Holzapfels in their family room, the only one they were allowed to have for the night." These soldiers were white.

In all wars and in all armies soldiers develop a penchant for looting. The black volunteers were no exception. "They loved to loot and shoot," said one white K Company veteran. But whites also participated in the looting of Germany. This was demonstrated in recent years by the return of artworks to their former German owners following the deaths of the white Americans who stole them. One white veteran admitted in a personal history sent to the Center for Military History in Carlisle, Pennsylvania, that he and his comrades were conquerors to whom no law pertained. "Stayed in houses and found we knew how to loot—without any training. No guilt feelings about it at all."

Strawder partook in the game as well. He carried a bag filled with diamonds and gold rings he had confiscated from the dead, from prisoners, or from any German who had anything valuable. He packed them all away in a small waterproof cigarette bag he carried in his left breast pocket.

"I must have had about twenty thousand dollars' worth of jewelry in that bag. I knew it was wrong, but I knew the war wasn't going to last that long and I wanted to get my life back together at home."

The Lord spoke to Strawder about his transgressions during a mortar attack while his squad advanced through a clearing in woods. "We had about three hundred to four hundred yards of open space to cross to get to the other woods and the Germans had us zeroed in. As soon as we started across they opened up and we hit the dirt and started crawling and I couldn't get close enough to the ground." Strawder was terrified and he began praying as mortar bombs exploded all around him.

"I was praying as loud as I could and hollering, 'Lord, please don't let me get hit, please don't let me get hit.' But there was the little matter of all the jewelry and gold and I knew the Lord was gonna punish me for having all that stuff so I took that bag out of my pocket and just threw it as far as I could. I am so glad I did because the good Lord didn't take me that day." Strawder's comrades laughed heartily and teased him about his newfound religion. "You sure was calling on the Lord."

The men of the 5th of K became adept at foraging for their chow, and scavenging parties set out through the villages and towns every night looking for food and animals. "In one village there were a lot of chickens running around when we arrived," Boris recalled. "When we left there was nothing but chicken feathers."

Boris and his comrades quickly learned where German hausfraus stored their food. "We'd go into houses and head right for the attic where they kept all the smoked hams and the eggs. The eggs were preserved in some kind of liquid in big crocks that kept them fresh."

Sometimes the former inhabitants were put to work cooking for the GIs. "There was an old German lady living in one house we took over who showed me how to fry potatoes with water," Ransom said. He recalled another evening when his squad commandeered a house and allowed the occupants to remain; then Ransom spent the rest of the night consoling the hausfrau, who was hysterical because she hadn't heard from her husband in months. He was in the Wehrmacht on the eastern front.

Lieutenant Ralston belatedly discovered that two of his men had been professional chefs in the States in high-class hotel restaurants. "We tried to stay in a house at night of course, and the search would begin for canned meats, potatoes, chickens, anything. When the food scavenging parties returned to his billet everyone was served a gourmet meal. A number of times I looked up to see white boys near us gaping at the really tasty food we were eating," Ralston said.

The evening's fare sometimes included women. Holmes said that German women weren't as enamored with the black troops as were many French women. But they would make themselves available on occasion as the 5th put into town for the night. "Sometimes it took some persuasion," Holmes said, "but not much. We were a conquering army and could get many things we wouldn't otherwise have gotten."

Fifth Platoon members were also adept at finding hidden stores of liquor. "I could have found a bottle of whiskey in the Sahara Desert," Strawder said. Men were constantly scavenging for schnapps, cognac, and wine in German cellars. One GI recalled that they would occasionally find wine stored in big tanks and they learned to put a bullet hole in the top of the tank, rather than near the bottom, so that all the wine wouldn't drain out at once.

In Giessen, the 5th Platoon hit the jackpot when someone discovered a warehouse filled with cognac. "That night turned into a fantastic drunk," Ransom said. Jack Dufalla remembered the night and wanted no part of the revelry with his black comrades. The 5th was ensconced in a large, beautifully appointed house in a village on the outskirts of Giessen where the party went well into the early-morning hours. Jeeploads of platoon members kept arriving with more alcohol to fuel the celebration. Eventually, however, the exhausted men drifted off to sleep with only one guard on duty.

The Americans had to be vigilant at night because the Germans lurked in nearby woods and liked to sneak out and attack unwary U.S. encampments. The sentry was stationed outside the house. In the calm and quiet just before dawn a rifle shot rang out. More shots followed as the groggy men of the 5th were roused from their stupor to grab rifles and rush outside. The sentry fired shots into a lane where he had seen a German patrol attempting to infiltrate into the platoon's area. He had a hole in his helmet to prove the intrusion, a cleanly punched circle on the front lip. The fusillade continued as men fired on a lane between their commandeered house and an adjacent building. Slowly the shooting died down until there was silence. Squad members probed the nearby yards and a field behind the houses, but there was no sign of Germans.

Daylight revealed some evidence of possible intruders: A German helmet and other pieces of enemy equipment were found in the field behind the house, but it looked to some as though the articles had been on the ground for some time. The men went about their business but later, a few pointed questions elicited the truth about the encounter. The sentry admitted to Ransom that there had been no German patrol. In his drunken state, he had fallen asleep over his rifle, which discharged into his helmet. Rudely awakened, he immediately assumed he had been hit by enemy fire. Once his comrades joined the fight against the imaginary enemy, the sentry regained his wits and realized he had shot himself, but he was too embarrassed to admit it.

25

•

MUTUAL SUPPORT

THE SENTRY HAD REASON to hide the truth about the night's fire-fight. Above all else, the men of the 5th of K judged one another by their combat proficiency. Some men might despise one another, but in a fight they needed complete confidence in one another at all times. Their safety and psychological well-being depended on it. And the men of the 5th Platoons knew they ultimately had only themselves to rely upon. They certainly would never seek the assistance of white boys.

For a man to fail at protecting his comrades was a cardinal sin in the infantry, and several members of the 5th admitted that any such laggard would have been disposed of with a shot in the back in the heat of combat. "If you weren't reliable you might be prone to having an accident," Ransom said.

Arthur Holmes didn't always get along with Pfc. Baker, but he had high praise for him in combat. The two had once nearly come to blows but that didn't change Holmes's trust in Baker in a firefight.

"Baker was very aggressive and good in combat," Holmes admitted. "Whenever we moved out on the attack Baker never fell back. He always moved forward. Everybody else hesitated before gathering up courage. We used to say to ourselves, 'Here goes nothing' as we prayed we wouldn't get hit." Baker would volunteer for the toughest assignments. Holmes remembered him going along with white members of K Company who sneaked into Honningen to kill or capture German troops before the Americans took the town.

Ransom was a good soldier and, like Baker, went beyond the call of duty when necessary. After a hard fight on the Ludwigs Canal in Bavaria, Ransom volunteered with three comrades to join the company chasing the fleeing Germans while 5th Platoon stayed behind and licked its wounds. "I wanted to be there when the last dog was dead," Ransom said.

Ransom had great confidence in the fighting ability of his neighborhood buddy Willie Pace. "Pace was a good BAR man and a solid fellow," Ransom said. "He kept his head at all times in combat."

There were squad members who some of the men believed should have been weeded from the unit before it reached the front. Holmes wondered how Pfc. Sampson Jones made it through the infantry training. To Holmes, Jones was too young and immature and didn't have the necessary qualities and instincts of a good combat soldier. Holmes's fears may have been justified. On the push to the Ruhr, Sampson Jones was in the wrong place at the wrong time.

Pfc. Ray Dexter was a good soldier, but several youthful indiscretions on the battlefield earned him the wrath of his comrades. Holmes recalled being dug in on a hilltop in the Ruhr Pocket awaiting orders to move out when the platoon was surprised to see a squad of German soldiers crest the top of the opposing hill and march toward the 5th. "They hadn't seen us and were going to walk right into our arms," Holmes said. "We wouldn't even have to open fire. We'd just surprise them and take them in."

Suddenly, without warning or explanation, Dexter rose from his position and waved his arms and screamed at the oncoming enemy troops: "Hey, over here you guys, over here!"

"What the hell are you doing?" Holmes yelled as the Germans scattered and the Americans opened fire. The ensuing firefight lasted five minutes and resulted in several German casualties. Holmes was certain the Germans would have surrendered without a fight because they wore their cloth caps instead of helmets.

"I wanted to kill Dexter," Holmes said. "I was never so mad in my life and I wanted to kick his head in." Holmes attributed Dexter's mistake to his age, a youthful seventeen.

Dexter later confided to Holmes that he was always terrified in combat, so scared in fact that he always followed behind Holmes. "I always walked right behind you because I didn't think you'd ever get hit." Dexter also complained that he had never killed anybody in combat, much to the amusement of platoon members, who reminded him that there had been plenty of targets.

There were those like Private First Class Richards who in Compiègne had accused Ransom of not having the stuff required to be an infantryman. But it was Richards who cracked in the last days of the war and had to be evacuated for shell shock.

Age was not necessarily a disadvantage in combat. Cloyce Blassingame was also a "kid" of seventeen like Sampson and Dexter but to Ransom he was a "very competent soldier." And Earl Jones at thirty-eight was the tough "old man" in 2nd Squad who often worked on point as a scout. To men like Holmes in their twenties and especially to the teenagers like Sampson Jones and Dexter, "thirty-eight might as well have been ninety-eight."

There were some in the 5th who seemed fearless. "It didn't bother me to get shot at," Des Journette said. Neither did combat perturb Lester Boudreau, who was always looking for a fight with the enemy.

Their initial days in combat revealed that the men of the 5th were brave soldiers, but some stood out in the fighting up to Giessen. James Oliver was something of a jokester but gained the respect of his comrades by being the best scout around. "He had his serious moments," Holmes remembers. "He had a knack for spotting Germans and once took out three of them preparing to ambush the squad. He paid attention to what he was doing and he saved us a lot of times when he was on point." Oliver had also distinguished himself in the platoon's first encounter with the enemy near Ariendorf when the 5th was searching for K Company just after crossing the Rhine.

Everyone respected David Skeeters, who replaced Oliver Sacco as platoon sergeant when Sacco was wounded shortly after the 5th arrived in the bridgehead. When Skeeters was put out of action with a leg wound, T. C. Williams took over. Everyone in 5th of K looked up to Williams, a quiet, competent soldier who had natural leadership qualities. He was fearless and "he kept us in line and he knew what he was doing," Ransom remembered.

The men regarded Lieutenant Ralston as a very competent combat officer. He was no-nonsense and chewed out his subordinates when necessary. Boris recalled Lieutenant Ralston's wrath after a particularly sharp fight in the Ruhr area because Boris had lost track of one of the members of his squad.

"A lot of us didn't have much contact with Lieutenant Ralston," Ransom said. "He was the platoon leader. I think he was somewhat fatalistic about his job and I think he said to himself, 'They played me this hand so I have to play it.' I had to respect Ralston for one thing. He was a white guy surrounded by all these black guys. He was victim, coach, and warden all in one. I always think of Lieutenant Ralston as a short white guy wearing an officer's overcoat and carrying a big plastic map case in his hands. He was such an obvious white guy among black guys that the Germans used to shoot at him like he was something good to eat. He was always up there with you. He wasn't one to stay in the background. He was always there."

The men learned quickly not to involve Lieutenant Ralston in their feuds and disputes. "Our philosophy was 'Don't bring him no problems and he won't bring you no problems,' " Ransom said. "If we were going to go upside each other's heads we would do it out of sight of white folks. We were not going to pass the dirty laundry up the line. We settled things down here with us."

One such incident involved Richards and Edwards. The strain of combat was showing on both men and exploded one night as the platoon settled into a commandeered house in a captured village. With numerous members of the 5th as audience the two argued and traded threats and Richards waved a .45 pistol, which discharged into a crock of peeled potatoes soaking in water. The bullet sprayed water and chunks of potato all over the room. Most of the men present, except Boris, erupted in laughter even as they dove for cover. Boris heard the report, felt the water splash on his face, and was sure he was dead and covered with his own blood. Lieutenant Ralston was never informed of the fracas.

But Lieutenant Ralston had ways of finding out about some of the goings-on in his platoon, and Holmes was convinced there were a few tattletales in the outfit. In one incident just days after the war had ended and the army had imposed a nonfraternization policy on the occupying American forces with the German population, Holmes and some of his comrades sneaked several German girls into their billet. Lieutenant Ralston suddenly appeared to confront his troops. Violating the nonfraternization policy was a serious infraction and often resulted in a reduction in rank.

"You have girls in your quarters," Lieutenant Ralston said to Holmes.

"How did you find out?" Holmes asked, figuring the informer was a platoon member.

"Never mind," Lieutenant Ralston replied.

"These girls were speaking French. They're not German," Holmes said. "Boudreau brought them in, since he speaks French."

"But Boudreau isn't even here," Lieutenant Ralston retorted.

The lieutenant was willing to overlook the incident, and the girls were sent home.

Lieutenant Ralston also knew that his men could be "bad," particularly on R and R. The men themselves knew it; some even thrived on it. Ransom singled out several platoon members as "professional bad actors" who reveled in their image of being miscreant and rebellious, but Holmes believed that being "bad" was part of the image that all black men wanted to project. "Being a bad actor was a way of surviving for young black men," Holmes observed. "They had been that way all their lives and it was their protection not only among themselves, but against a hostile white world."

"As a group we were badder," Ransom said. "We were isolated so we had to stick together. We had to prove that we could do what we had to do." In short, the men of the 5th had to present a facade among their white comrades that they were tougher than anyone else. In the end, they proved their point.

26

•

INTO THE FLAK HILLS

THE 99TH DIVISION SOLDIERS who fought it called the fight for the Ruhr Pocket the Battle of the Flak Hills, and this industrial area was now the objective of the Allied advance into Germany. Next to Berlin, the Ruhr was the Allies' most coveted target, described by historian Russell Weigley as "the indispensable nexus whose conquest would deprive Germany of the means to resist the final drive to Berlin." By March 1945, however, the Ruhr had lost much of its strategic value because of the Allied bombing raids, which had cut its steel production by nearly 30 percent. "But the image of the Ruhr as the great German workshop, along with the lure of bags of prisoners, still drew Bradley, and Eisenhower as well, toward the Ruhr as an objective overshadowing even Berlin," Weigley wrote.

In the first week of April the 99th, along with the 9th Infantry and 7th Armored Divisions, comprising III Corps, began advancing out of the Giessen area towards this industrial heart of Germany that included the cities of Essen, Dusseldorf, Bouchum, Gelsenkirchen and Oberhausen. The attack followed weeks of new allied bombing raids in "Operation Clarion" that crippled many of the important rail centers that connected the Ruhr to the rest of Germany.

V and VII Corps joined the 99th and III Corps in what military historian Charles MacDonald called, in the official army history, *The Last Offensive*, "the great wheel to the north." The plan was to link First and Third Armies, advancing from the south, with the Ninth Army (and British forces in Field Marshal Bernard Montgomery's 21st Army Group) advancing from the north, to encircle the Ruhr.

By early April Generalfeldmarshall Model recognized that his position in the Ruhr was hopeless, so he attempted a breakout eastward toward Kassel, where he planned to link up with German forces attacking westward in an attempt to form a corridor through which Model's forces could escape. The two German armies would meet and fashion a defense against the eastward advance of the Allies toward Berlin. But the plan was doomed, and by April 1 the Allied envelopment of the Ruhr was complete, with the Wehrmacht troops effectively trapped. The job for the

Allies and the 99th now was to go in and root out and destroy the enemy. But despite the ravaged condition of the German army, it remained dogged and determined even when facing defeat.

The terrain over which the 99th Division advanced into the Ruhr was breathtakingly beautiful, more a wonderland than a battleground. "It is a scenic land," General Lauer observed, "beautiful but rugged. For more than fifty miles in the direction of our drive cross-country were hills and more hills, ridges and valleys, one piled on another like the pleats of an accordion which had been opened and stepped on, so that the ridge lines ran in all different directions.

"This is ideal country in which to spend a vacation, fishing and hunting. I am sure that every man who fought over that area, at some time or other, longed for an opportunity to try his skill with a 'Royal Coachman' in the crystal clear babbling brooks. That longing, however, was but a passing fancy, for the business in hand was hunting—hunting down the German army!"

The 99th began the final assault on April 5. There were few roads leading to the objective, and those that existed passed through dense woods and over narrow gorges and deep-cut streams that were spanned by seemingly countless bridges. K Company, with the 394th, started its attack at 8 A.M. and advanced to capture the village of Latrop after a short, stiff fight, and then moved to take the forested high ground just beyond.

The fight for Latrop typified the kind of combat the men of the 5th of K encountered in the Ruhr. "After Giessen we just stopped moving forward and started going up and down this high ground in the pocket," Ransom remembered. "We generally moved out every day more or less spread out in formation and kept moving until we hit something and had a fight.

"The Germans would often make a stand in a village; they'd set up a machine gun in one spot, fire it until we got too close, and then retire to the next machine gun that was set and ready to fire," Ransom said. "It was mostly the Volkssturm, old men and young kids, but sometimes you'd run into hard-core German army officers who would make the Volkssturm fight. If they had enough tanks they'd put up a good fight, and we'd have at least one good fight a day."

When driven from the villages the Germans would retreat to fortifications in the hills, which were covered with planted pine forests. Here they concealed themselves among the trees in deep trenches, and every nook and cranny in the forest was a potential gun emplacement.

"The branches could be knee high or over your head and the trees were planted in rows and the Germans would put a machine gun down one of those rows and you had a problem," Ransom said. The rows of stately pines became shooting galleries, with the Americans as targets.

"At night we'd dig holes and sit there," Ransom said. "It was very disconcerting to be up there in front of everyone in the dark without armored protection. German armor often would take advantage of our vulnerability and every time you made a sound or shone a light enemy tanks would fire on you. We were waiting and praying for daylight, when we could get an air strike. This characterized our drive in the pocket."

The Germans made excellent use of all calibers of flak guns that were dug in at ground level and hidden in woods or in towns. The Americans would learn of their presence by the sudden bark that erupted when they were fired, often with devastating effect. Ransom remembered seeing numerous captured Russian 76-mm guns, which were lightweight and fired a high-velocity projectile.

Whenever possible the 5th of K tried to avoid a fight. "Sometimes we would mount a loudspeaker and a white flag on a tank and send it down to a village and ask them to surrender," Boris said. "We would meet with the burgermeister and try and persuade him to give up the town."

Sometimes the persuasion worked; sometimes it didn't. When it didn't, 5th Platoon called in artillery fire and air strikes to blast the Germans out of their positions. "The artillery would send over a white phosphorous shell to mark the town," Boris said. "Then the flyboys would do their thing and blow the town to pieces." The 5th would then advance into utter destruction, and the aftermath of the bombing was unsettling. Boris can't forget the "smell of scorched flesh of animals and sometimes people" that was left in the wake of the P-47s.

The 5th of K had a particularly costly fight for the village of Wormbach two days after jumping off on the attack to the Ruhr. The town was situated near an important highway and G-2 (intelligence) reported light resistance in the vicinity.

The men began a wary advance on Wormbach just after dawn on April 8 spread out in a long skirmish line that moved forward through an open field dotted with haystacks. A thick forest of pine trees swept down from a steep rise on the right to border the field and offered concealment to the enemy. The men were abreast of one of the white platoons on their left flank that was led by a Sherman tank whose commander rode exposed in the turret. Beyond the Sherman, lying in a crumpled heap, were the weathered and rusted remains of an Air Corps A-20 light bomber. On their right flank an M-36 tank destroyer moved out with the platoon.

Frost sparkled in the grass and frail wisps of mist lingered just above the earth as the men moved out silently except for the occasional barked orders of noncoms and the muffled clinks and clonks of their equipment. The tank-destroyer engine revved in a whiny roar as the machine lumbered over the open ground, its tracks flinging up clods of muddy earth as they spun.

"It was just before we got to a hedge of planted pines between us and the village that they opened up," Ransom said. The platoon hit the ground as machine-gun bullets cut the air above them. The men hugged the earth and looked to their squad leaders. Holmes remembered that morning's briefing: "Just a few Germans. Go in and get them." He was experienced enough now as a squad leader to know that the enemy fire had been high. No one was hit, and Holmes figured the Germans were probably some of the new Volkssturm, down deep in their holes, afraid to show themselves and unable to properly aim their guns.

The order came down from Lieutenant Ralston: "Marching fire." Holmes stood up. "Let's go." First Squad rose with the rest of 5th Platoon and the men moved forward with their rifles held at hip level. As the skirmish line advanced, the men opened up, and waves of rifle fire ripped across the landscape and echoed down the valley as the men of K Company spewed out a hail of bullets to keep the enemy down in their holes. As they finished one clip they reloaded and marched on. Below on the open field the sharp slapping crack of American tank cannon fire split the morning air and tracer rounds from tanks' machine guns flashed over the open field.

"Lordy, how can that uncle lose with all that stuff he use," Ransom recalled big Sam Wade bellowing gleefully as he marched along toting his BAR, watching the volumes of American fire pour in on the German positions. The fire slackened as K Company approached the edge of Wormbach. For a moment there was a lull on the battlefield. Then came the chilling "short, flat bang" of an enemy SP (self-propelled) gun.

Boris heard the gun as it opened fire one hundred yards in front from a concealed position in a tree line just in front of the village. Bang! Bang! Bang! Artillery shells, possibly from a 76-mm antiaircraft gun, tore through the chilly morning air. Ransom felt the wake of a projectile as it zipped past him. Others suddenly realized their exposed position.

"Fall back! Fall back!" men screamed from Boris's right. The tank and tank destroyer on both flanks had suddenly stopped and were backing up in retreat. Boris knew that he and his men were completely exposed out in front of the company. As 2nd Squad leader he ordered his men to retreat behind some haystacks to the rear.

Ransom ducked behind a hedge with other members of 1st Squad and observed the fight as it unraveled, his senses absorbing fragmentary slices of the real and the absurd that flashed in front of him. A haystack on the right flank suddenly exploded in a plume of flame revealing a hidden drum of gasoline. Ransom watched as the lid flew through the air,

hit the ground, and rolled like a wobbling automobile tire down the in-
clined field. Shells whined through the tree line, showering the Americans
with twigs and scattering pine needles. To his left a shell hit a pump house.
Another burst near the Sherman in a cloud of black smoke that blew a
squad of white infantrymen off the back of the tank just as it wheeled in
retreat. Des Journette was hit by the same salvos and crumpled under the
weight of his radio. A round had nearly severed his arm and sprayed him
with shrapnel that also struck him in the head. Ransom watched helplessly
as he saw D.J. crawl to the rear, then heard frantic calls: "Medic! Medic!"
The man who had gone AWOL to go into combat would never fight
again.

Holmes saw rounds exploding near the Sherman and heard the whine
of more shells as they came right at him. As the tank and TD went into
reverse Holmes yelled to his men, "Get back! Get back!" He began running for cover. The man behind him was Sampson Jones. What the hell
was Jones doing there? He was in Boris's squad and supposed to be farther
up on the right flank.

Boris was watching Jones at the same instant. "I saw Sampson Jones
get hit in a big red flash around his legs." Ransom saw it too. "We were
lying on the ground behind a hedge and a round exploded out front. It
hit Sampson Jones in both legs and blew them to pieces and threw him
up into the air. Here's Sam, twenty yards out front, floatin' up in the air
on his back, his helmet going one way, his rifle going the other way, and
there's a big cloud of dust and blood," Ransom said. "Sam Jones was lying
on his back with his arms stretched out looking at where his legs had been
and he was trying to pull his glove liners off."

Ransom looked to the side. "Lieutenant Ralston was lying there with
a gob of meat, it looked like a chunk of stew meat that had been part of
Jones's leg, right in front of his nose, and he was just staring at it."

Nearby something landed six feet in front of Robinson's position with
a thud. It was Sampson Jones's boot, which oozed blood from the protruding and jagged flesh. "That's somebody's foot in there!" Robinson
exclaimed.

"Sampson got up trying to walk and somebody hollered for a medic,"
Robinson said. Ransom also was screaming for a medic. "I can't go out
there!" the white medic yelled back. This was a response Harold Robinson
would remember for the rest of his life. A white medic was refusing to
go out and take care of a badly wounded black infantryman.

Jones's screams and cries could be heard above the din of rifle and
artillery fire. The men watched transfixed and were afraid to expose themselves to the enemy. Streams of German machine-gun tracer bullets
streaked over the field and flak-gun shells continued to explode around

the platoon. Holmes could see that one of Jones's legs was nothing but fleshy strands. The kid who Holmes never thought was qualified for the infantry was clearly going to die unless he got immediate medical help.

Holmes rose to his feet. "I need somebody to go out there with me and bring him back." Robinson also got up and rushed with Holmes out to the wounded man, both running low to avoid German fire. They scooped Jones off the ground and cradled him as they carried him back to the safety of the 5th's position. The men looked on silently and in horror as Holmes and Robinson brought him back. For an instant the battleground was quiet as the German defenders withheld their fire while the two Americans came to the aid of a comrade.

Holmes and Robinson laid Jones down and screamed for medics. Their rescue efforts, however, were in vain. Jones's legs had been severed. "He didn't die right away, but he was gone by the next morning," Holmes said. Holmes was saddened by the death of this likable young kid, but infantrymen learn not to mourn. Death in combat is a fact of life, and besides, Jones had been a member of another squad. The squad was the family unit in the army, and what happened in other squads didn't have the same impact as what happened in your own.

As the medics tended to the dying Jones, K Company's weapons platoon moved up with its mortars and began lobbing bombs on the German positions. Jack Dufalla was one of the members who were experienced mortar men after months in combat. One, two, three rounds with a 60-mm mortar and the flak gun began to blow up in the distant tree line.

Holmes believed, once again, that fate had somehow interceded to save his life. "Sampson was where he wasn't supposed to be," Holmes said. "He was in my squad area and behind me and I don't know how he got hit and I didn't get hit. I may have moved at the right time."

Robinson wrestled with the fact that Jones might have survived had the medics rushed out to administer aid. He had his orders, the medic said. He wasn't supposed to expose himself to enemy fire when the unit was retreating, or at least that was his excuse. Robinson raced back to an ambulance crew. Opening the back doors to the vehicle he found white medics playing cards. They too refused to come to the wounded man's aid. "Sampson Jones bled to death because nobody got to him in time," Robinson said.

The platoon was readying to move out on Wormbach when Boris realized they were missing another man, Cloyce Blassingame. A search was mounted and Blassingame's body was found behind a haystack near where the antiaircraft shells had impacted. There were no visible entry wounds on his body, and the men suspected that he'd been killed either by the concussive force of an explosion or by a minuscule sliver of steel hitting a vital organ.

The casualty list was high. Two from the 5th of K Company had been killed along with a white machine gunner from one of the other platoons. Several members of the company had been wounded, including Des Jour-nette, who would spend the next five months in a Paris hospital. He would never regain full use of his arm.

Fifth Platoon regrouped and advanced cautiously, past the bodies of the German gunners, past the burning hulk of the SP gun, and into the village. Enemy troops had taken cover in the houses and were firing on the Americans. Ransom and Pace rushed into the village post office and found the first floor empty. There were sounds from the basement and Ransom hurled a grenade down the steps. The blast rocked the building and Ransom quickly started down into the unlighted gloom. Halfway down he saw the form of a German soldier emerge and Ransom raised his M1. The rifle fire reverberated through the darkened rooms. *Blam! Blam! Blam! Ping!*

The last was the tinny, metallic sound of the clip being ejected from the rifle breech—Ransom was out of ammunition while his enemy still was not down. He stood staring at the ghostly form of the German soldier when he was deafened by blasts from Pace's M1 fired over Ransom's shoulder and within inches of his ear. Pace got off several shots in quick succession and the German fell dead.

Pace was first down the steps and was searching the German's body as Ransom approached. Pace stepped back and held up his prize, a German Luger. As the two Americans admired the trophy two forms appeared in a doorway. Ransom swung his rifle around and aimed it at two surren-dering Germans. Pace covered the two as Ransom searched them and came away with a set of binoculars. These were Ransom's prize, and he has them to this day.

Fifth Platoon chased the remaining Germans from the village. They later learned that at Wormbach they had run into hard-core Nazis. One high-ranking German officer calmly related after capture why the resis-tance had been stiff in front of the village. "At Wormbach I shot several officers and men who attempted to pull back. Court-martials are much too slow. . . . We are proud of our outfit. Its presence on the line boosts the morale of the men near it." His unit was the Panzer Lehr Division, one of the best in the German army. Though badly depleted, it fought on.

"We were mad as hell about what had happened there and wanted to go in and get the Germans," Holmes said. Boudreau had to be restrained from killing just about every German he encountered in Wormbach.

Jack Dufalla, a white in the heavy weapons platoon, noticed something during the fight that he always remembered. "I was sent up as a mortar man to clean out that gun that did the damage and I happened to see Jones's legs. That made me believe there is significantly little difference between blacks and whites. His flesh was red and his blood was also red."

27

•

ISERLOHN–STRANGE TWISTS OF WAR

BY MID-APRIL THE FIGHT for the Ruhr was nearing an end as the Allied armies advanced on avenues of attack that Lieutenant Ralston likened to the spokes of a wheel. Hundreds of thousands of Allied soldiers along with thousands of vehicles and tanks pressed inward on the Germans. "All kinds of vehicles, tanks, trucks, and jeeps were concentrating on the last of the pocket," Ralston said. "It was a real smorgasbord. There were traffic jams way back in the hills."

German resistance was crumbling on all fronts. Strawder recalled moving through village after village clearing the enemy, who usually threw down their arms and surrendered. Strawder remembered one village in particular because of two deaths that day: the German he killed, and President Franklin Roosevelt. The 5th of E was ordered to clear the village of all resisting enemy and Strawder moved through the streets with the advance guard, flushing Germans. As he approached the corner of a house he came face-to-face with a field-gray-clad German infantryman skulking around the same corner. Strawder reacted first, clubbing the man on the head with the full force of his rifle butt. The soldier fell dead at Strawder's feet just as an amazed E Company comrade approached to gawk at the corpse. "Man, you mashed that helmet clear down to his collar bone."

There were still times, however when the Germans fought back savagely and resistance stiffened as the Americans closed with the German units and positions protecting the Ruhr Pocket. Harry Arnold remembered enemy resistance as being "determined" with the Americans having to use artillery to help break through the defenses. Arnold recalled one harrowing fight in the rugged hills for the village of Oberhundem as E Company advanced along a road that dipped down a hillside and then observed white sheets of surrender hanging from the windows of houses in the village. All seemed tranquil.

Strawder was reconnoitering for his squad as E Company approached Oberhundem. "The sun was real bright, and I could see sunlight flickering off the barrels and movement in one of the gun emplacements as they were getting the guns in position to fire on us," Strawder remembered. Suddenly massive amounts of fire erupted from the guns across the valley.

To veteran infantryman Harry Arnold, it seemed as though every weapon in the German arsenal was pouring fire on the Americans as they approached the village."

Strawder was lying down when the guns began firing, but a sergeant next to him stood up and was hit almost immediately. Some of the men hit the dirt alongside the road while others raced up the hillside hoping to find shelter and the low growth on the heights. To Arnold, it was a perfect killing ground. If the men stayed out on the road, they were visible to the enemy. If they raced up the slope, they exposed themselves to deadly fusillade.

Arnold pondered his fate as the barrage of bullets and shells continued; then he instinctively rose and dashed up the slope. He had never encountered such dense fire, and most of it came from flat trajectory weapons. "We were impaled on the hillside before it in the fashion of a target on a dartboard. . . . Identifiable among the weapons were 20mm Oerlikons, the rapid fire 47mm antitank guns, and a number of conventional machine guns. . . ."

"The Oerlikon's impacts and explosions could be heard faintly to the sides, increasing as they approached, and dwindling after they passed, *fram-fram-fram-FRAM-FRAM-FRAM-FRAM-FRAM-FRAM-FRAM-Fram-Fram*," Arnold said. The 47s were deeper and spaced greater, *blam-blam-BLAM-BLAM-BLAM-BLAM-Blam-Blam*. The machine guns stitched rapidly by and returned as rapidly, though they could hardly be heard in the din of weaponry. "With each sweep of each weapon our bodies tensed involuntarily, awaiting the bit of hot steel."

The Germans kept up the fire for what seemed like hours before the rain of shells and bullets slackened. But their attacks on E Company doomed Oberhundem. The Americans poured artillery fire on the town and called in flights of P-47s that swooped down strafing and bombing.

Strawder himself was hit in the same bombardment when he was struck on the head and back by shell fragments. "I thought it was rocks hitting me." Later, when the troops had moved into the village, he removed his helmet and felt his head. A steel sliver was stuck in his scalp.

E Company cautiously moved into Oberhundem at nightfall. Buildings smoldered while others blazed as E Company mingled with farm animals that had broken loose and were running in the streets. The light of the fires illuminated the Americans and made them easy targets, but it appeared that most of the Germans had withdrawn. E Company secured the town and dug in in case of counterattack. The night was cold, and many of the infantrymen lit fires around their foxholes for warmth. Some even dragged overstuffed chairs and couches from the houses to bed down in comfort for the night. The odor of the burning town barely registered on their senses—they were used to it after months of combat. The Americans now owned Oberhundem, but the enemy troops who had battered them had escaped to fight another day.

The last major bastion of resistance in the Ruhr in the 99th's sector was the city of Iserlohn some thirty miles southeast of Cologne, and the 5th of K was involved in the fight. Ralston remembered Iserlohn as one of the strangest experiences of the 5th of K's war.

The weather was foggy and cool as Lieutenant Ralston's infantrymen prepared for the final assault on the city. By April 15 the men had advanced to within two miles of Iserlohn when they came under heavy fire from a German SP gun. "That was a bad scene for a couple of hours in a field on the outskirts," Ralston remembered. "We were sitting around six or so of the tanks, and we were held up for some reason, when all of a sudden we started getting hit by 88s and other artillery fire coming straight up the valley from the city. The high-velocity 88 shell hits and explodes before you hear it coming. So first thing you have is an explosion in your midst with the cone of shrapnel mostly straight ahead. We got some hits on the tanks and some injuries as we crouched and hid behind the tanks as they moved around for cover."

The men fought on through roadblocks, tank fire, and determined bands of enemy troops who held up the advance with burp guns and machine guns. Thousands of enemy soldiers surrendered, creating a vast logistical problem for the Americans. All POWs had to be escorted to the rear. It was clear to the enemy troops in the line that their war would soon be over; and on April 16 the 99th alone captured 23,884 Germans. As night fell on April 16 the men dug in on the outskirts of Iserlohn amid talk of an impending truce.

The next morning the platoon continued the attack, and after advancing several blocks into the heart of Iserlohn the 5th received orders to cease all action until noon. The Germans and Americans had struck a surrender deal to make Iserlohn an open city because it was the site of three hospitals, one that housed American wounded. "There also were a hell of a lot of German generals in the city, even an admiral, so that was part of the political process of the truce," Ralston said. "It would also take several days to get those guys organized to turn in their weapons and get them behind barbed wire."

The truce brought an eerie silence. Americans and Germans, cautiously at first, peered over their defenses and moved into the open. It was like Christmas Eve, 1914, when German and British troops celebrated together in no-man's-land between the trenches. Lieutenant Ralston and his men found themselves mingling with armed German soldiers on the streets of Iserlohn. "We were wandering around town with our rifles over our shoulders while the surrender was being coordinated," Ralston remembered. "There were too many Germans to disarm that quickly, so it was really spooky and weird to walk along, eyeing each other warily and turn around and find they'd also turned around and were looking at us too.

"Sometimes you'd be looking in the same store window—they're talking in German, you're talking in English. There were no fights and I didn't see Germans and Americans stopping to talk. But there were smiles exchanged and shoulders shrugged, sometimes in disgust, dismay, and even joy with the expression of 'it's about time.'"

Even before the German surrender in Iserlohn was negotiated, the enemy was laying down its arms. "Great numbers of enemy soldiers, too impatient to reach our POW cage to wait for negotiations, poured into our lines in ever increasing numbers, much to the chagrin of the Nazi 'die-hards' who wished to continue the hopeless fight," General Lauer wrote. The numbers of Germans caused consternation at headquarters.

Lauer received a distress call from Lt. Col. Thomas N. Griffin, commander of the 395th Regiment. Griffin had two battalions of infantry stretched thin along high ground overlooking a wide valley immediately to the west of Iserlohn. "I need help!" Griffin radioed General Lauer. "The whole damned German army is flowing down the valley right at my position."

"Sure enough," General Lauer wrote. "The entire countryside was alive in gray-blue uniforms. Marching troops, motor vehicles loaded with troops, SP guns in columns, and still more columns of troops moving down every road and trail across the valley as far as the eye could see, coming toward us at the slow, regular plodding rate of foot troops. No bands playing, no fanfare, just subdued ranks of troops marching as though they were coming from a big review. On they came, slowly, ceaselessly, doggedly.

"There was no fight in them. All they wanted to know is 'where is the POW cage?' The drag of their feet, the slump of their shoulders, the vanquished look in their eyes, their attitude of finality and resignation, cried aloud. On they came, slowly, ceaselessly, doggedly."

At the end, the number of German prisoners captured in the Battle of the Ruhr Pocket far exceeded the number of enemy troops Allied intelligence had first estimated was holed up in the pocket. XVIII Corps alone took 160,000 prisoners, and the final count of POWs was 317,000, including twenty-five generals. For General Bradley and the Allies the catch of Germans was greater than the number of POWs from the Afrika Corps captured at the end of the North African campaign in 1943, and was far more than the estimated 90,000 prisoners taken by the Russians at Stalingrad also in 1943.

The number of German generals captured in Iserlohn was impressive. Among them was General der Panzertruppen von Luttwitz, who had commanded the German Seventh Army in the Battle of the Bulge.

The 99th also captured what was believed to be a counterfeit American general among the POWs, a soldier claiming to be Brigadier General Gjelsteen, artillery commander of the 86th Division, which had been operating on the 99th's left flank. His American captors figured he was just another Kraut trying to escape unnoticed. No amount of persuasion would assure his release, but the MPs relented and brought him to 99th headquarters under armed escort. The prisoner was taken before Brig. Gen. Frederick H. Black, the 99th's artillery commander. When Gjelsteen saw Black he exclaimed: "Hey, Freddie, for Crissake tell 'em who I am!"

General Black welcomed his prisoner back into the fold and wined and dined him before sending him back to the 86th Division.

28

•

ONE HELLUVA WALK–WITH PATTON

THE 5TH OF K had no time to catch its breath. Within twenty-four hours of Iserlohn's surrender the 99th was ordered south to join Third Army in a drive to destroy Wehrmacht forces in Bavaria. It was an assignment that in later years would carry great honor. The 5th of K, along with the 99th Division, would have the distinction of serving under Gen. George S. Patton, commander of the U.S. Third Army, that was racing through southern Germany.

For the journey south the troops of the 99th were loaded into every type of vehicle imaginable. "The day the Germans surrendered in the Ruhr they piled the entire III Corps into trucks and shifted us from First Army to Third Army," Ransom said. "I mean they loaded us into trucks. Forty guys in the back of a deuce-and-a-half, people riding on the bumper and everything else."

The vast convoy plodded through countryside that the division had captured just weeks before. It drove on, down the banks of the Lenne River to the town of Grevenbroich and on to Ople, where it turned south to roll through Siegen and Limburg and through the Westerwald. The route continued down toward Frankfurt am Main, on to Hanau and Bad Ord, through Lohr and Schweinfurt to Bamberg. Once again the troops remarked on the beauty of the landscape.

The greatest excitement during the journey was a nighttime strafing attack by German fighters. The planes swooped low over the convoy with their guns blinking and tracers arced and ricocheted all around the convoy, but there were no casualties. The attack came in the early-morning hours under a brilliant full moon that had the men yearning for home.

For the 99th, the luxury of motor transport ended in the city of Furth near Nuremberg. From then on they marched south to the Danube and beyond. "That was one helluva walk," Ransom remembered. The early spring brought rain or sleet one hour and eighty-degree temperatures the next, and the men were up to their knees in mud and slowed by the "runs." "The farther south we got the higher the hills, and by the time the war was over it was good that it had ended because we'd all had it with walking," Ransom said.

The men limped and staggered after weeks of forced marches and the ranks of the platoon began to thin as men fell out from exhaustion and injuries. Harry Lucky dropped out. Holmes too fell back with a leg injury and the company medic gave him permission to rest and catch up later. He attached himself to the 14th Armored Division, which was moving along with the 99th.

The marching continued. "25-April-45: At 0545 this morning, Company was up and moving out of positions? . . . Most of this day was spent on the road hoofing it out. Weather being hot, made it hard marching," wrote S. Sgt. Harold Adkins in F Company, 394th.

"26-April-45: At 0500, Company got up and in short time was moving out again across country. Reaching the end of 12 miles, the town of Dietfurt could be seen by the troops as they gazed down in the valley," Staff Sergeant Adkins added. The company's next move would be to cross the Ludwigs Canal.

The enemy was elusive and nearly invisible as the advance toward the Danube continued on April 24. Their presence was noted mostly by the blown bridges and mined roads they left behind, but bands of enemy soldiers would also come out at night to fall on unsuspecting Americans sleeping in their billets and foxholes. Vigilance was the watchword for all.

On the twenty-fifth the advance moved through open countryside, pastureland, vineyards, and hop fields, and over seas of colorful wildflowers in uncultivated areas, all blossoming in the early spring. The Danube was not far away, but the 99th had to cross the Ludwigs Canal and the Altmühl River.

The approach to the Ludwigs Canal in the 5th of K's sector was from high wooded ground that overlooked a sprawling saucerlike valley. A dirt road with an adjacent drainage ditch ran in front of the forested area from which fields, planted with six-inch-high rye grass, stretched away several hundred yards down an incline to the canal. The canal banks were lined with bushes and occasional stands of trees, and the waterway was spanned by a weir, or dam, wide enough for only one soldier to cross at a time. On the opposite bank were several farm buildings behind which were forested, low hills that gave the Germans excellent cover. Behind these wooded hills was the village of Dietfurt, the 5th's objective for the day.

Lieutenant Ralston had orders to force a crossing on the weir, which showed up on their maps as a thin line across the canal. The Germans had blown all the bridges over the Ludwigs, and the Americans were looking for any place to cross. Sister companies were fighting to gain crossings a thousand yards to the right and left when Lieutenant Ralston received his orders to cross in the 5th of K sector.

"I looked at the situation with great anxiety," Ralston said. "I just knew we would come under fire, and that even if we somehow had enough backup to gain the weir, the Germans would just blow it up and render the fighting useless anyway."

The men also sized up the situation and were alarmed at the order for a frontal assault. Boris reminded Lieutenant Ralston that there was a machine gun chattering away across the canal and the men would have to attack directly into its fire. "I said to Lieutenant Ralston, 'You can hear that machine gun going off over there,' and he winked at me and said, 'You didn't hear nothing.' "

Lieutenant Ralston had an additional worry. The platoon had just been assigned a new, white forward observer (FO), whose job was to direct artillery fire in support of the platoon, but his abilities were questionable. "I went over the target area with him, explained that I felt sure the Jerries would be in and around those farm buildings and that they would fire on us. I wanted to use smoke first from one battery when we were about halfway across the field, firing spaced so as to give us as much cover as possible. I told him to cover the weir area and out onto the field for 150 feet or so. I went over the coordinates with him and helped work out the smoke fire problem, and then the HE [high-explosive] firing if necessary, and pleaded with him to promptly file his fire problems with the gun battery, so they would have them all set when he gave them the fire orders."

Lieutenant Ralston told the FO that he would radio for him to switch to HE rounds from 12 guns if the platoon got pinned down. He then left the observer to his own devices and gathered the squad leaders to prepare the 5th for the advance to the canal. It was a sunny late afternoon as the men spread out in formation and began the march to the canal. They moved quickly, almost at a trot, as they closed on the Ludwigs, every man praying the advance would be uncontested. At the midway point Lieutenant Ralston looked around and waited for the unmistakable whine of American artillery shells bearing smoke. There was only silence and the sound of heavy footfalls crunching in the rye grass.

Lieutenant Ralston radioed back and received a garbled message that the FO was working on the problem. Four hundred feet from the weir, Lieutenant Ralston called again, but the radio only crackled in silence. The men were now almost at a run and closing on the Ludwigs when the first enemy bullets sliced through the air followed by the ripping sound of German machine guns.

"Shit!" Lieutenant Ralston exclaimed, and he screamed into the radio for the HE rounds. Again there was silence. The men hit the ground and began firing rapidly at the unseen enemy across the Ludwigs. Harold Robinson winced when he heard the unmistakable bark of flak guns hurling their lethal projectiles at the Americans, and mortar shells began exploding in their midst. Robinson looked up to see a comrade being spun like a top from the force of an exploding shell.

Ransom was just behind Oliver on point as the platoon approached the canal. They heard voices from the opposite bank and barely had time to react before the fusillade began. Both men dove for the water of the canal as the bullets and shells cut the air above their heads. They would stay pinned down there for several hours to remain hidden from the Germans.

Farther back in the field the men hugged the ground and waited for the HE rounds to scramble the Germans and give 5th Platoon time to make a run for it back to the protection of the woods. Boris found himself being singled out by the German machine gunners. "Every time I moved I'd hear the grass being cut all around me and I wondered how the Germans were seeing me. I'd make another move and *tat, tat, tat, tat.* Then it dawned on me!" Boris was carrying his squad's rifle-cleaning rods in his backpack, which protruded above the low-lying rye grass, and the Germans were sighting on his pack. Slowly he removed his bandoliers of M1 clips, his grenades, and then the backpack. The shooting stopped.

Harold Robinson decided to stay put until relief came. To stand up and run was suicide. He lay in the grass listening as the enemy sprayed bullets across the field and 20-mm shells hummed overhead and mortar rounds exploded nearby.

Lieutenant Ralston realized he had no alternative but to withdraw the platoon back to the tree line. "I started the platoon crawling back in threes and fours as the rest kept up the firing across the canal." It was a slow, painstaking operation with groups of men offering covering fire while others bolted a few yards farther back.

Ransom and Oliver slowly dragged themselves from the canal waters and worked their way back. "I'll run, you cover me," Ransom told Oliver. "Then you run and I'll cover you."

As the action unfolded and with no place to go except deeper in the ground, Robinson fell sound asleep in the rye and was awakened by a comrade gingerly poking at his foot with the muzzle of his BAR. "You OK?" the man softly cried out. He was bug-eyed when Robinson stirred and turned around, a dead man come to life.

Robinson rose and the two men ran, ducked, and dodged their way back to the top of the field. Boris and Baker did the same, slowly working their way back. After one quick dash to gain a few yards Boris and Baker clung to the earth and Baker pulled out a stick of Juicy Fruit gum. "I'll never forget that," Boris remembered. "He broke it into two pieces and we chewed it. To this day I can taste the grit and the gum stuck to our lips because our mouths were so dry."

Boris and Baker made one last dash for the road by the woods. As they came upon the road a shell landed off to the side. The force of the blast lifted Baker into the air and laid him flat on the road. He survived with scratches although both men were exhausted by the ordeal.

When Lieutenant Ralston was satisfied that his men would make it back safely he too started crawling back. He had gone only a few yards when the soldier on his right screamed as he was hit. "Blood gushed out of the leg of his pants; he had taken one in the thigh," Ralston said. With the help of another soldier Lieutenant Ralston wrestled the wounded man back toward safety, dodging intensified German machine-gun fire when they rose and rushed forward, then fell to the ground before the German machine gunners could take aim. Lieutenant Ralston rose up and began to run when he felt a heavy blow to his leg. "It felt like someone had swung a golf driver at it," he remembered. "It hurt for a while, quit, and I thought it had happily gone numb."

Ransom and Oliver worked their way back to the ditch just as a distant American artillery battery dropped a few smoke shells near the German positions. "We got about 6 rounds of WP [white phosphorus] smoke and they weren't very smoky," Ransom remembered. The Germans kept up their machine-gun fire.

"In the gathering darkness I couldn't tell whether I had ten or thirty men, and we started receiving mortar fire. The Germans adjusted fire fairly quickly and I knew it was time to keep moving," Ralston remembered. He wrestled the wounded soldier up to the ditch, where they jumped in and crawled along before taking refuge in a large drainage pipe that ran underneath the road. It was narrow and uncomfortable but Lieutenant Ralston could do nothing but wait for darkness before getting the wounded soldier back to the safety of the woods.

A brilliant moon rose as Robinson and the BAR man worked their way back across the field and dove into the drainage ditch headfirst. Robinson remembered seeing the BAR burying itself muzzle first in the mud and sticking up like a lance. "You get that thing cleaned 'cause we're going to need it real soon," Robinson said. He could hear the Germans screaming at the retreating Americans, "Come on out, we can see you!" Robinson peered out over the field from the edge of the ditch as the mortar rounds still crashed down around them and the machine-gun fire continued to spew from the distant woods.

Robinson and his BAR man had begun crawling through the ditch when they heard somebody call out. "I didn't see nobody," Robinson said. "I'm crawling along this ditch and came to a drainage pipe through the road. Lieutenant Ralston was in there. He'd been shot in the foot and was in there with a wounded guy."

"What's you doing there?" Robinson asked.

"I got a wounded man in here and I'm shot in the foot. Who are you?" Lieutenant Ralston asked.

"Pfc. Robinson."

Robinson helped both Lieutenant Ralston and the wounded soldier from the pipe and checked Lieutenant Ralston's foot. There was no blood and Robinson discovered a wooden bullet sticking out of the seam between the sole and the leather. The four soldiers were now in the ditch, in bright moonlight. "What bad timing on the moon's part!" Ralston remembered thinking.

Lieutenant Ralston heard more voices in the distance and assumed Germans had crossed the Ludwigs and were advancing through the field. "If we had only stayed put, they wouldn't have seen us. It occurred to me what a stupid move I had just made. Then I heard the unmistakable sound of black platoon talk! Happy, delirious. I looked up and saw two of them and yelled at them to get down in the ditch." Lieutenant Ralston had forgotten that the blacks had a way of keeping their sense of humor even in combat. "They laughed, and said, 'What's the matter Lieutenant, you chicken?' "

Lieutenant Ralston and Robinson carried and dragged the wounded soldier back to the tree line under bursts of machine-gun fire from across the canal. Once in the safety of several farm buildings Lieutenant Ralston took stock of his platoon. There were no dead, but sixteen men had received shrapnel and bullet wounds during the fight.

Ransom recalled scenes of the battered platoon: a wounded white sergeant pleading with the medic to extract a protruding piece of shrapnel from his back; the medic refusing, and sticking the soldier with morphine to ease the pain. In another scene Private First Class Adams bared his battered buttocks, which had sustained bullet wounds. And then there was Richards. Ransom was surprised to see his old nemesis staring ahead in a catatonic state, an obvious case of battle fatigue. Boris noticed Richards too. "You could tell by his eyes there was something wrong. When you spoke to him he looked right through you." Richards was sent back for medical care.

Lieutenant Ralston couldn't believe the casualties from the day's fight had been so light. "God had his hand around us out there on the field in the waning light of the afternoon. One would have thought we would have mostly all been killed or wounded," he said. His only other explanation: "Maybe there had been very green makeshift troops firing at us."

The men were still jittery and grabbed their weapons when they heard voices coming down the hillside toward their position. The guard was relaxed when it turned out to be a patrol from K Company trying to reestablish contact with 5th Platoon. Headquarters had not heard from them since noon. The company was moving out with the battalion that had already sent troops across the Ludwigs at several locations. "So our struggle had been for naught anyway," Ralston said.

29

•

THE WAR IS OVER

MOST OF 5TH PLATOON stayed behind when K Company advanced over the Ludwigs Canal in pursuit of the enemy that night. Lieutenant Ralston rested his men and caught up the following day. "We were a burden, exhausted, wounded, and some of us were weaponless." But he told his troops that any who wanted to cross with K Company could do so. Ransom, Francis, Day, and Oliver elected to join their white comrades in a race through the German countryside.

"The Germans had pulled back from the canal when the battalion forced the crossings," Ransom said. "So we started through various villages trying to surprise the rear guard before they could alert the others by ringing the church bells." The company took village after village without a fight as the disintegrating Wehrmacht fled.

K Company encountered only civilians who stayed behind. "We came to this little town and the four of us blacks went through some houses looking for German soldiers," Ransom recalled. "Me and Francis go up the stairs in a three-story house. The barn was on the first floor for the animals and the people lived on the floors above, where it's warmest. We went up an outside stairway. We didn't say anything, just knocked on the door. Someone opens the door and we are yelling 'Raus, raus, raus' [out, out, out], and the entire family, including an old lady who was probably the grandmother, leave the house and go down the stairs. They get to the bottom and the old lady turns around and looks at Francis. Now Francis was short and stocky and very dark complexioned for a black. The moon is shining but she can't see anything of Francis under his helmet except the whites of his eyes and the white from his grinning teeth. She took one look at Francis, threw up her arms, and fainted dead away into a big manure pile by the side of the barn."

K Company caught up with the main body of the 394th the next day and the 99th crossed the Altmühl River, despite pockets of resistance, and pushed on toward the Danube, about sixteen miles distant. Boris remembered approaching enemy artillery emplacements where the crews were packed and waiting in front of their guns to be taken prisoner.

By April 26 much of the division was on the north bank of the famed

Danube. "The Beautiful Blue Danube was in reality a muddy, dirty, yellow colored, fast flowing, smelly river," General Lauer observed. "Its banks were marshy, its valley flat and unattractive, and its towns ratty appearing." And within hours of their approach the 99th would have its last big fight of the war on the banks of the Danube.

The 394th reconnoitered for fording sites and let the 393rd Regiment pass through to make the crossing at several locations. The 395th Regiment also made preparations for the crossing, and just after noon on the twenty-seventh Company F of the 395th started across. But once on the opposite bank the company ran into intense fire from machine guns, mortars, and flak guns, so thick that the rest of the battalion could not make the crossing. F Company was reduced to sixty-seven men from a normal complement of around 150 combatants.

The black platoon, E Company, 395th Regiment, was largely responsible for rescuing F Company. "They routed out the well concealed enemy in cold fury and drove them away screaming for mercy," General Lauer wrote.

The black platoon's CO, Lieutenant Gerdes, recalled the fight. "We pulled out at night, just at dusk, and then walked down to the Danube River. I can still see a little white church that we passed. The moon was out and it had been raining for awhile. We crossed over the river . . . then came back up the other side. The terrain was just like a pool table—level and real green. We encountered quite a bit of resistance from those SS boys. We knocked hell out of them."

The 5th of K crossed the Danube near the town of Kienheim and once on the south bank began receiving heavy fire from entrenched Germans in the town of Eining. "There was a large flak nest there and this stuff put a lot of fire on us," Ransom said.

On April 29, the 99th resumed its advance and by nightfall had moved more than twenty miles deeper into Bavaria. "After we crossed the Danube it was more of the same, you'd run into Germans, they'd fight and give up. We were pretty well worn out marching and marching and having several firefights a day. It didn't help when you're going uphill most of the way," Ransom remembered.

For the German civilians in the path of the 99th the Americans offered a strange contrast to their own soldiers. In a personal memoir one civilian remarked on the division's passage:

> The roads were dry by now. The moving vehicles and men raised thick clouds of dust, which clung to the soldiers' uniforms, weapons and equipment. Under the blazing sun, the young soldiers looked hot, sweaty, grimy and tired. Their clothing and equipment were novel and

strange to us. In contrast to the tight, neat uniforms of the Germans, the Americans' khaki uniforms clung loosely and casually on them. They wore rounded helmets as opposed to the sharply angled helmets of the Germans, their knapsacks held no blankets that German soldiers usually carried, and their belts and webbing were made of canvas instead of leather that the Germans used. Their rubber-soled combat ankle boots were tied with shoelaces and had straps over the ankles and appeared to be lighter and more comfortable than the knee-high nail-shod boots of German soldiers. The Americans carried modern semi-automatic rifles that packed much greater firepower than the old bolt-action, single shot rifles of the Germans. Gas masks were part of a German infantryman's standard equipment, but the Americans had none.

Compared with Germans, the American soldiers were much less formal and much more casual with their officers. Again in contrast to the Germans, they constantly smoked cigarettes and were chewing something, which we soon discovered to be gum. The soldiers of the three other armies that I had seen previously often sang traditional songs to counteract and hasten the passage of time, but we never heard the American soldiers singing. Their language was full of rounded vowels and sounded nasal, indistinct and incomplete, as if spoken lazily, and behind their backs the villagers laughed at them and said it was just like German spoken while eating a hot potato.

There was little fight left in the German regular army and the Volkssturm, and even SS units were demoralized and ready to give up the fight. "The bitter humor of the surrendered and captured Wehrmacht, the only kind of humor which was left them, was well illustrated by a theme song, sung in our cages by prisoners of war from the 17th SS Panzer Grenadier Division," General Lauer wrote. "It went like this:
"Do you fellows know the Avanti step, forward one and back three?
"Yes, yes, yes we do, ever since the Invasion!"
Boys as young as twelve fought on fanatically even as the veterans of the Wehrmacht were surrendering. Infantryman John Kuhn remembered that the Americans humiliated one kid captured by K Company. "We cut off his pant legs above the knees, gave him two chocolate bars and sent him back to his commanding officer with this message: 'Tell your captain we Americans don't shoot children.' "
But often there was no alternative but to shoot armed children. Holmes was almost killed in a firefight with a group of boys in an SS outfit. "We came across a bunch of kids. The oldest was lucky to be seventeen. They were down in a covered dugout and I said I'd go and get them. So I went out and stood over this hole and told these kids in

German to come out with their hands up. They didn't come out; they opened fire at me," Holmes said.

Holmes was accustomed to a tommy gun, but he had picked up a "grease gun," a fully automatic, cheaper version of a tommy. He tried to return fire but the safety latch stuck and he had to dive for cover. "I was shot through the helmet, through my trouser leg, and through the left epaulet of my field jacket. I don't know how they could have missed me."

When the firing ceased, a tanker approached the kids and talked all but one out of the dugout. Then the Americans opened fire and cut down the lone enemy soldier in a hail of fire.

Strawder awoke one morning to a sniper firing random shots into the E Company's bivouac area. "I couldn't go to breakfast and I told the fellas that if I got my hands on that so-and-so I'd kill him. Finally the sniper ran out of ammunition and came down from a tree and he wasn't more than fifteen with a uniform that was way too big for him. Because I said I'd blow his brains out they handed him over to me. I was mad and I grabbed that little son of a bitch by the arm to take him back to the POW cage and he turned around and put his fists up. I had my rifle on my shoulder and a German Luger in my hand and instinctively shot him in the head. That hole takes a little while for blood to come out. I saw the hole before I heard the gunshot.

"That hole came on to me for years afterward. I'd wake up shaking in the middle of the night. I suffered mental anguish because of that. It took a lot of praying before I removed it. He was just a little kid who wanted to be in the SS."

The 5th of K pushed on to the Isar River. The weather was mild and Lieutenant Ralston allowed himself to notice and absorb the coming spring. "Another nice day, and the storks are in some of the chimney tops," Ralston wrote. The company crossed the Isar, where the 99th liberated a sprawling German prisoner of war camp at Moosburg. Among the prisoners released were members of the 99th who had been captured during the Battle of the Bulge. "We greeted some of the men of our own battalion who had been captured on December 17 at Buchholz Station at the start of the Battle of the Bulge. Do you know what they wanted more than food? Flea powder."

The Americans found themselves having to process thousands of Allied POWs along with thousands of German prisoners giving up the fight. "We were ass deep in all these miserable stiffs," Ransom said.

Ransom recalled coming across hundreds of U.S. gold certificates that German guards had frantically tried to rip up. "These people had been tearing them up and throwing them in the mud and a POW column was walking right over them—certificates with green faces and a gold seal on the back. Later on I said to myself, 'My gosh, if we had stopped to pick them up we could have gotten rich off them.' But we were too beat. It was go, go, go. I wouldn't have stopped for a diamond ring if it had been there."

On May 1 a light snow was falling as the 394th prepared for a spearhead into Austria. The scuttlebutt was that a cease-fire had been arranged. Some Germans were resisting but most were surrendering, with many of them packed and ready to be taken prisoner.

As K Company approached the Inn River the rumors continued all day that the war was over. "We passed through a town where we ran into some American soldiers," Boris remembered. "They said, 'Where are you guys going? Don't you know the war is over?'

"When I reached my men they were sitting on the side of the road and we could see the Harz Mountains in the distance and I said we would have to go fight there. I also told them I had heard the war was over and they couldn't believe it."

Despite the rumors and the hopeless plight of the Wehrmacht, the killing continued. "It was the day they said cease all forward movement— it may have been the last time the 5th was engaged with the enemy— that we took fire from three German kids, probably members of the Hitler Youth," Ransom said. "The company had moved out on one side of a highway, across some fields in the hills and brush. The heavy-weapons companies were over on the highway and we had light tanks moving along with us. These crazy little German kids came out of a woods in the fog, first thing in the morning, yelling 'Heil Hitler' or some sort of trash and firing machine guns from the hip. They were so small they could hardly hold them up and immediately there was a whole lot of firing from our units. Those German kids took enough lead that they practically sank into the ground."

That same day a German fighter plane swooped over low to strafe the company and was shot down by American antiaircraft gunners. The pilot bailed out and floated down in the midst of K Company. Instead of throwing up his hands in surrender he pulled out his pistol and started shooting. "That was suicide," recalled John Kuhn. "The machine gunner opened fire along with the riflemen. When his body hit the ground, there was not much left to bury. In trying to figure out his logic, we reached the conclusion that he was probably one of Hitler's fanatical 'SS' troopers and knew that they had lost the war and could not face defeat and wanted to go out in a blaze of glory."

"The rumors of the war's end trickled down to the company commander and Lieutenant Ralston asked us why we were spreading rumors about the war being over," Boris remembered. "I said I'm not spreading rumors, it's only what I heard. There was a column of tanks coming right through our position and Lieutenant Ralston said, 'If you think the war is over why are those tanks going through?'

"Later that afternoon those tanks came back up the road and now there was buzzing going on and we got orders to pull back. They said something was going on and we fell back three miles," Boris said.

As the men retraced their steps they passed the site where earlier that day the three kids had fired on them. The local civilian population had buried them. "We passed the crosses on the hillside where they got shot dead. Silly kids!" Ransom said.

But the killing had ended. The war in Europe was over.

There was great joy and celebration in the ranks of the 5th. But the first order of business was to find a good billet for the night. Thousands of other members of the 394th and the 99th had the same thought. Lieutenant Ralston eyed a small village about a half mile from K Company's position. "I radioed the captain and said that soon that town would certainly have troops in it. Couldn't I get started now with a quartering party to secure the company a place to stay? Captain Simmons came back, 'Go,' so I took about six men and we started sauntering off in that direction like with nothing on our minds. About 100 yards from the road I turned around and looked, two or three more little groups from other companies were starting out. We picked up our pace considerably, and after another 100 yards we saw dozens now running at us. So we ran the rest of the way and posted men at five good houses."

One of the billets was a large barn and K Company shared it with three tanks from an armored division that carried powerful radios. Lieutenant Ralston will never forget that night, and neither will his men. "It was warm and we were tired and sweaty and thirsty. Nowhere could we find food of any kind, nor a beer or bottle of wine," Ralston said.

Every man reflected on his good fortune at surviving the war, and at the misfortune of those like Sampson Jones, Cloyce Blassingame, Eddy Hunter, and the others who had been killed or wounded. Holmes, in particular, wondered how he had survived so many close calls.

For the first time in months Lieutenant Ralston relaxed with his men. "We sat in the dark, gathered round the tanks in the barn, sitting in the dust and straw listening to the revelries taking place in New York, Chicago, and Los Angeles. The wild celebrations, drinks flowing, dance bands playing. We were finally beginning to believe it was really the end of the fighting. So as we sat there listening to all that joy and celebration at home, we were the ones that had fought and earned it, and here we were tired, dirty, hungry, and thirsty—just sitting and listening to them back home. . . .

"We lay there gradually understanding what we had done—done it all. Lay there shaking our heads and smiling at each other, tapping the next guy on the shoulder in sleepy exhaustion. We had won, and the enormous relief flowed over us. Let them celebrate at home, we were having a much larger one. And we slept."

30

•

WE ARE COMBAT VETERANS

THE WAR WAS OVER, but not life in the army. Shortly after the fighting ceased, 5th Platoon and K Company were loaded onto trucks and taken to Bamberg, then to the town of Aub, where they were stationed as occupation forces. Peace brought an almost immediate return to garrison-type duty: inspections, classes, guard duty, and lectures on the new policy of nonfraternization with the German people. It also meant a return of hot food at every meal and the right to sleep late in the morning—until at least 7 A.M.

"11-May-45: Weather clear and warm. Company up at 0700. Hot meals all day. Company on interior guard duty with two platoons out on outposts. Hot meals were taken out by motor to outposts. Morale very high. Pfc. Sykes received 7 day furlough to Riviera, France," Sergeant Adkins in F Company, one of K Company's sister units, commented in his diary.

Strawder's E Company also experienced the same routine. "Reveille, retreat, etc. and saluting officers were restored. There were conditioning marches and even lectures on the nomenclature and operation of the Garand or M1 rifle. But there was some fun, too. We had our own beer parlor," wrote Harry Arnold.

E Company was stationed near the town of Haibach and Strawder's squad was on occupation duty in the nearby village of Schlasbechenbach. "Life was pretty good there," Strawder remembered. There were women and plenty of liquor and the duty was light, mostly police and traffic duties. No one bothered the squad that far out in the country.

Willfred Strange's platoon was quartered in individual homes and he was assigned to a house with a woman who was terrified her three young daughters would be violated by Strange and his comrades. The men assured her the girls were safe and the woman became the squad's personal cook during the three weeks' tour of duty in the town.

But with peace and occupation duty came the quick, insidious return of segregation. Strange's unit experienced it within days of the war's end. In the last week of the fighting his company captured a large country estate near Leipzig that had been used as an exclusive club during the war for the SS. After V-E Day Strange's company was stationed in the same area and used the club as a recreation facility for its men. But when a truckload of black troops from the 5th Platoon rolled up to the entrance, the MP on duty told them bluntly: "No niggers are allowed in here!"

"We went back and told the company commander," Strange said. The captain immediately ordered the first sergeant to call the company out, full field packs, rifles and ammo, locked and loaded. "He put us all in trucks and drove us to the club and went up to the guard and asked, 'Who runs this place?' The guard said Major So-and-So. The captain said, 'You tell him Captain Herbert Pickett is here and to bring his ass out here.' The guard said, 'He's a major.' Pickett said, 'I don't give a damn.'

"The major came down and Pickett says: 'Know who I am? I'm Captain Herbert Pickett, commanding officer of K Company. We fought for this town thirteen days ago. We took it and God damn it, if we have to we'll take it again. When my men come in here you treat them with respect.' He turned and walked away and said, 'You men go in there.' " Pickett later explained to his men in 5th Platoon: "I'm a southerner, but you are in the army and I'll go to hell with you!"

The most devastating blow to the black infantry volunteers came in July 1945. The men were unsuspecting at first. "All of a sudden we were told to pack up and they put us in trucks and started moving us out. I thought the whole company was going, but I found out it was nobody but us blacks. We were being separated out of the company," Strawder said.

"I cussed and raised Cain. I was having a rage I was so upset. I said, 'I knew it. All this mess was for nothing. How could they be so indifferent as to kick us out of our infantry divisions?' "

Strawder believed the order came from the 99th and pertained only to the blacks in the division; only years later did he learn it was an order from the SHAFE. All the black platoons were being detached from their combat divisions and sent back to segregated service outfits. The men were outraged. They had volunteered for infantry duty when their country needed them most. They had fought and died alongside their white comrades. They had proven themselves to be skilled and valiant warriors. They had even given up their old rank to join the infantry. The new orders proved once again to the blacks that the army and the country would use them when they needed them and then reassign them to the scrap heap afterward.

The men in Willfred Strange's platoon were so angered by orders removing them from the 69th Division that they armed themselves and set up a perimeter around their barracks. "We told the army they would have to come and get us and we warned that the first white guy that crossed our line would be buried," Strange said. The division called in Lt.

Gen. John C. Lee, COM Z commander and the originator of the black platoon experiment. He spoke to Strange's platoon. "I know how you boys feel."

"How the hell do you know how we feel?" Strange interrupted. "How long have you been black?" General Lee was able to mollify the troops by promising that they would return to the States as members of the 69th Division.

Most of the other platoons, however, were separated from their combat divisions and reassigned to service units, and many of the men staged sit-down strikes or threatened mutiny. Some actually mutinied. "They got us all together and told us the blacks we weren't going back with our outfit, the 99th," Harold Robinson said. "They told us we were being sent back to our old outfits. We said we're not going back to where we came from."

Robinson recalled that several of the 99th volunteers traveled to Frankfurt to speak to Eisenhower, who agreed that the orders weren't right. SHAFE then arranged for the blacks to be flown back to the States from one of the Lucky Strike camps. These were large separation centers for the European theater around Le Havre, France, from which GIs in the ETO were sent home. "Now we all knew they weren't going to fly blacks home to the States," Robinson said.

Strawder had contemplated a career in the army after the war but was so incensed by the transfers that he dismissed the idea. "From then on I wasn't going to be bothered by the military. I had no more interest even in the 99th." He recalled the hope he had once had in high school that someday he would be accepted in white America by putting his life on the line for his country.

With various units of black volunteers threatening mutiny, the situation rapidly deteriorated at camps and separation centers in Europe where the black infantrymen were housed. When Strawder and some two hundred black infantry volunteers from the 99th reached a Lucky Strike camp in northern France they refused to comply with all orders and requests for duty. The immediate order was for the former volunteers to grab picks and shovels and help build barracks for the servicemen being processed for the voyage home.

"Somebody said, 'We're not going to do anything.' So we didn't do anything," Strawder said. One of the organizers said, 'We'll sit on our duffel bags, boys. We ain't going out there to work with German POWs building camps for the white soldier!'

"The army was trying to get us to cooperate, like get up at reveille and so forth, but we would do nothing," Strawder said. "They called in the MPs and they threatened to put us all in the guardhouse, but they couldn't discipline us. We got up and got into formation and marched down in front of the guardhouse and staged a sit-down strike. I was scared to death.

"Everybody had pistols and everybody was watching everybody. One peep out of anybody and they were dead. The war wasn't over for a very long time and this was mutiny and that charge carries an automatic death sentence."

To placate the rebellious black infantry vets in the camp, the army put them on trucks and shipped them to Paris on a three-day pass in hopes the matter would blow over by the time the men returned. But when they came back they were far from mollified. The army brought in General Davis to talk to the men and allow them to express their grievances. "We said to him that we were combat veterans and we were going home with a combat outfit, not some service unit," Strawder said. Through the efforts of Davis, many of the men from the 99th were assigned to the 69th and were brought home with that division.

Harold Robinson theorized as to why the black volunteers were kicked out of their divisions at war's end in the ETO. The 99th was slated for service in the Pacific once it returned to the States, as were many other divisions that had fought in Europe. "They separated us from the 99th because it had not been decided if blacks would fight side by side with whites in the Pacific," Robinson said. "That was a decision to be left to the commanders like MacArthur."

The determination to remove the black troops from their divisions caught some of the white troops by surprise. Curtis Whiteway, with the 99th, remembered returning from a special operations assignment behind enemy lines at war's end and wondering what had happened to the black troops. "I remember asking where they were but no one had seen them."

Bradford Tatum expressed the opinions of many of the volunteers separated from the 12th Armored Division in a letter to General Davis on July 28, 1945.

I am writing to bring to your attention a most unfortunate situation. Seven months ago when the call went out for volunteer infantrymen, you came to France to the 47th Replacement Battalion and saw the result. What you saw far exceeded anyone's expectation but those present were only a portion of those who wanted to come. We came to the Infantry, were trained and sent forward. We were assigned to the Seventh U.S. Army, 12th Armored Division. We fought exceptionally well, so say our Divisional Commander, our Battalion Commander, our Task Force Commander, our Company Commander. And even what is more important to us, the veteran fighters with whom we fought praised us highly, wanted to fight with us, accepted us as real combat men.

Now that the war is over, we have been transferred to a Quartermaster Service Company. This isn't the way they reward a man for a
job well done! I hope not, for it seems as if we have been used, and
now we are no longer wanted. All that our fellows who are no longer
here sacrificed, all that we offered for sacrifice, seems to have been done
in one great futile gesture. On returning to civilian status, our thought
of the army and its policies will be greatly affected by this latest move.

While some of the men from the black platoons went home with the
69th Division, many others returned home with black service units. "I
was shipped out to an ordnance unit to come back home," Holmes said.
"I didn't much like that because we couldn't come back and march down
Fifth Avenue with the rest of the 99th." Foremost in Holmes's mind,
however, was the fact that he had survived the war and could once again
gaze on the Statue of Liberty as his ship came into New York Harbor. He
also learned later that the 99th never made it down Fifth Avenue. The
division departed from Europe at Marseilles, France, and arrived back in
the United States at Newport News, Virginia, with other contingents
arriving in Massachusetts.

General Davis knew the profound effect the army's separation policy
had on many of his black comrades, and he said at the time, "These men
appear to be broken in spirit. They feel that the high command that
offered them the privilege of combat has broken faith with them."

He was right, and the army didn't take steps to restore that faith for
another five years.

31

•

THE BEST TROOPS IN THE ETO

"THEY WERE THE BEST platoon in the regiment. I wish I could get a presidential citation for them." This was the assessment of the performance of the black infantry volunteers by the commander of an infantry company that included a black platoon.

"They are very aggressive as fighters—really good at fighting in woods and at close quarters work. The only trouble is getting them to stop: they just keep pushing," said another officer who commanded black volunteers.

These officers could have been describing the 5th of K. The glowing evaluations of the black infantry volunteers were part of an army study conducted by the Research Branch, Information and Education Division, Headquarters, U.S. Army, European Theater of Operations, that was released in June 1945. As soon as the war ended the army was eager to know and analyze the performance of the black infantry platoons and the black soldiers.

The report was commissioned in May 1945 and included interviews with 250 white officers and men who commanded or served with the black volunteers. The interviews were conducted with men in the 1st, 2nd, 9th, 69th, 99th, and 104th Divisions, all of which had black platoons in each of the divisions' three regiments.

The Research Branch also conducted interviews with an additional 1,700 white enlisted men in other units who served with or near the black infantrymen. These white soldiers filled out anonymous questionnaires to gather "their personal attitudes toward the utilization of colored platoons." The authors of the report noted the "striking similarities" in the attitudes of white enlisted men and officers. The men interviewed for the report were approached independently and few had an opportunity to "compare notes."

Considering the year, 1945, and the entrenched, prevailing attitudes of race in the United States, the Research Branch study was revolutionary. The report was so favorable that the army's high command refused to release the report immediately, no doubt because it didn't conform to age-old racial stereotypes and attitudes. Many Americans also would have rejected the report's conclusions.

Chief among the findings: "White officers and enlisted men in companies containing Negro platoons agree that the colored soldiers performed well in combat. (Eighty-four percent of the officers say the colored troops did 'very well,' and the remainder say 'fairly well.' In no instance was the performance rated as poor.)"

The reported added: "Many of the platoon lieutenants, company commanders and other officers interviewed, gave detailed accounts of specific actions in which the colored platoons had proved themselves. Qualities particularly mentioned include aggressiveness in attack, effective use of firepower, adeptness at close-in fighting, teamwork in battle.

"Two main reservations were mentioned in a number of the interviews: (1) that the colored soldiers are volunteers and may therefore have exceptional combat qualities, and (2) that some of the platoons have not experienced the most severe types of fighting, e.g., sustained attacks under heavy mortar and artillery fire."

As for the issue of whether the blacks had "exceptional combat qualities," few had such qualities when they arrived for training at Compiègne. Some, in fact, had little prior infantry-type training. What they had was an exceptional determination to prove themselves.

The army's conclusion also belies the fact that many of the volunteers had prior reputations as troublemakers and malcontents in their former service units. Many, like Ransom and Strawder, were "volunteered" for the infantry platoons by officers who were glad to see them go.

The report also failed to note that because of the terrible attrition rates in the ETO in the fall and winter of 1944–45, many white combat troops, if not the majority, were equally inexperienced around mortar and artillery fire. Thousands were individual replacements fresh from the United States.

Several divisions fighting in Germany near the end of the war had only arrived in Europe in late 1944 or early 1945 and had experienced very little heavy combat before war's end. The 16th Armored Division served only three days in combat and suffered only twelve casualties, all wounded, none killed. The 20th Armored Division experienced only eight days in combat and suffered only seventy-six casualties with nine killed in action. The 13th Armored Division served sixteen days in combat in the ETO, the 97th Division served thirty-one days, and the 86th Division served thirty-four days in combat, all less time in the lines than many of the black platoons.

Many white troops did not stand up well under intense artillery fire. One need only cite the experience of the 106th Division, the Golden Lions, an untried division that arrived at the front just days before the German attack in the Battle of the Bulge. The 106th was in the direct path of the enemy assault and was destroyed in the first hours of the attack.

Massive artillery barrages played a major role in the German breakthrough in the Ardennes, and two of the 106th Division's three regiments were decimated in the first days of the Bulge. The 106th was composed of inexperienced white soldiers who had been in the front line, in the supposedly quiet sector of the Ardennes, for about a week.

Ironically, the performance of the 106th was overlooked, even glorified. Despite its disastrous showing, the division was eulogized in a 1946 *Saturday Evening Post* article titled "The Glorious Collapse of the 106th." Black troops received no such forgiveness.

Brig. Gen. H. T. Mayberry, assistant division commander of the 99th Division in the spring of 1945, countered the argument that the black volunteers did not experience heavy fighting. Mayberry stated: "True, we had the Germans on the run but we had to cross several rivers and fighting at the crossings, particularly the Danube, was hot. The Negroes participated in some intense fighting. They were subjected on occasion to some artillery and mortar fire. All in all, the fighting in which they took part was of such character as to give them a pretty good test. They would go anywhere their leaders would take them. Their performance was consistently good. . . . One of the platoon leaders said to me, 'I'll take these people anytime.' "

The report quoted a number of officers who had fought with the black platoons:

Battalion Commander (Lieutenant Colonel): "The colored troops did well in combat. We have had consistently good reports on them. It has been a surprise to many of us." (From Minnesota).

Company Commander (Captain): "They have had real battle testing, and have done well. . . . Good on teamwork. This colored platoon of 35 men with no prepared positions was counterattacked by 90 Germans. The platoon commander had just been captured. They killed 46 and took 35 prisoners, without losing any ground or having any casualties." (From Virginia.)

Platoon Commander (Second Lieutenant): "Once we ran into 4 MGs and a tank firing direct fire. We found a covered route, and they went in, took the Jerries by surprise, and cleaned out the whole business. These men are aggressive and they really lay down the firepower—shoot more than any platoon in the company." (From California.)

Another startling finding—for the era—in the report was that "a majority of both officers and enlisted men endorse the idea of having colored soldiers used as infantry troops." In fact, the report stated that many white infantrymen who had served with the black platoons would "just as soon have a colored platoon in their own company. Furthermore, men in other companies in the same regiment are more likely to express a favorable attitude than are men in other units with the same divisions, or a cross-section of Field Forces units not having colored platoons."

As the war ground on and casualties in infantry platoons and companies mounted, there was actual integration in the ranks as white squads were sometimes assigned to black platoons and vice versa. Some whites were reported to have refused to leave their black comrades when offered a transfer back to a white platoon.

When the strength of 5th Platoon, Company B, 16th Infantry Regiment, 1st Infantry Division, "fell too low to operate as a platoon the Negro riflemen were used as a squad or squads in a white platoon," wrote historian Lee.

A black reporter for the *Pittsburgh Courier* wrote about the informal integration in the ranks. He interviewed a white soldier who said "some of the colored boys fought in white platoons right along with white soldiers. He told me of one platoon, which was made up largely of Texans who voted to receive the Negroes. I understand that there was never any friction between the two groups, and that the colored boys gave an excellent account of themselves." The white infantrymen liked fighting with them because of their aggressiveness and the high volume of fire they laid down whenever they were in action.

Strawder fought alongside "Calvados," the white southern redneck, for the last three months of the war, and Calvados never asked to be reassigned to a white outfit. The 5th of K had a white medic named Banks who was transferred to a white infantry unit. "He raised so much Cain they had to bring him back," Boris said. "Banks was a southern fellow too, a nice fellow. We got used to him and he got used to us."

The postwar report found that "the effectiveness of the colored platoons in combat is judged by a majority of the white officers and men to be at least equal to that of the white platoons." And the report also stated that "colored and white soldiers in the same infantry companies have gotten along well together. Cooperation during the period of combat is said to have been excellent, and good relations on the whole have continued since V–E Day."

Other findings in the report: "Nearly all of the officers and men questioned say that the relations between white and colored soldiers have been better than was expected.

"Most of the white enlisted men report that their initial attitude toward having colored soldiers in their company was that of reluctance, apprehension, or dislike. Three-fourths of the men say that their feeling toward the colored soldiers has changed since first serving with them in combat. They report increased respect and friendliness."

The report quoted a number of white soldiers on their relations with black volunteers:

Platoon Commander (Second Lieutenant): "Got along fine in combat—teamwork couldn't have been better. A lot of boys from the South didn't like the idea at first, but a few days fighting along with them changed their minds. Since we've been out of combat we haven't had any trouble and don't expect any." (From Rhode Island.)

Company Commander (Captain): "Never have had a bit of trouble in the company. Once in a while some white soldiers from other outfits have acted towards them like they were rear-echelon colored, which of course isn't good." (From Pennsylvania.)

Company Commander (Captain): "Relations are very good. They have their pictures taken together, go to church services, movies, play ball together. For a time there in combat our platoons got so small that we had to put a white squad in the colored platoon. You might think that wouldn't have worked well, but it did. The white squad didn't want to leave the platoon. I've never seen anything like it." (From Nevada.)

Platoon Sergeant: "They sort of group together and us the same—friendly, but don't mix as freely. Everybody respects them, they're good combat men."

Good combat men or not, the report did not sit well with many in high places in the army hierarchy. Gen. Brehon B. Somervell, commanding general of the Army's Service Forces, questioned the advisability of releasing the report. He asserted that the conclusions drawn by the report were based on too small a sampling of opinions. He also argued that release of the report might encourage the NAACP to pressure the army for similar experiments with troops in training commands in the United States and even those engaged in the fighting in the Pacific. He stated that many in Congress, newspaper editors, and others in positions of influence were opposed to integration in the armed forces under any conditions, and their opposition would hurt the war effort.

Gen. Omar Bradley, in whose 12th Army Group in the ETO many of the black platoons fought, discounted the significance of the black platoons. Most, he believed, had been involved in mopping-up operations or in combat against a disorganized enemy. Bradley also asserted that the black troops were atypical because they were volunteers of above average intelligence. (While their AGCT test scores were generally higher than those of other blacks in the army, they were generally lower than those of white troops.) Bradley also believed that while blacks and whites had lived side by side in harmony in combat, they would not fare well in rear areas.

Nevertheless, Bradley agreed that the platoons' performance had been satisfactory enough to warrant a continuation of the experiment, but he recommended draftees, with average qualifications, be used in the future. He discouraged complete integration by suggesting that blacks be formed into infantry companies rather than platoons, in an effort to avoid some of the rear-echelon friction between whites and blacks.

Gen. George C. Marshall, the chief of staff of the armed services, expressed interest in continuing the experiment of integrating black soldiers into white units. But Marshall did not believe the report should be made public, because the conditions under which the black platoons were organized were "most unusual," and many of the circumstances of the experiment were special. In short, Marshall and the others believed the black volunteers were a cut above the average black soldier. He also believed that, while integrated by platoon, some degree of segregation had been maintained in the ranks.

It seems clear that despite the excellent performance of the black platoons, many high-ranking officers still clung to stereotypes and past attitudes and judged blacks by a different standard. It is difficult to comprehend today the plague of virulent racism that infected otherwise decent, fair-minded Americans in 1945, and its influence, particularly in the military, where segregation had been institutionalized and attitudes about race hardened.

Only twenty years before the formation of the black platoons, in 1925, the highly respected Army War College in Carlisle, Pennsylvania, issued a report called "Negro Manpower." It stated in part: "In the process of evolution . . . the American Negro has not progressed as far as other sub species of the human family. . . . The cranial cavity of the Negro is smaller than whites'. . . . The psychology of the Negro, based on heredity derived from mediocre African ancestors, cultivated by generations of slavery, is one from which we cannot expect to draw leadership material. . . . In general the Negro is jolly, docile, tractable, and lively. . . . In physical courage [he] falls well back of whites. . . . He is most susceptible to 'Crowd Psychology.' He cannot control himself in fear of danger. . . . He is a rank coward in the dark."

32

•

RECOGNITION—FINALLY

IT WASN'T UNTIL THE 1990s that the men of the 5th Platoons were recognized for their pioneering service to the army and to the country. President Bill Clinton lauded their service, as did the chairman of the Joint Chiefs of Staff, Gen. Colin Powell.

The man behind efforts to honor the volunteers was a former black platoon member, J. Cameron Wade of Irving, Texas, a former business manager for *Ebony* magazine who served with the 1st Infantry Division in Germany and was wounded in the fighting along the Rhine in March 1945. Wade founded the Association of the 2221 Negro Volunteers in 1991 to publicize the exploits of the platoons and to gain belated recognition for these infantrymen. "Nobody would know about us at all without the association," Wade said.

Wade set out to locate as many members of the 5th Platoons as possible and to obtain for them the combat medals many had never received. He also wanted the army to restore the rank that many gave up to become volunteers.

As a result of a request from the Association of the 2221 to the Army Board for Correction of Military Records, the board turned to the National Archives and Records Agency (NARA) for help. With NARA's assistance records were found for 763 of the 2,600 men who had served as volunteers, and forty-six Bronze Stars were awarded, most posthumously. In addition, these 763 soldiers were reinstated to the same rank they had held before transferring to the infantry.

According to figures released by NARA nearly 1.2 million African-Americans served in World War II. A NARA report added: "Yet for the tens of millions of moviegoers watching the epic D-Day battle in *Saving Private Ryan,* not a single African American soldier is presented. But black soldiers fought at Normandy. Black artillery units provided fire support and air defense from Normandy beaches to the heart of Germany. Black soldiers earned many individual awards for valor and several unit commendations, including a distinguished unit citation. And in the last 2 months of the war, black volunteer infantry replacements, who had been serving in combat support roles, joined and fought alongside white infantry and armored units . . . in separate all-black platoons."

In 1993 General Powell wrote to the men of the "2221," telling them: "In a time of segregation in the ranks, your service came alongside your white brothers, fully integrated with them, fighting with them, living with them, dying with them—proof if ever it were needed that segregation in the military was not only wrong, it reduced effectiveness and denied manpower when manpower was sorely needed. . . . Your story would be untold for the most part, but you should take great pride in what you did. . . . Each of you had a strong hand in the making of the future and I am proud of you all. On behalf of the men and women of America's Armed Forces, thank you for all you have accomplished."

President Bill Clinton honored the volunteers in 1994 for "their two-front war." "Even as you fought the persistent scourge of racism and prejudice, nearly 50 platoons of African-Americans stood shoulder to shoulder with white soldiers, your bravery and valor [helped] to turn back Germany's offensive," wrote the commander in chief. "Today, you hold a distinguished place among the proud leaders of integration in our Armed Forces. From your exemplary service flowed the landmark decision that led the military to desegregate. For your heroism, your courage, and your pioneering role, 'A Grateful Nation remembers.' "

33

·

WORLD WAR II CHANGED AMERICA

ARTHUR HOLMES IS THE typical retired World War II veteran living "comfortably" in a new 1,600-square-foot one-story house in the suburb of Alta Loma, California, near Los Angeles. The San Gabriel Mountains soar a few miles to the west. White children play next door and white neighbors wave to Holmes as they pass by in new SUVs.

Like so many Americans of his generation, Holmes migrated to California with his wife, Marge, whom he met during the war, in the years after World War II. He had lived in California for several years as a youth and went off to war from the Golden State, but returned from World War II to spend most of his working life in New York City. When he retired in 1976, California beckoned, and he worked for a decade in Los Angeles in real estate management before again retiring. His wife died in 2001; Holmes, at eighty-five, lives with his dog, Buddy, and remains active.

As an African-American Holmes never expected to achieve even this modest a slice of the American dream. After the war Holmes went to work for the U.S. government because of its policy of hiring veterans without regard to race. His status as a wounded veteran helped him secure employment with the Post Office Department in New York City in the late 1940s. But employment did not mean promotion, and it wasn't until the late 1960s, when the civil rights movement gained momentum, that blacks were elevated to supervisory positions.

Nevertheless, Holmes was determined to succeed and directed his energies to self-improvement. He joined the Army Reserve and enrolled at Fordham University in New York, receiving a B.A. degree in sociology in 1975. By the time Holmes retired from the Post Office Department he was a supervisor and was prospering.

In August 2002, Holmes was recognized for his military service when California Congressman David Dreier "officially" awarded him his medals for World War II service. These included the Combat Infantry Badge, given to soldiers who have participated in combat; the Purple Heart, awarded for wounds suffered in combat against the enemy; the Bronze Star, given for meritorious achievement in ground operations against the enemy; the American Campaign Medal; medals for the campaigns in

Northern France, the Rhineland, and Central Europe; the Good Conduct Medal, and the World War II Victory Medal.

For most white Americans the achievements of Arthur Holmes are a birthright. But Holmes's birthright was segregation. What changed? Was it the civil rights movement? Yes, Holmes says, but only to a degree. He also does not discount his own energy and determination to better himself, nor his Purple Heart and his status as a veteran, which helped open doors to a better life. But he believes that there was one overriding force that changed life in America for blacks. "It was World War II that changed things," he says.

The historian Doris Kearns Goodwin noted in her book *No Ordinary Time* that the war was a turning point in the struggle for civil rights. She called it "a watershed experience in which the seeds of the protest movements of the succeeding decades were sown. Looking back on the 1940s, historian Carey McWilliams observed that 'more has happened in the field of race relations in this country; more interest has been aroused; more has been said and written; more proposed and accomplished than in the entire span of years from the end of the Civil War to 1940.' These years, historian Richard Dalfiume confirms, constitute 'the forgotten years of the Negro revolution.' "

Many of the men who served in the 5th Platoons did well after the war and were afforded opportunities that their forefathers would have been considered fantasy. Waymon Ransom was mustered out of the army in 1946 but returned a year later to make a career of the military. He was assigned to the 24th Infantry Regiment in Korea in the early, desperate days of the fighting as the North Koreans swept south and almost drove the Americans from the peninsula. He was wounded in action.

He also served a tour in Vietnam and retired from the army in 1973 after twenty-five years of service. He worked for the U.S. Customs Service for ten years and retired in 1984. Today he lives with his wife, Yukie, whom he met while on occupation duty in Japan. The couple were married in 1953 and have three children, Ann, Linda, and Waymon junior. The Ransoms live in a suburban neighborhood in Burlington, New Jersey.

Lawrence Boris, a widower, returned to work for the Otis Elevator Company in Yonkers, New York, for three years, but found himself being bumped into lesser jobs as returning veterans claimed their old jobs back. He went into the construction industry until 1967 when he began work for the Post Office Department. He retired in 1983 and lives in Mt. Vernon, New York. His wife Lenore, died in 2001. He has three children, two girls and a boy.

Harold Robinson, also a widower, worked for the Post Office Department for about ten years after World War II and then joined the assembly line at a Ford Motor Company plant near Buffalo, New York. He retired in 1984. Robinson died in July 2002, shortly after a trip he and Boris made to visit Ransom in New Jersey.

Clayton Des Journette started with the Post Office Department after the war and later went to work for the Chrysler Corporation, where he was a shipper. He retired in 1974.

James Oliver was in construction work and now resides in a nursing home in New York State.

David Skeeters returned to Baltimore and worked for forty years as a longshoreman in the Port of Baltimore. He died in 2000.

James Strawder became a truck driver and a member of the Teamsters union. The years have muted but not erased the anger of his youth. Today he lives in a quiet residential area of Washington, D.C., near Catholic University with his second wife, Rezelia. He has five children.

Strawder never gave up fighting. Later in life his cause was integration, particularly in the Teamsters. When he started in the union whites drove the best truck routes and the blacks were relegated to dump and cement trucks. He also found religion. "The church changed my way of living and thinking. I'm not a religious fanatic," Strawder said, "but the religious side really restructured me. I cut out drinking and that was really a salvation because I always thought I was going to hell anyhow."

Bradford Tatum taught school in Washington, D.C., for many years, rising to become a school principal. He lives in the District of Columbia.

Willfred Strange came home to Washington, D.C. to help found what became the second-largest minority real estate firm in the country. He was also associated with the State Department as a host to hundreds of foreign visitors to the United States every year. He lives in Washington, D.C., with his wife, Dora. They have one daughter, Cheryl.

Herbert Pugh, who never went beyond the fourth grade before quitting school to help his parents raise a family, came home to found his own construction firm. But he first returned to school to obtain a high school equivalency degree and then went on to college at the Tuskegee Institute. He moved to Colorado from Louisiana and worked in the Pueblo area and did contracting jobs for the Air Force Academy. He is retired in Colorado.

Bill Windley, who served with the 1st Division, returned to finish college at A & T University of North Carolina and received a master's degree in industrial arts. He taught at the Morrison Training School for Delinquent Boys, became the director of the McCain Training School, and later joined the Central Office Division of North Carolina's Department of Youth Services, where he was appointed director in the 1970s. He retired in the early 1990s after thirty years' service. He lives today in Raleigh, North Carolina.

Bruce Wright, the poet-infantryman with the 1st Division, graduated from law school in 1950 and went to work for a number of black law firms specializing in appeals and estates. He also worked in the growing field of civil rights, which led to posts with the New York Urban League and to the position of assistant administrator for legal affairs of the New York City Human Resources Administration. In 1971 Wright was appointed a judge in the New York Supreme Court. It was on the bench that Judge Wright made a name for himself in the realm of the law.

Wright believed that blacks entering the nation's criminal justice systems are judged by white standards that do not reflect the problems that many blacks encounter in their lives. He consistently angered white colleagues on the bench and law enforcement officials with his decisions and was banished from the criminal bench to serve only in civil cases.

Wright was the subject of a lengthy *New Yorker* article in 1976 which noted that "even the *News* [New York *Daily News*], which often attacks him editorially as 'Judge Wrong,' described him in 1974 as 'an articulate lawyer with a grasp of Constitutional law that few can match.' Wright has attained substantial literary and social recognition. He is, for example, the only member of the New York judiciary to have published a volume of poetry—'From the Shaken Tower,' which came out in 1944. In 1954, he helped Langston Hughes, the celebrated black author, edit an anthology of Lincoln University poets. More recently, the Judge has restricted himself to writing articles for legal publications, but in one of these, published in the *North Carolina Central Law Journal,* his extralegal citations began with Spinoza and progressed through Edmund Burke, T. S. Eliot, Oscar Wilde, Lewis Carroll, George Bernard Shaw, George Orwell, Sebastien-Roch Nicolas Chamfort, George Jackson, Edward Gibbon, Henry Steele Commager, Pablo Neruda, James Madison, Peter De Vries, Catherine D. Bowen, Cyril Connolly, and Shakespeare."

Judge Wright made the front page of the *New York Times* in June 2001, when he was made an honorary member by the class of 2001 at Princeton University. The award was in recognition for his work in civil rights and to atone, in some small way, for his rejection by the university in 1937 because of his race. In his piercing way, Wright noted that this recognition came from the class of 2001 and not the university.

Wright is now retired with his wife, Elizabeth Davidson, a former New York City schoolteacher, in Old Saybrook, Connecticut.

Lt. Richard Ralston returned to Oregon after the war to work for his father-in-law in the heating and air conditioning business. Over the years the business thrived and today focuses mainly on steel fabrication and framing. Ralston ran the business until 1990, when he retired. His son is now president of the company. Ralston lives in Portland, Oregon, with his wife, Marianne. His four children and five grandchildren live within twenty-two miles of the family homestead.

Ralston never realized the bond he had developed with his men in the 5th of K until long after the war. It was 1982 when an old comrade paid him a visit.

> I was working in our steel company then, as president. The front door opened, and in walked this black guy in a nice sports jacket. I turned and looked at him, and started to say "Yes, may I help you?" Suddenly, a shock of recognition shot through me, and I gasped, "D.J.?!!"
>
> When [Des Journette] heard me say his name and saw the look of joy on my face, he beamed. I took the five steps or so to reach him on the run and threw my arms around him in a tight bear hug.
>
> I let go of him and turned to my employees, standing there with amazed expressions on their faces, and explained that this was one of my sergeants during WWII and that he and I had been through a lot of hell together.
>
> It was noon and I asked him to lunch and we chatted for a long time. There was something so satisfying about doing it, like a real need being taken care of. He had to go, and as we started to shake hands, we knew it would be the last we would see one another. I gave D.J. a quick hug of good-bye.
>
> I sometimes think about D.J., and our meeting 20 years ago. Yes, we had been bonded, and probably only vaguely realized it. We were Brothers.

34

•

I'M YOUR DAUGHTER

IN JULY 1992, MARGARET Stanley Scobbie was awakened at 2 A.M. in her home in Manchester, England, by a telephone call she had waited a lifetime to receive. When she heard the caller's voice, she sobbed with joy. Her search was finally over.

The caller was Clayton Des Journette, telephoning from his home in Los Angeles. He was Margaret Scobbie's father.

Indeed, Margaret had been looking for him for twelve years. She was born November 1, 1944, in Wales and grew up with only snippets of information about her father. She knew his name, and that he was African-American and not much more. Her mother said that he was dead. Nevertheless, Margaret wanted to know more.

Margaret was a love child. Her mother, Gladys Stanley, had met Des Journette in her hometown of New Inn Panteg, Wales, where he was stationed. The two were lovers, and Gladys became pregnant. In the summer of 1944, Des Journette was shipped to France with his engineering unit, and he never saw nor heard from Gladys again.

When Margaret began the search for her father, she was a "founder member" of TRACE (TRansAtlantic Children's Endeavor) that assists other young British men and women search for their American fathers, servicemen who had either been killed in the war or had returned to the United States and never been heard from again. She investigated every possible lead but to no avail. She even consulted a psychic who didn't reveal the whereabouts of her father but who was prescient enough to declare that he would be found with the help of a retired colonel in the military.

In the early 1990s, Margaret had all but given up the search when Pamela Winfield, who founded TRACE, asked her to relate the story of her search for her father for a book Winfield was compiling. Margaret sat down and tape-recorded her story with such passion that it caught the eye of a retired Royal Air Force lieutenant colonel who was a TRACE volunteer. "I'll find that guy," he said.

And he did. The retired officer found Des Journette living in Los Angeles and gave Margaret the information. Unable to locate a telephone number, she wrote him asking if he was the same man who knew Gladys

Stanley in New Inn Panteg during World War II. If he was, she was his daughter.

Margaret posted the letter and waited expectantly for a reply, but heard nothing. Finally she called a neighbor of Des Journette's in Los Angeles. "Please don't put the phone down on me," she pleaded to the young man who answered. Margaret explained that she was looking for a Clayton Des Journette who had served in Wales during the war. She said he was her father.

The young man said that Clayton Des Journette lived next door and that he would relay the information. "Someone in England by the name of Margaret Scobbie is looking for you," the neighbor told Des Journette. The neighbor handed Des Journette the woman's number.

Margaret believes that Clayton always knew, or at least suspected, that he had a child in England. Certainly, her letter the week before informed him that Margaret might be his daughter. Des Journette dialed the overseas number, and Margaret answered.

"You've been looking for me for a long time," Des Journette said.

"Then you know who I am," Margaret said.

"Yes, honey, I do."

"I am Margaret Stanley, and I am your daughter," Margaret said as she burst into tears.

Hattie Des Journette said that Clayton was stunned yet overjoyed by the news. "I have a daughter, I have a daughter," Clayton wistfully repeated. He had been married four times but had no children. "He was so delighted," Hattie said.

Within two weeks Margaret visited Des Journette in Los Angeles. She refused publicity in Britain, wanting a private reunion of father and daughter. But when she arrived at the Los Angeles airport, there was great celebration with balloons and cameras. "Clayton loved every minute of it," Hattie said.

If the reunion revived wartime memories, Des Journette didn't reveal them all to Margaret. His recollections of combat haunted him, and he rarely spoke of the war even to Hattie. "He would start talking about his experiences during the war and then just stop talking," Hattie said. "It was about a foxhole he was in and the dead bodies that were around him. He said he could see it all and smell the odor, and he couldn't scream out to see if anyone else was near because it could be the enemy. It really disturbed him. I had to beg him to see a psychiatrist to help him walk through this and release his mind of these things. He went, but it didn't help."

His wounds, physical and psychological, plagued him for the rest of his life. "His arm was nearly severed when he was hit by shrapnel," Hattie said. "Clayton was a very proud man, and he would be suffering so bad from the pain and you'd never know it. He wouldn't say anything."

Des Journette, Hattie, Margaret, and her son, Mark, saw each other twice a year until Des Journette's death. He died July 21, 1999, at the age of eighty-one. Today, Margaret Scobbie has returned to Wales to be closer to home. She now lives two miles from New Inn Panteg in Cwmbran, Wales. She remains in close contact with Hattie and pays frequent visits to her stepmother in Los Angeles.

35

•

FINALLY–INTEGRATION IN THE MILITARY

HOW IMPORTANT WERE THE black platoons in the future of the military and the future of American life following World War II?

In retrospect, they played a role, possibly a significant one, in the later integration of the U.S. Army. The experiment of the black volunteers demonstrated that blacks and whites could live and fight together and make a powerful team. During the years between the end of World War II and the Korean War, the army could not escape the lessons of the platoons.

The Gillem Board, established by the military at the end of World War II to find a solution to the problems of segregation in the armed forces, studied the platoons and described them as "eminently successful." In a circular known as "Army Talk," the War Department in 1947 noted: "The Gillem Board found that 'experiments and other successful experiences of World War II indicate that the most successful employment of Negro units occurred when they were employed as units closely associated with white units on similar tasks.' "

The Gillem Board's recommended solutions proved half measures at best, but were based, in part, on the positive results of the platoon experiment. "In calling for the integration of small black units instead of individuals, the Gillem Board obviously had in mind the remarkably effective black platoons in Europe in the last months of World War II," wrote Morris J. MacGregor in the army's official history, *Integration of the Armed Forces, 1940–1965,* published by the Center for Military History.

By the outbreak of the Korean War, when integration of the armed forces was accelerated by necessity, high-ranking commanders could look back on the achievements of the black platoons and know that integration worked, particularly on the battlefield.

Nevertheless, until the Korean War, blacks in the army continued to serve, for the most part, in segregated units. In the army the problem was largely one of tradition. The high command, composed of officers who had been seasoned with old assumptions of black inferiority in combat and the fear of unrest when the two races were mixed, refused to alter their opinions about the ineffectiveness of black troops and denied the advantages of integration for military efficiency. As they saw it, "segregation was necessary to preserve the internal stability of the Army," MacGregor stated. "Since society separated the races, it followed that if the Army allowed black and white soldiers to live and socialize together it ran the very real risk of riots and racial disturbances which could disrupt its vital functions.

"Remembering the contributions of black platoons to the war in Europe, General Eisenhower (in testimony before a Senate committee in 1948), for his part, was willing to accept the risk and integrate the race by platoons, believing that the social problems 'can be handled,' particularly on large posts. Nevertheless he made no move toward integrating by platoons while he was Chief of Staff," MacGregor wrote.

Even General Lee, who was largely responsible for the black platoons, "wanted the Army to avoid social integration because of the disturbances he believed would attend it. General Omar N. Bradley believed the Army could integrate its training programs but not the soldiers' social life. Hope of progress would be destroyed if integration were pushed too fast, he believed. Bradley summed up his post war attitude very simply: 'I said let's go easy—as fast as we can,' " MacGregor wrote.

According to MacGregor, the army truly believed that "segregation was the only way to provide equal treatment and opportunity for black troops. Defending this paternalistic argument, Eisenhower told the Senate: 'In general, the Negro is less well educated . . . and if you make a complete amalgamation, what you are going to have is in every company the Negro is going to be relegated to the minor jobs, and he is never going to get his promotion to such grades as technical sergeant, master sergeant, and so on, because the competition is too tough. If, on the other hand, he is in smaller units of his own, he can go up to that rate, and I believe he is entitled to the chance to show his own wares.' "

The army was also very cognizant of the power of Congress's southern delegations, who were violently opposed to integration in the ranks of the military. "Any change in the army would be a big step in the south," said General Bradley. "I thought in 1948 that they were ready in the North [for integration in the army], but not in the South."

The manifestations of segregation in the postwar army, and the military in general continued to demonstrate their absurdity and inefficiency. In 1946, for example, the quartermaster general became involved in a controversy related to the integration of the national cemeteries. Some cemeteries were segregated by race, and when the quartermaster general recommended integrating all cemeteries there were objections. "The Army Air Forces commander . . . opposed integrating the cemeteries, as did the Chief of Staff, who on 22 February rejected the proposal. The existing policy [of segregated national cemeteries] was reconfirmed by the Under Secretary of War three days later, and there the matter rested," wrote MacGregor.

The army still struggled with the issue of where to train its black troops. In 1946 the army reorganized its training centers and sent all white troops to facilities near where they lived. But all black troops were shipped to Fort Jackson, South Carolina, because the army couldn't afford to maintain segregated training battalions at every one of its training centers. So black troops continued to be sent to the South, contravening a recommendation of the Gillem Board that "called for the assignment of Negroes to localities where community attitudes were favorable." The practice of sending black recruits to the South elicited protests from black organizations, that warned that continuation of the practice would have the effect of "crystallizing Negro objections to the enlistment of qualified men and also Universal Military Training."

To be sure, there was progress for black troops in the late 1940s. Very significant was a change in attitude among enlisted personnel about segregation. In 1946 the Gillem Board found "substantial agreement" among enlisted men in favor of segregation. Three years later "less than a third of those questioned were opposed to integrated working conditions and 40 percent were not 'definitely opposed' to complete integration of both working and living arrangements." The survey found that the better educated the soldier, the more receptive he was to integration.

By 1948 black troops were no longer restricted to certain positions in the army. Blacks "could be found in a majority of military occupational fields. The officer corps was open to all without restrictions of a racial quota."

A major breakthrough came on July 26, 1948, when President Harry S. Truman issued Executive Order 9981, which declared, in part, "that there shall be equality of treatment and opportunity for all persons in the armed services without regard to race, color, religion or national origin. This policy will be put into effect as rapidly as possible."

While the term *integration* was not used in the order, the president later clarified his intentions by stating that he expected the order to abolish racial segregation in the armed forces. Truman established the Fahy Committee to oversee the presidential directive.

But implementing the president's new policy would not be easy. Even General Bradley declared that "the Army would have to retain segregation as long as it was the national pattern." The army's traditionalists also continued to fight against integration within the ranks. But time was running out on those who wished to maintain a segregated army.

June 25, 1950, the day North Korea invaded South Korea, was a milestone in race relations in the army, as well as in America. The Korean War, more than any other event in midcentury America, spelled the end of segregation in the armed forces of the United States. Within the space of five months the army doubled in size, and by June 1951 it numbered 1.6 million men, with 230,000 serving in Korea in the Eighth Army. The vast expansion severely tested the army's racial policy as the number of blacks in the ranks rose from 10.2 percent of total strength to 13.2 percent in December 1952. The percentage of blacks enlisting in the army rose from 8.2 percent in March 1950 to 25.2 percent in August and constituted about 18 percent of all first-time enlistments.

MacGregor pointed out that about 22 percent of blacks served in combat-related units during World War II, about half the percentage of white troops. By 1950 some 30 percent of blacks in the army served in combat units, and by 1951 "they were being assigned to the combat branches in approximately the same percentage as white soldiers, 41 percent."

The effect of these increases on a segregated army was tremendous. As black troops were shipped to Korea local commanders found that black combat units were overstrength, while white ones were understrength. The army quickly began assigning black troops to white combat units and vice versa. "The practice of assigning individual blacks throughout white units in Korea accelerated during early 1951. . . . By this time the practice was so spread that 9.4 percent of all Negroes in the theater were serving in some forty-one newly and unofficially integrated units," MacGregor wrote. By 1951 some 61 percent of the Eighth Army's infantry companies were integrated.

"Though still limited, the conversion to integrated units was permanent. The Korean expedient, adopted out of battlefield necessity, carried out haphazardly, and based on such imponderables as casualties and the draft, passed the ultimate test of traditional American pragmatism: it worked. And according to reports from Korea, it worked well. The performance of integrated troops was praiseworthy with no report of racial friction," MacGregor stated.

The changes also took place at a time of changing social attitudes. The army was discovering that segregation "did not represent the views of younger Americans whose attitudes were much more relaxed than those of the senior officers who established policy." Even some of the older officers were emboldened to speak out against segregation in the army. Gen. Matthew Ridgeway, Far East commander, spoke out against segregation as "wholly inefficient, not to say improper."

The white combat soldiers in the Eighth Army were learning what white soldiers in World War II had discovered about the black platoons: that blacks were as competent and courageous as whites. The army found the conclusions about black soldiers by their white comrades illuminating: "Far as I'm concerned it [integration] worked pretty good. . . . When it comes to life or death, race does not mean any difference. . . . It's like one big family. . . . Got a colored guy on our machine gun crew—after a while I wouldn't do without him. . . . Concerning combat, what I've seen, an American is an American. . . . Each guy is like your own brother—we treated all the same. . . . Had a colored platoon leader. They are as good as any people. . . . We [an integrated squad] had something great in common, sleeping, guarding each other—sometimes body against body as we slept in bunkers. . . . Takes all kinds to fight a war."

In the years that followed the Korean War the American army and the armed forces of the United States were completely integrated. A half century after World War II the issue of integration in the military is forgotten. There was no one specific effort or event that changed the direction of the American Army away from segregation. There were many. But the volunteer black infantry platoons that fought in Germany in the closing days of World War II proved for anyone who wished to see that blacks were competent and brave soldiers. They were men.

SELECTED BIBLIOGRAPHY

BOOKS

Allen, Col. Robert S. *Drive to Victory*. New York: Berkley Publishing, 1947.

Ambrose, Stephen E. *D-Day, June 6, 1944: The Climactic Battle of World War II*. New York: Simon & Schuster, 1994.

Astor, Gerald. *The Right to Fight*. New York: Da Capo Press, 2001.

Beck, Alfred M. *The Corps of Engineers: The War Against Germany*. Washington, D.C.: Office of the Chief of Military History, Department of the Army, 1985.

Binkin, Martin, and Mark Eitelberg. *Blacks and the Military*. Washington, D.C.: Brookings Institute, 1982.

Blumenson Martin. *The Patton Papers*. Boston: Houghton Mifflin, 1974.

Bogart, Leo, ed. *Project Clear*. Somerset, N.J.: Transaction Publishers, 1991.

Bradley, Omar, with Clay Blair. *A General's Life*. New York: Simon & Schuster, 1983.

Buchanan, Russell A. *Black Americans in World War II*. Santa Barbara, Calif.: Clio Books, 1977.

Buckley, Gail Lumet. *American Patriots*. New York: Random House, 2001.

Bykofsky, Joseph, and Harold Larson. *The Transportation Corps: Operations Overseas*. Washington, D.C.: Office of the Chief of Military History, Department of the Army, 1954.

Carter, Joseph. *The History of the 14th Armored Division*. Atlanta: Love, 1945.

Cavanaugh, William C. C., Richard Byers, and Jeffrey W Phillips. *Dauntless: A History of the 99th Infantry Division*. Dallas: Taylor, 1994.

Cole, Hugh Marshall. *The Ardennes: Battle of the Bulge*. Washington, D.C.: Office of the Chief of Military History, Department of the Army, 1983.

———. *The Lorraine Campaign*. Washington, D.C.: Office of the Chief of Military History, Department of the Army, 1950.

Colley, David. *The Road to Victory: The Untold Story of the Red Ball Express*. Washington D.C.: Brassey's, 2000.

David, John. *The American Negro Reference Book*. Englewood Cliffs, N.J.: Prentice-Hall, 1966.

D'Este, Carlo. *Patton: A Genius for War*. New York: HarperCollins, 1995.

Eisenhower, Dwight D. *Crusade in Europe*. Garden City, N.Y.: Doubleday & Company, 1948.

Doyle, Howard, and Leo Hoegh. *Timberwolf Tracks: The History of the 104th Infantry Division, 1942–1945*. Washington, D.C.: Infantry Journal Press, 1946.

Esposito, Brig. Gen. Vincent J. *The West Point Atlas of American Wars*. New York: Frederick A. Praeger, 1964.

Farago, Ladislas. *Patton: Ordeal and Triumph*. New York: Ivan Obolensky, 1963.

Fletcher, Marvin E. *America's First Black General: Benjamin O. Davis, Sr.* Lawrence: University Press of Kansas, 1999.

Freidin, Seymour, and William Richardson, eds. *The Fatal Decisions*. New York: Berkley Publishing, 1958.

Fuller, Maj. Gen. J. F. C. *The Second World War*. New York: Duell, Sloan and Pearce, 1962.

Goodwin, Doris Kearns. *No Ordinary Time*. New York: Simon & Schuster, 1994.

Hart, B. H. Liddell. *History of the Second World War*. New York: G. P. Putman's Sons, 1970.

Keegan, John. *The Second World War*. New York: Penguin Books, 1989.

Lauer, Walter E. *Battle Babies: The Story of the Ninety-ninth Infantry Division*. Nashville: Battery Press, 1985.

Lee, Ulysses. *The Employment of Negro Troops*. Washington, D.C.: Office of the Chief of Military History, Department of the Army, 1966.

Leckie, Robert. *Delivered from Evil*. New York: Harper & Row, 1987.

Longmate, Norman. *The G.I.s: The Americans in Britain, 1942–1945*. New York: Charles Scribner's Sons, 1975.

MacDonald, Charles. *The Last Offensive*. Washington, D.C.: U.S. Army in World War II, Government Printing Office, 1954.

MacGregor, Morris J., Jr. *Integration of the Armed Forces, 1940–1965*. Washington, D.C.: Center for Military History, United States Army, 1981.

Mandelbaum, David. *Soldier Groups and Negro Soldiers*. Berkeley, University of California Press, 1952.

Mayo, Lida. *The Ordnance Department on Beachhead and Battlefront*. Washington, D.C.: Office of the Chief of Military History, Department of the Army, 1966.

Men of Trespass Blue King. *Co. K, 271st Infantry (69th Infantry Division), Our Story*. July 1945.

Mershon, Sherrie, and Stever Schlossman. *Foxholes and Color Lines*. Baltimore: Johns Hopkins University Press, 1998.

Mittleman, Capt. Joseph B. *Eight Stars to Victory: A History of the Veteran 9th Infantry Division*. Columbus, Ohio: Herr, 1948.

Moore, Brenda. *To Serve My Country, to Serve My Race*. New York: New York University Press, 1996.

Motley, Mary Penick. *The Invisible Soldier: The Experience of the Black Soldier in World War II*. Detroit: Wayne State University Press, 1975.

Nalty, Bernard. *Strength for the Fight*. New York: Free Press, 1989.

Nichols, David. *Ernie's War: The Best of Ernie Pyle's World War II Dispatches*. New York: Simon & Schuster, 1986.

Nichols, Lee. *Breakthrough on the Color Front*. Boulder, Colo.: Reinner, Lynne Publishers, 1993.

Patton, George S. *War As I Knew It*. Boston: Houghton Mifflin, 1947.

Pergrin, David. *First Across The Rhine*. New York: Simon & Schuster, 1989.

Pogue, Forrest C. *The Supreme Command*. Washington, D.C.: Office of the Chief of Military History, Department of the Army, 1954.

Reynolds, David. *Rich Relations: The American Occupation of Britain, 1942–1945*. London: HarperCollins, 1995.

Risch, Erna, and Chester Kieffer. *The Quartermaster Corps: Organization, Supply and Services*. Vols. 1 and 2. Washington, D.C.: Office of the Chief of Military History, Department of the Army, 1953–55.

Rooney, Andy. *My War*. New York: Public Affairs, 2000.

Ross, William F. and Charles F. Romanus. *The Quartermaster Corps: Operations in the War Against Germany*. Washington, D.C.: Office of the Chief of Military History, Department of the Army, 1965.

Ruppenthal, Roland. *Logistical Support of the Armies*. Vol. 1. Washington, D.C.: Office of the Chief of Military History, Department of the Army, 1953.

———. *Logistical Support of the Armies*. Vol. 2. Washington, D.C.: Office of the Chief of Military History, Department of the Army, 1959.

Silvera, John. *The Negro in World War II*. New York: Arno Press, 1969.

Thomason, John W. *Fix Bayonets*. Annapolis, Md.: Naval Institute Press, 1994.

Thompson, Harry C., and Lida Mayo. *The Ordnance Department: Procurement and Supply*. Washington, D.C.: Office of the Chief of Military History, Department of the Army, 1960.

Weigley, Russell F. *Eisenhower's Lieutenants*. Bloomington: Indiana University Press, 1981.

Wilmot, Chester. *The Struggle for Europe*. New York: Harper & Brothers, 1952.

Wright, Bruce. *Black Robes, White Justice.* New York: Carol Publishing Group, 1987.

Wynn, Neil. *The Afro-American and the Second World War.* New York: Holmes & Meier, 1976.

PERSONAL HISTORIES/MEMOIRS

Adkins, Harold E. *Company F, 394th Infantry Regiment, 99th Division.* Personal Memoir.

Arnold, Harry. *The Way It Was.* Carlisle, Penn.: U.S. Army Military History Institute. Personal memoir.

Brice, Cpl. Edwin L. *Journal of the 3909th QM Truck Company, 1945.*

Howe, Capt. John S. (2nd Information and Historical Sv. III Corps). *The Remagen Bridgehead: The Battle for Honningen, 15–17 March 1945* (after action report, April 3, 1945). Carlisle, Penn.: U.S. Army Military History Institute.

Kuhn, Rev. John L. *Memories of Yesteryear.* Carlisle, Penn.: U.S. Army Military History Institute, 1988.

Lombardo, Samuel. *Memoir.* Carlisle, Penn.: U.S. Army Military History Institute.

Priscus, V. J. *Bavarian Spring: A Memoir of Lithuanian Family's "Adventures" from January to June, 1945.* Carlisle, Penn.: U.S. Army Military History Institute.

Ralston, Richard. *A Short History of the Black Platoon Assigned to K Co., 394th Inf.* Personal memoir (typescript).

Roland, Charles. *Memoir.* Carlisle, Penn.: U.S. Army Military History Institute.

Unknown. *Combat History of the 394th Infantry Regiment.*

LETTERS

Davis, Brig. Gen. Benjamin O. Letters to his wife, Sadie, 1944, 1945. Carlisle, Penn.: U.S. Army Military History Institute.

Whiteway, Curtis. Letters to author, 2002.

ORAL HISTORIES

Williams, Col. Bruce H. Conversations between Gen. James A. Van Fleet and Col. Williams. Senior Army Debriefing Program. Carlisle, Penn.: U.S. Army Military History Institute, March 3, 1973.

PAMPHLETS/ARTICLES

Army Service Forces Manual. *Leadership and the Negro Soldier.* 1944.

Army Talk. *Negro Manpower in the Army.* Washington, D.C.: War Department, 1947.

Bogart, Leo. "The Army and Its Negro Soldiers." *The Reporter,* December 30, 1954, pp. 3–11.

Daily Reports, 394th Infantry Regiment, March, April 1945. National Archives.

Journal of Negro History, vol. 38 (April 1953); pp. 194–215.

Our Local Correspondents. "Judge Wright." *New Yorker,* September 6, 1976.

War Department Pamphlet no. 20-6, *Command of Negro Troops.* 1944.

Welliver, Warman. "Report on the Negro Soldier." *Harper's,* April 1946, pp. 333–39.

NEWS ARTICLES

Catledge, Turner. "Behind Our Menacing Race Problem." *New York Times Magazine,* August 8, 1943.

Deutsche, Albert. "Army Camp Letters Arouse Negro Resentment." *PM* (Detroit), August 13, 1943.

Pittsburgh Courier, articles, 1943–1945.

"A Soldier's Story." *U.S. News & World Report,* May 31, 1999.

Stark, Louis. "Says Foes Exploit Our Race Divisions." *New York Times Magazine,* September 16, 1943.

Stars & Stripes, articles, November 1944–May 1945.

Washington Times Herald, Washington, D.C.: Sept. 14, 1944.

INTERVIEWS

Bailey, James. Phone interview with author, 1997.

Betts, Arthur. Phone interview with author, 2000.

Blackwell, James. Phone interviews, personal interviews with author, 1996, 1997.

Boris, Lawrence. Phone interviews, personal interviews with author, 1999–2002.

Brown, Neil. Phone interviews with author, 2002.

Chappelle, James. Phone interviews, personal interviews with author, 1996, 1997.

Des Journette, Clayton. Phone interviews with author, 1999.

Des Journette, Hattie. Phone interviews with author, 2001–2002.

Hall, Marvin. Phone interviews, personal interviews with author, 1996, 1997.

Harnist, William. Phone interviews with author, 1997.

Heard, Herman. Phone interviews, personal interviews with author, 1996–1997.

Holmes, Arthur. Phone interviews, personal interviews with author, 1999–2002.

Houston, John. Phone interviews with author, 1998.

Jackson, Edward. Phone interviews with author, 1999–2002.

Nance, Booker. Phone interview with author, 1995.

Oliver, James. Phone interviews, personal interviews with author, 1999–2002.

Pugh, Herbert. Phone interviews with author, 1999–2002.

Ralston, Richard. Phone interviews with author, 1999–2002.

Ransom, Waymon. Phone interviews, personal interviews with author, 1999–2002.

Rector, Washington. Phone interviews with author, 1995.

Rife, Leonard. Phone interview with author, 2000.

Robinson, Harold. Phone interviews with author, 1999–2002.

Roland, Charles. Phone interview with author, 2002.

Rookard, James. Phone interviews, personal interviews with author, 1996, 1997.

Sacco, Oliver. Phone interview with author, 1999.

Scobbie, Margaret. Phone interviews with author, 2002.

Simmons, Mrs. Ann. Phone interviews with author, 1999–2002.

Skeeters, David. Phone interview with author, 1999.

Stevenson, Charles. Phone interviews with author, 1995, 1996.

Strange, Willfred. Phone interviews with author, 1999–2002.

Strawder, James. Phone interviews, personal interviews with author, 1999–2002.

Tatum, Bradford. Phone interviews with author, 1999–2002.

Watt, Fred. Phone interview with author, 2000.

Windley, William. Phone interviews with author, 1999–2002.

Wright, Bruce, personal interview with author, 2001.

INDEX